PREVAILING
WORLDVIEWS

OF WESTERN SOCIETY SINCE 1500

PREVAILING WORLDVIEWS

OF WESTERN SOCIETY SINCE 1500

by Glenn R. Martin

Triangle Publishing
Marion, Indiana

Prevailing Worldviews of Western Society Since 1500
by Glenn R. Martin

Third Printing

Direct correspondence and permission requests to one of the following:

Triangle Publishing
Indiana Wesleyan University
1900 West 50th Street
Marion, Indiana 46953

Web site: www.trianglepublishing.com
E-mail: info@trianglepublishing.com

Glenn R. Martin (1935–2004)
Prevailing Worldviews of Western Society Since 1500
Compiled by Linda MacKay
Compilation assistance by Scott Shepherd

ISBN: 1-931283-16-8

Graphic design: Lyn Rayn

TABLE OF CONTENTS

PREFACE

CELEBRATING THE LIFE AND TEACHING MINISTRY OF DR. GLENN R. MARTIN

For more than thirty years, Dr. Glenn Martin chaired the Division of Social Sciences at Indiana Wesleyan University (IWU). Along with his wife Betty, the Martins conducted a teaching ministry impacting thousands of students, many of whom are engaged today in scholarship, teaching, pastoral leadership, law, and government service in the United States and around the world. Prior to Dr. Martin's untimely death to cancer in 2004, hundreds of students attended IWU as a direct result of his international outreach. Dr. Martin offered these students a full-spectrum analysis of the historic record, especially as it relates to Western/American history.

The attraction to Dr. Martin's teaching came from his insistence on several primary principles, or presuppositions, and their application to academic study: The centrality of an infinite, personal, sovereign God; the advent of God-in-Christ; and the transforming ministry of God's Spirit as our Comforter and Companion, offering meaning and purpose even in this Post-Modern Age. In the words of St. Augustine, whom Dr. Martin greatly admired, "In You [God] we live and move and have our being. You move us to delight in praising You, for You have made us for Yourself, and our hearts are restless until they find rest in You."[1]

With this brief volume, we have tried to offer a representative sampling of Dr. Martin's teaching. With its use, we hope to produce another generation of scholars willing, as the Bible commands, to bring "into captivity every thought to the obedience of Christ" (2 Corinthians 10:5 KJV). These few lessons, selected from among many, provide the essential tools of Biblical reinterpretation and, studied as a succession of worldviews, offer a model for faith-learning integration.

Throughout his teaching career, Dr. Martin insisted that no interpretative system should be "absolutized," including this reinterpretation—only God is absolute.[2] Even so, Dr. Martin's analysis is a valuable starting point for ongoing research, the culmination of his lifelong observations and prayerful insights, and a provocative challenge to scholars who look to the Bible as Truth and subscribe to the Lordship of Christ.

David Daniel Bartley

July 2006

NOTES

1. Augustine, Aurelius, <u>Confessions</u>, Doubleday, 1960, Ch. 1, p. 43.
2. A Glossary has been included as an appendix to this study, to acquaint students and scholars with the terminology employed by Dr. Martin.

COMPILER'S NOTES

We have attempted to format this material for use in a variety of courses: general college level (or advanced high school level) courses in government, law, economics, international politics, business, history, and social science. We would welcome suggestions for future editions, particularly from teachers using the material and from former students who are sharing it with their children and grandchildren. We have done our best to acknowledge sources and check the accuracy of data. Please advise us of any corrections.

Although abridgement results in word alteration and lost continuity, we have worked diligently so you will still find this "vintage Martin." It is compiled from various sources of Dr. Martin's lectures including audio tapes and transcriptions of his courses and tapes of his basic series of lectures based on his Western/American Intellectual and Social History course. The compiler would like to thank all those who helped to make these materials available. Portions of the basic series which are not included here are Darwinism, Pragmatism, Freudianism, Existentialism, Occultism/Satanism, and most worldview applications in the areas of education, the church, and the arts.

Also, although some of our good friends prefer inclusive language, we have retained Dr. Martin's use of the word "man" in reference to humanity in general (a decision for which there is Biblical precedent--see Genesis 5:2).

Scores of people gave their time to assist with reviewing, editing, proofreading, and encouraging over the years as the material has been in process. It is simply not possible to thank each one here. We plan to do so in the larger unabridged textbook which is being prepared. May the One who rewards our work reward each one richly in ways far beyond what we are able to provide.

The dates of individuals' lives and biographical background information found in the text and the notes at the end of each chapter are, unless otherwise noted, adapted from entries in Webster's Biographical Dictionary.[1] Likewise, general background information or historical dates or details, particularly relative to political matters, are from The World Almanac and Book of Facts 1994.[2]

Notes on terminology, unless otherwise referenced, are from Webster's International Dictionary of the English Language,[3] 1903. Occasionally, a word is used in the text which you will not find in any dictionary; no available word was suited to the idea being expressed, so it seemed best to Dr. Martin to coin a new word. One such word is hypothecate, which is not equivalent to hypothesize. The Glossary may assist those who find new words or usages dancing on the pages.

Audio Lectures: We are preparing an accompanying CD which will contain the audio lectures from which this material is taken. Also, in the near future, the entire basic lecture series will be available in CD and/or DVD format.

Timeline/Maps: For an excellent grouping of historical maps to use as reference while reading, the out-of-print Historical Atlas by William R. Shepherd is recommended (New York: Barnes & Noble, 1956). Also, an accompanying CD will include an interactive timeline and animated maps.

Companion Projects: Additional projects by Dr. Martin and, also, by his students who are reinterpreting and teaching in various areas of life and various disciplines of study, are being prepared. One is a brief treatment of economic principles and procedures. Another is Dr. Martin's lectures on domestic and international politics. We will attempt to keep these projects posted on our division website: http://cas.indwes.edu/Social_ Sciences/GlennMartinWritings.htm.

Linda MacKay, compiler

NOTES

1. <u>Webster's Biographical Dictionary</u>, G. & C. Merriam Co., Publishers, Springfield, Massachusetts, First Edition, 1969.
2. <u>The World Almanac and Book of Facts 1994</u>, Funk and Wagnalls Corporation, New Jersey, 1993.
3. <u>Webster's International Dictionary of the English Language</u>, G. & C. Merriam Co., Publishers, Springfield, Massachusetts, 1903.

INTRODUCTION

DR. MARTIN'S ASSUMPTIONS (ABRIDGED)

I presuppose [hold as a basic assumption] that ideas have consequences, that thoughts produce actions. "As a man thinketh so is he,"[1] and so, ultimately, will he act. It is, of course, more fashionable today, given the influence of environmental determinism, to assume that consequences result in ideas.

Additionally, I presuppose that we can and should know, not only **what** we believe but also **why** we believe it, and that we cannot really know what we believe and why without simultaneously knowing what we do **not** believe and why, for nothing is ultimately knowable in a vacuum.

Therefore, it would appear that every person who has lived, is living, or will live in this age, without exception, will either know what he or she believes and why in contrast to what he or she does not believe and why, or will be led or victimized by those who do. Thus, each person is either a leader or led, influential or influenced.

It is apparent, moreover, from a historical perspective that, at any given point in time, a relatively small number of people are the prime movers in the affairs of men. That is, there are only a relatively small number of people who consciously know what they believe and why in contrast to what they do not believe and why. (Most who appear to be leaders today have not thought through what they believe and why but are, rather, trying to put into practice what they have been taught by those few who have done so.)

Of course, true leadership demands, not only that we know what we believe and why, but that we be fully committed to living existentially, that is, moment by moment, our world and life view. It is one thing to know; it is another thing to act on the basis of what we know. We must combine the intellectual content with an experiential commitment. An intellectual content without an experiential practice leaves us with an immobilizing scholasticism. On the other hand, an experiential practice not anchored in an intellectual content leaves us with an impotent mysticism.

DR. MARTIN'S STORY

The material you are about to read was born out of a struggle out of which God brought me to an understanding of Himself as applicable to all of life. I was privileged to be born into a devout Christian family. It was not until I was a senior in high school that I became a Christian. At that point, mine was, without question, a conversion. Whereas in my thinking I had been headed in one direction, now I was headed in the opposite direction.

After graduating from high school, I went on to university... majoring in history, philosophy and religion, psychology and education, and minoring in literature. I graduated with honors and was well prepared academically (though not, as we shall see, Biblically) for graduate school.

For the first time, in graduate school, I met people who were very effective in their teaching and were hostile to Christianity. They were teaching, by implication and by explication, that the only way a person could be a Christian was either to have a second-rate mind or to be willing to turn his or her mind off. I was a professing Christian, but coming under that teaching and being significantly influenced thereby, I reached a crisis in my life. I realized that to be intellectually honest and consistent with what I was being taught and coming to believe, I either had to renounce Christianity as a cruel hoax, or I had to rethink all of life—and I mean the whole of existence. By the grace of God and the prayers of devout parents, I did the latter.

This took me through five years of "hell" on earth, as it were, as I read virtually everything I could get my hands on, probably a minimum of five hundred volumes. I read the "left" and the "right" and I finally read the Bible. The result of my search is a testimony to God's faithfulness. We are told Biblically, that those who truly seek God will surely find Him (Proverbs 8:17b).

Is that not right? It is true! My life gives witness to that reality. I was sincerely searching for the truth of what is... Moreover, God brought me through to an understanding of what I share as the Biblical Christian worldview. God does, indeed, apply to all of life. He is Lord of all. There is a Biblical view of politics, a Biblical view of the arts, as well as law and the whole spectrum of life. It is comprehensible, it can be articulated, and it can be practiced! What I share is not an applicability which I concocted; rather, the key to comprehending it was and is Biblical Christian thinking...

When I share what I went through over that five-year period, I use the analogy of the peeling of an onion which, I believe, is a very good analogy. What happened to me was very simply this. I was seeking the truth, wanting to understand the what-is-ness-of-what-is, and God knew my heart. Consequently, as I reflected on the Bible and the other volumes I was reading, God would bring me to a point where I realized that I had to renounce what I had been taught. That is difficult to do, because we are attached to that which we have been taught. We are emotionally attached to it, often to the extent that we will argue in support of that to which we are attached, even irrationally. God would make clear, however, that I had to abandon it. Usually I would do so kicking and screaming. Finally, I would throw it overboard.

Then, I would think, "Aha, I have finally arrived." Oh, no! God then had to make me aware that there was another layer. This was so because I was born into a naturalistic age. Virtually everything I had been taught was contrary to the truth of what-is, just as virtually everything you have been taught is contrary to the truth of what-is. And so it went on, layer after layer after layer after layer until, finally, I stood completely naked before God. At that point, and only at that point, could He begin renewing my mind. We cannot have a renewed mind if there is any naturalistic clutter between God and ourselves. Only after having thrown out everything we have been taught can God begin to renew our minds so we can learn to think His thoughts after Him, to begin and end with Him in our thinking.

How long will it take for God to peel a person's onion? I do not know. A student once suggested that, in the case of the Apostle Paul on the road to Damascus, his onion was peeled rather quickly. I think ours would be, too, if we caught a glimpse of God-in-Christ as he did. It is also true, however, that the Apostle Paul's onion was not altogether peeled at that point. You will recall that the he had a wilderness experience for a number of years. God was peeling his onion! You and I must consciously submit to God all that we are. He will then, in His own way, peel our onion and renew our mind.

NOTES

1. Bible Reference: *Proverbs 23:6-7 (NASB)*: Do not eat the bread of a selfish man, Or desire his delicacies; for as he thinks within himself, so he is.

1 WHAT IS A PREVAILING WORLDVIEW OR PARADIGM?

All thinking is from presuppositions. There can be no thinking without presuppositions, and therefore, all respectable thinking is from sound presuppositions. Any "neutrality" in science, philosophy or religion is fictional. The only respectable procedure is to admit that one thinks from presuppositions and to choose those presuppositions in a responsible manner.

Dr. Bernard Ramm[1]

COMPONENTS OF A WORLDVIEW

Our objective is to explore the impact of successive worldviews on society, in particular on government, law, economics, and international politics. This is not possible, however, unless we first understand what a worldview is. In this chapter, we will examine at length the components of a worldview. Of what does a worldview consist?

We will also respond briefly to two additional questions: What is the difference between a worldview and views of lesser significance? How does a worldview become influential in a community, nation, or civilization, working its way into the very fabric of society?

We suggest that a worldview has three components, each of which is an important question to be answered. The first two are referred to as the primary questions of God, man, and the cosmos. The primary questions are as follows: What is the origin, nature, and destiny of the cosmos? What is the origin, nature, role, and destiny of man?

FIRST PRIMARY QUESTION: WHAT IS THE ORIGIN, NATURE, AND DESTINY OF THE COSMOS?

The first primary question is "What is the origin, nature, and destiny of the cosmos?" The word *cosmos* is chosen deliberately (instead of *world*, *universe*, *galaxy*, etc.) to refer, simply, to everything. It refers to everything that exists because we are raising a most basic question, "What is the origin, nature, and destiny of everything?" No question is more important than the cosmological question.

SECOND PRIMARY QUESTION: WHAT IS THE ORIGIN, NATURE, ROLE, AND DESTINY OF MAN?

The second primary question, "What is the origin, nature, role, and destiny of man?" is sometimes termed the anthropological question. Subsumed under it are several basic subsidiary questions, such as the following: Is man basically free or determined? Is man basically good or evil? Is man rational, intuitive, or neither?

FOUR SIMPLE, SUBSIDIARY "PHILOSOPHICAL" QUESTIONS

In order to answer what I call the primary questions of God, man, and the cosmos—the cosmological question and the anthropological question—it is first necessary to raise and answer four very basic, yet simple, so-called philosophical questions. Everyone who has lived, is living, or will live in this age has raised these questions. Not a person has failed to ask them at one time or another during the course of his life. Who has not asked, "Who am I?" "Where did I come from?" "Why am I here?" "Where am I going?" and "How do I know?"

Philosophers through the ages have wrestled with these questions. Philosophically, they are spelled *ontology, epistemology, axiology,* and *teleology* (words being derived from the Greek words meaning *being, knowing, worth,* and *destiny*). The ontological question is the question of being. The epistemological question is the question of knowing. The axiological question is the question of value, and the teleological question is the question of destiny. A careful look at each in turn assists one in coming to grips with the primary questions of God, man, and the cosmos.

1) The Ontological Question: Who am I? How do we exist?

How do we exist? Theoretically, there are innumerable ontological possibilities. In the final analysis, however, they can be reduced to a relatively few categories. Two of the more significant categories among these would be a presupposed supernatural ontology in contrast to a presupposed non-supernatural or so-called natural ontology.

What is a supernatural ontology? It is the position that there is some force, power, or agent greater, above, beyond, larger than man which is explanatory of all that exists, including man. **Super** simply means **above**, so supernatural causation means that some power, force, or agency outside of, greater than, above, beyond, outside of the visible or seen world including man brought everything into being that exists. For example, the first view we will be discussing, the worldview which flowed out of the Reformation, holds that the God of the Bible created all that exists including man, hence a Biblical supernatural ontology.

The alternative to a supernatural ontology is that the non-supernatural—some yet-to-be-discovered naturalistic force, power, or agent—is productive or explanatory of all that is, including man. This would be a naturalistic ontology. The worldview which flowed out of the Enlightenment takes this position.

Historically, philosophers have termed these alternative starting points the *ground of grace* vs. the *ground of nature.*

Supernatural versus *Natural*

Ground of Grace (God) versus *Ground of Nature*

This, without question, is the most basic of all questions. What is the starting point? The truth is that you and I cannot finish other than where we start, ontologically speaking. Our starting point will ultimately determine our terminal point! We will either have the ground or starting point of grace or the ground or starting point of nature.

2) The Epistemological Question: How do we know?

The second of the philosophical questions is the question, "How do we know?" It includes the further inquiry, "How do we know that we know?" Again, theoretically there are innumerable epistemological possibilities, but, in the final analysis, there are relatively few categories. It can be presupposed that we know, **ultimately**, on the basis of revelation **or** on the basis of reason **or** on the basis of intuition:

- revelation (authoritative outside force)
- reason (autonomous human thought; rationalism)
- intuition (divine knowledge residing ontologically within man)

The first category contains all views which hold that man knows the answers to the primary questions of God, man, and the cosmos on the basis of some authoritative outside force disclosing the truth of what is—that is, itself—to man, whereby man may know. Historically, this has been called *revelation*, hence a revelational epistemology. Again, the first view which we will discuss holds that the God of the Bible has disclosed of Himself and of the-truth-of-what-is to man in verbal, propositional form in the Bible, whereby man may know, hence, a Biblical revelation epistemology.

Another category consists of views which assume that man knows simply by exercising his intellect. It is assumed that man, by starting with himself autonomously and taking thought, can come into a possession of knowledge and truth. Usually it is assumed that this knowledge, if acted upon, will enable him to achieve progressive or gradual perfection. Thus, we have an epistemology grounded in human reason or, to use a more accurate term, *rationalism.*

What Is the Difference Between Rationality and Rational*ism*?

In order to differentiate between the epistemological possibilities of revelation and reason, it is necessary to distinguish between rationality and rationalism.

The alternative to rationality is irrationality. Presumably, a revelation epistemology could presuppose rational or irrational man, but revelation presupposes rational communication, and rational communication is impossible if man is irrational. Thus, in the final analysis, **communication presupposes rationality**. If we are not rational, communication as we know it is impossible. Every historically significant revelation epistemology, including a Biblical Christian revelation epistemology, presupposes rational man. Reason or rationality, then, is not negated by revelation but, on the contrary, is indispensable to it. By its very nature, a revelational epistemology presupposes rationality and rational man.

> Whenever we see the postfix **"ism"** being added to any term, all that is usually being suggested, if only inadvertently, is the absolutizing of what precedes it.

An epistemology which presupposes not revelation, but the supremacy of the human intellect in knowing, presupposes rational*ism* rather than rationality, rational*istic* man rather than rational man. Whenever we see the postfix "ism" being added to any term, all that is usually being suggested, if only inadvertently, is the absolutizing of what precedes it—in this case, rationality or reason. Rational*ism*, therefore, asserts that man does not need an outside source for knowing because, at the most basic level, his own reason, being absolute, is sufficient. A rationalistic epistemology is the view that rationalistic man, starting from himself alone has the cognitive ability by taking thought to come to a knowledge of the truth of what is. There is no need for revelation. Indeed, for the rationalist, any imagined belief in revelation is, ultimately, a hindrance to true knowledge.

The third epistemological possibility is that man knows simply because he exists. He knows on the basis of intuition. This necessarily presupposes a pantheistic ontology, that man, ontologically speaking, is god, that is, part and parcel of god. If the divine resides within man, then, theoretically, he does not need revelation to know, nor does he even necessarily need to think to know. He knows simply because he is. He "intuits." When we discuss Romanticism/Transcendentalism (1770s-1860s), we will discuss the particular intuitional epistemology that came into being at that time.

3) The Axiological Question: What, if anything, is the ultimate value?

What, if anything, is the ultimate value? Once again, there are theoretically innumerable axiological possibilities, but it would appear that, in the final analysis, relatively few categories. Three of the most significant among those categories would include: 1) **a theistic axiology**, that a god who is above or beyond man is the ultimate value; 2) **a humanistic axiology**, that man is the ultimate value; or 3) **a materialistic axiology**, that matter is the ultimate value.

The first possibility is that there is an ultimate value greater than, higher than, beyond man. That which we would refer to as the *supernatural* or *god* is presumed to be the ultimate value. One such possibility would be the Reformation view that the God of the Bible is the ultimate value, hence a Biblical theistic axiology. Others, as was the case during the Enlightenment, hold that man is the ultimate value, a humanistic axiology. The other alternative, held by many during the twentieth century, is that matter is the ultimate value, a materialistic axiology.

4) The Teleological Question: Where are we going?

With respect to the fourth and final philosophical question, the question of destiny, we ask the question, "Where, if anywhere, are we going?" Most views of God, man and the cosmos are teleological, holding that there is definite direction or design to time. It is believed that time or history is going somewhere, moving toward some object or objective. Most views hold that there is meaning to the flow of history and most anticipate, ultimately, perfection.

Theoretically, once again, there are innumerable teleological possibilities, but, in the final analysis, relatively few categories. Two of the most important among them would be what are here termed a Kingdom of God teleology in contrast to a Kingdom of Earth teleology.

Kingdom of God versus *Kingdom of Earth*

What is the Kingdom of God? By definition, it would include God and His rule. Thus, a Kingdom of God teleology is the view that God and His rule are in ultimate control and are determinative of direction in time.

The other teleological possibility holds the view that some yet-to-be discovered non-supernatural force, power, or agency is in ultimate control and is determinative of direction in time, what is here being called, in a generalized sense, a Kingdom of Earth teleology. Many, if not most, Kingdom of Earth teleologies also hold that there is direction in time and that history will ultimately by some means usher in perfection.

ANSWERS TO THE SUBSIDIARY QUESTIONS HELP ANSWER THE PRIMARY QUESTIONS

Having raised and answered the basic philosophical questions, we are in a position to raise and answer the two primary questions of God, man, and the cosmos (as we shall hereafter refer to them). That is, knowing the ontology, epistemology, axiology, and teleology of a paradigm enables us to articulate its presuppositions and determine how it raises and answers the cosmological and anthropological questions. Beyond this, as we shall see, the answers we give to the primary questions will determine the way we propose to live.

THIRD QUESTION: WHAT IS THE INSTITUTIONAL STRUCTURE AND PROCEDURE OF THE WORLDVIEW?

We will now consider the third component of a worldview. It was suggested at the outset that a worldview consists of three components or questions. To answer the first two (primary) questions, we found it necessary to raise and answer the basic yet simple philosophical questions—ontological, epistemological, axiological, teleological—which then determined the answers given to the two primary questions. Next we will see that the answers we give to the two primary questions will, in turn, determine the answer we give to the third component: What is the institutional structure and procedure of the worldview?

The third question is, put simply, "How shall we then live?" To be a worldview, in addition to answering the *cosmological question* and the *anthropological question*, a view must answer the question, "How do we propose to structure and proceed with the respect to the whole—that is, every area—of our lives?" What is the institutional structure or procedure? For want of better terminology, we are calling this the **institutional structure and procedure** of the worldview.

The answers which, by design or default, are given to the two primary questions will necessarily determine how one proposes to structure and proceed institutionally in the whole of life. There is an institutional structure and procedure which flows from each worldview.

For purposes of analysis and discussion, we are arbitrarily dividing life or the institutional spectrum into seven areas. It could be divided as profitably in other ways, but, as some breakdown is necessary for the sake of analysis, the following has been selected:

1) The **civil-social** will refer to all of the corporate relationships of man, including marriage, the family, local and national government, etc. 2) The **ecclesiastical** has reference to the affairs of the church. 3) The **educational** area refers to the means of acquiring information, including the schools, both formal and informal, and the media. 4) The **legal** has reference to the law order, the cement that holds everything together. We have to be careful here because, when a civilization is disintegrating, as the modern West and world most certainly is, we tend to think of law in terms of criminal law. We should, rather, think of law as the law order, that is, the cement which holds everything together. 5) **Economics** refers to the relations between and among men in the marketplace. 6) **Aesthetics** involves all of the art forms, expressive of the ultimate beauty, ranging from the literary arts such as literature and history on the one hand, to the audiovisual arts including music, painting, and sculpturing as examples on the other. Finally, 7) **international politics** has reference to the relations between and/or among nations or civilizations.

Thus, to repeat what we have said, the answers that we give to the so-called philosophical questions will determine the answers we give to the primary questions of God, man, and the cosmos, which will determine how we will propose institutionally to structure and proceed in all of life.

EVERY PERSON RAISES AND ANSWERS THE BASIC QUESTIONS

I would like to emphasize that each one of us answers the primary questions of God, man, and the cosmos. The significance of worldviews applies, not only to nations and civilizations, but to every single person who lives. Each person either consciously raises and answers these questions for himself or herself or allows, if only by default, someone else to answer them for him or her. They may not raise them in the philosophical terms we have used, but they raise the questions. This is to recognize that every single person—there never has been and there never will be an exception in this age—is either a leader or is led. Each one of us is either influential or influenced.

HOW A WORLDVIEW'S ANSWERS DETERMINE ITS INSTITUTIONAL STRUCTURE AND PROCEDURE

It is helpful at this point to demonstrate with two examples how the answers given to the primary questions determine one's institutional structure and procedure.

First, as in the case of the Biblical Christian worldview, we could hypothecate that one presupposes a **Biblical supernatural ontology**. How do all things exist? The God of the Bible created everything that exists including man. Such a person would hold a **Biblical revelation epistemology**. How does man (ultimately) know? On the basis of God's disclosure of the truth of Himself and what exists in verbal, propositional form, the Bible. This one would also hold a **Biblical theistic axiology**, that the God of the Bible is the ultimate value but that man, created in the image of God, is of infinite, eternal value. Finally, he or she would presuppose a **Kingdom of God teleology**, that God and His rule are in ultimate control and determinative of direction in time.

It is apparent that, if we propose to structure and live on the basis of such presuppositions and conclusions, we will propose to structure all of life vertically, orienting man to God. Man, in all of his practices individually and corporately, that is, in all of his institutions, will be oriented to God as the focus, the center, the measure, the infinite reference point, the absolute. This will be just as true of the social, the educational, the legal, the economic, the arts… as it will be of the ecclesiastical sphere.

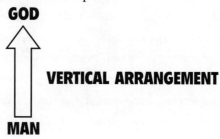

Conversely, one could presuppose a **naturalistic ontology**, that man and everything else exist on the basis of some yet undiscovered non-supernatural or naturalistic force; a **rationalistic epistemology**, that man knows simply by exercising his intellect; a **humanistic axiology**, that man and, particularly, the awesome potential of his intellect, is the ultimate value; and a **Kingdom of Earth teleology**, that some yet-to-be-discovered non-supernatural force is in ultimate control and determinative of direction in time.

If we propose to live on the basis of these presuppositions, we will logically attempt to structure and proceed institutionally in a horizontal fashion, orienting man to man. Man will be the focus, the center, the measure, the reference point, the absolute—particularly, as we have noted, the human intellect with all of its possibilities. Thus, whether speaking in terms of law, education, or the church, the effort will be made to proceed on the basis that man is, if only by default, the absolute.

CHARACTERISTICS OF WORLDVIEWS

Several signal characteristics help us identify the prevailing worldviews in a nation or civilization. Indeed, to qualify as a worldview at all, any view must have the following characteristics.

First, a worldview must deal with the larger questions. That is, it must supply answers to the primary questions of God, man, and the cosmos. Views which do not penetrate to the basic questions can be dismissed as relatively insignificant.

Secondly, a worldview must be universally applicable. This is to say that the answers which a worldview gives to the primary questions must be capable of application across the entire spectrum of life. A view, for example, which presupposes an absolutely materialistic axiology and, therefore, has nothing to say about personality, love, hope, justice, or faith, could not qualify as a worldview on this basis because, by its very presuppositions, it is incapable of raising—let alone answering—very basic subsidiary questions with which men and women must deal in their everyday lives.

Evangelical Christianity is a view which is often dismissed in intellectual circles because it makes no pretension of being universally applicable. It views certain areas, such as the church and the means of man's individual salvation as significant, but with respect to the other areas, such as the arts, law, economics, government, international relations, it appears to be silent.

The universal applicability of a view can be determined both theoretically and actually or historically. We are, in this book, proposing to analyze the impact of successive worldviews on government, law, economics, and international politics.

Thirdly, a worldview must provide lasting answers. It is not necessary to chronologically define "lasting." It might be a half millennium (500 years), it might be a century (100 years), it certainly will be at least as short as a generation (20 years). For various reasons worldviews are implemented over longer or shorter periods of time. The point is that a view which is only momentarily fashionable intellectually speaking, what might be called an intellectual flash in the pan, is not a worldview. Thus, a worldview must have sufficient durability so as to provide lasting answers.

In summary, then, a worldview must provide **enduring** answers to the **larger** questions which are **applicable to the whole of life**.

LEVELS OF APPLICATION OF A WORLDVIEW

Elsewhere I go into detail with respect to how a worldview comes into being and how it works its way from the intellectual community into the local community, into the warp and woof of an entire civilization. In this book, suffice it to say that there are always some individuals who labor to answer the primary questions of God, man, and the cosmos, repackaging what exists in some manner so as to offer an explanation for what exists and how we should live. These I call abstractions.

Many of these abstractions, of course, never become widely known or influential. In some cases, however, another person or group will buy the abstraction and attempt to market it. This I call the level of sociological application. For there to have been a Marx, there must have been a Lenin; for there to have been a Darwin, there must have been a Spencer; for a Freud, a Jung, and on we could go.

Most college and university faculty members operate at a third level, the eclectic level of application. They make eclectic selection from the packages which have already been marketed, which they then present to their students. Usually, they select whichever packages prevailed during the time of their professional birth, that is, as they worked their way through to their graduate or terminal degrees.

The fourth level is the level at which most people find themselves. I call it the conglomerate level. Most people do not have a consciously held consistent worldview which they have thought through and, therefore, could propound. Rather, they operate fragmentally, on the basis of contradictory bits and pieces (from such sources as family, cultural traditions, customs, teachers, politicians, peers at school, Hollywood, the media, church), or on the basis of the prevailing worldview. Why do most not have a consistent worldview?

From my own experience, I would suggest that we do not have a consistent worldview because, whenever we attempt to make a sincere and serious effort to raise and answer the basic questions, we are confronted with inconsistencies which are difficult, if not impossible, to overcome. To resolve such a confrontation it is necessary, first, to acknowledge that we are wrong in some area of our lives, which goes against our human nature. Secondly, we must change. This, also, is difficult—if not impossible—because we become emotionally attached to our positions. Most people, when confronted with inconsistencies, back off and give up the enterprise. They simply resign themselves to living in a conglomerated fashion.

Sadly, this renders them incapable of leadership. They are manipulated and manipulable. I am convinced, however, that any person can, by the grace of God, penetrate through to a consistent worldview.

GRADUAL RISING AND SETTING OF PREVAILING WORLDVIEWS

Beliefs change very, very slowly, particularly in the case of nations and civilizations. It is not the case that one worldview is center stage at one moment and at the next moment another worldview appears and drives the first view off center stage. Rather, there is always a gradual superinterposition of the new upon the old. There is a twilight period, a lengthy time of intellectual transition, during which the old worldview is setting and the new worldview is rising.

The twentieth century has been such a period. The Biblical Christian worldview of the Reformation was pushed off center stage during the eighteenth century by the Rationalist worldview. The Rationalist view was challenged and displaced by its derivatives, Romanticism and process philosophy. Today, what remains of the Rationalist worldview itself and its derivatives have been setting, and we do not yet know what worldview will replace it.

SUMMARY: WHAT IS A WORLDVIEW?

To summarize the skeletal framework of a worldview as presented in this chapter, we would recognize that a worldview is a full-orbed, rationally considered, and articulated view of God, man, and the cosmos, which answers both the cosmological and the anthropological questions (addressing to that end the four subsidiary questions: ontology, epistemology, axiology, and teleology) and applies those answers to all of life generally and to every area of life specifically in terms of the institutional structure and procedure flowing from those answers. Additionally, to be a worldview, a view must address the larger questions of life, must be universally applicable across the entire spectrum of life, and must have demonstrated that it has sufficient durability to provide lasting answers.

NOTES

1. Citation: Ramm, Bernard, in his chapter on Abraham Kuyper, <u>The Christian College in the Twentieth Century</u>, Grand Rapids, MI: Eerdmans, 1963, p. 93.

2 THE BIBLICAL CHRISTIAN WORLDVIEW (REFORMATION RESTATEMENT 1517–1688)

Just as... those who have bad eyesight, if you put before them the finest book, although they recognize that something is written, can yet scarcely put two words together, but if they are helped by the interposition of [glasses] will begin to read distinctly, so the Scriptures, gathering together the knowledge of God in our minds which is otherwise confused, disperses the darkness and clearly shows to us the true God.

John Calvin[1]

The first worldview to be discussed is the Biblical Christian worldview, which flowed out of the Reformation (A.D. 1517-1688).

Background: The Reformation

The Reformation is dated variously, but most historians begin it with the posting of Martin Luther's 95 Theses on the church door in Wittenberg, Germany in 1517 and continue it through the following century. It could easily be extended to 1700 in terms of the flow of its intensity.

The Reformation was led by such men as Luther, Calvin, Zwingli, Farel, and Knox.[2] It had been anticipated, however, well over a century and a half earlier by the Englishman, John Wycliffe[3] (1320?-1384), a professor at Oxford University, and the Bohemian, John Huss[4] (1374-1415), a professor in Prague at what is today Charles University. Huss, by the way, was highly influenced by the writings of St. Aurelius Augustine (391-427), whose teaching and prolific Biblically based writing, particularly The City of God, had provided the intellectual foundation for Western civilization in its infancy after the collapse of the Roman empire. Both of these men, like Augustine, held that the Bible, not the church, is the final authority. This would cost Wycliffe his position and his reputation and Huss his life as he would be burned at the stake.

The Reformation was in reality a counter-revolution, an effort to oppose the current flowing from the re-injection of the Hellenic tradition into the Western thought stream. Thus, the reformers were engaged in what we have called the Three-R Method. They were attempting to reaffirm, restate, and reapply Biblical Christianity. (This is in opposition to the One-R Method, which is to reconcile that which you are attempting to preserve with what is coming to prevail.)

As such, the reformers were concerned with two issues: **heresy** and **apostasy**. Heresy, very simply, is **addition** to the truth, and apostasy is **subtraction** therefrom.

First, the reformers had to take a stand against the heresies which had sprung up within the church. Although the Roman Catholic church had once been a dynamic center of Biblical Christianity, there had come to be super-added to the Bible over a period of many, many centuries what came gradually to take precedence over the Bible in the form of *canon* (or church) *law*. This crystallized into non-Biblical, extra-Biblical and, even, anti-Biblical teachings, customs, practices, and traditions such as sacramentalism and sacerdotalism and the efficacy of the purchase of indulgences in procuring grace. Indeed, it solidified into what we could correctly call a religion [which Dr. Martin defines as a system which begins with man reaching out to God rather than with God reaching down to men], the religion of Roman Catholic*ism*.

CANON LAW

BIBLE

By the time of the sixteenth century (1500s), without question, the church had come to interpose itself between God and man. Indeed, it was widely presupposed that the only way one could get to God was through the church or the priesthood of the church. The church had, as it were, a monopoly on salvation. Against the heresy of ecclesiastical absolutism, led, in this case, by Dr. Martin Luther (1483-1546), the Reformers reasserted the central Biblical teaching of **the priesthood of all believers.**

The Reformers were equally concerned, if not more so, with apostasy. Indeed, one could argue that the apostasy of the day was of greater concern to them than the heresy of ecclesiastical absolutism. Any person who reads Martin Luther (whose writings such as <u>The Three Treatises</u>,[5] should be required reading in any history of civilization course), will quickly realize that Luther was as concerned with apostasy as he was with heresy. Of course, deviation from the truth of any kind, whether adding to the truth or subtracting from it, is necessarily a matter of significant concern. Today, however, we usually discuss the Reformation only in conjunction with heresy. How did they address the apostasy?

The Reformers, led in this case by such individuals as John Calvin, re-asserted against the apostasy of Renaissance Humanism the central Biblical teachings of the sovereignty of God and the depravity of man. Not only is man not central or sovereign, God alone being sovereign, but man is, indeed, depraved, being completely dependent upon the work and will of God for his deliverance.

THE BIBLICAL CHRISTIAN WORLDVIEW

What, then, was the faith and vision or worldview propounded by the Reformers? Was their view, which we are calling the Biblical Christian worldview, truly a worldview as per our discussion in the previous chapter?

Does it both raise and answer the primary questions of God, man, and the cosmos? Does it do so in a manner which can actually be lived?

How does it answer the basic philosophical questions: ontological, epistemological, axiological, and teleological? Is there an institutional structure and procedure which flows from the Biblical Christian worldview? Are there general principles and procedures applicable to such? If so, what does the Biblical view have to say about how we structure and operate within civil-society (marriage, family, government)? How do we structure and proceed relative to law? Is there a Biblical view of economics? What does this view have to say about international politics?

THREE BASIC PRESUPPOSITIONS

In order to discuss the Biblical Christian worldview, as with any worldview, it is necessary to discover its presuppositions. The three basic presuppositions of the Biblical Christian worldview, I suggest, are as follows:

- The Kingdom of God is spiritual,
- Man is prophet, priest, and king under sovereign God, and
- There is no institutional interposition between God and man.

The Kingdom of God is Spiritual

The first presupposition is that the Kingdom of God is spiritual. The starting point for the Biblical Christian is God and His rule. The basic reality is God. Therefore, the center of all things is God. God is the final authority; He is ultimate. The first four words of the Bible are, without question, the most instructive of the words of God to man. "In the beginning God..."

Accordingly, the Biblical Christian holds that God, who has always been, is now, and will always be, reigns over all that exists. His rule is spiritual in that it includes the totality of all things, seen and unseen, temporal and eternal. Other worldviews may begin with the visible or temporal realm in their effort to grapple with the basic questions, but a Biblical worldview, with a spiritual King as its center, begins with God and His all-encompassing spiritual Kingdom, of which the visible realm is only a part.

The fifth word in the Bible is the second of the most instructive of the words God has given us: *"... created...."* It was God plus zero, and God "created." Therefore, Biblical Christians understand the what-is-ness-of-what-is; it is creation. God is not to be confused with creation because God did not create from Himself. He created something from nothing. The time-space-continuum is not a part of God; we do not have a "pantheistic" scheme; rather, God created something from nothing.

The Kingdom of God, then, while including time and space (which are created), cannot be circumscribed or defined in terms of time and space. For the Biblical Christian, the Kingdom of God is eternal, perfect, triumphant, and coming. It is eternal because it has always existed, exists now, and will always exist. It is perfect. It is triumphant over Satan, sin, and death on the basis of the shed blood of Jesus Christ. Finally, it is coming to reign in full power and glory over all that exists.[6]

Accordingly, institutionally speaking, the Kingdom of God is not to be equated or confused with any single temporal institution as, for example, the church. It most certainly includes the church because, being spiritual, it includes the totality of what is, but it includes every other institution as well. Thus, for those who hold to a Biblical Christian worldview, God and His Kingdom are over every area of life, without exception. Every area of life is a place of nearness to and service of and unto God.

The Kingdom of God is spiritual. Nothing is more significant than this basic presupposition for the Biblical Christian. God and His Kingdom is the starting point and the terminal point.

Man is Prophet, Priest, and King Under Sovereign God

The second presupposition of the Biblical Christian worldview is that man is prophet, priest, and king under sovereign God. The Biblical Christian does not begin with man, but he begins with God, for God is Alpha and Omega; and if He is Alpha and Omega, He is everything in between as well.

Nevertheless, as we shall see, the Biblical view of man is a high view of man. Let us examine each component of this significant presupposition.

Man as Priest Under God: All men, on the basis of the finished work of God-in-Christ, have direct access to God. Therefore, the Biblical Christian recognizes the priesthood of all believers.

The priesthood of all believers had been an integral part of the Augustinian Biblical Christian worldview which, as we know, had provided the consensus for Western society for well over five hundred years. Gradually, however, there had been a shift in focus from God to man until, by the sixteenth century (1500s), the Roman Catholic Church had interposed itself between God and man. It was believed that individuals did not have access to God excepting through the priesthood of the church. Moreover, salvation was [not of the work of God-in-Christ but] of works. When one practiced the rituals and sacraments of the Church in the prescribed fashion, one was able to work one's way to God. Finally, the Biblical truth broke through to Martin Luther and other reformers.

Luther was reading Romans, with the help of the Augustinian commentaries, when it struck him forcefully that "The just shall live by faith," (Romans 1:17 KJV) that salvation is by grace through faith in the Biblical God, which is to say, through faith in the once-and-for-all finished Work of God-in-Christ. He came to the Biblical realization that man does not have to go through a church or a priesthood to get to God, but every person has direct access to God on the basis of the finished Work of God-in-Christ alone.

In opposition to the mediation of the priesthood of the church, the great reformers rediscovered, rearticulated, and reapplied the liberating recognition of the priesthood of all believers.

Man as King Under God: Secondly, under sovereign God, the Biblical Christian views man as king. Every person under sovereign God is a king. The starting point is always God, but the secondary reality is creation. The Biblical view is that God created the heavens and the earth and gave man dominion over creation, calling upon man to exercise godly exploration, knowledge, and usage of creation.

The view that man is king, created by God to make responsible use of creation is the basis for the Biblical view of science and the motivation for scientific endeavor. The Biblical Christian does not, on the one hand, despise, debunk, or deny science, because man is called upon to make use of and enjoy what God has given him. On the other hand, the Biblical Christian does not absolutize or worship science, succumbing to scientism, which leads to all manner of difficulty and problems. For the Biblical Christian, science is not despised or worshipped, but reverenced as God's means to the end of man's exercising dominion over creation under a sovereign God.

This view of man is clearly articulated in the first chapter of Genesis. It is often called the *dominion mandate*. Every person under God is a king.

Man as Prophet Under God: Finally, the third component of this presupposition is that every person under sovereign God is a prophet. This is very little understood today.

We tend to think of the Biblical view of man as prophet only in connection with the *gift of prophecy* which the Holy Spirit gives to select individuals in order to disclose His purposes at particular times and places or, even, in the narrower sense of foretelling particular future events. Biblically, there is a gift of prophecy, which is a very important gift.

What is meant, however, by man as prophet, is the reality that God lets us know. Biblical Christians believe that all men are prophets because God gives man knowledge of the Truth. Every person, without exception, can know Truth—absolute Truth—from God. Therefore, as prophets, all people without exception may know what has happened and why, what is happening and why, and what will happen and why—not exhaustively in terms of every detail, but truly. This being the case, Biblical Christians are never caught by surprise.

What, for the Biblical Christian, is the source of this knowledge from God? The Bible. God is Truth, and the Bible is God's revelation of Himself and what-is in verbal, propositional form. Therefore, on the basis of the

Bible every person can know—truly, though not exhaustively. In the Bible, God has disclosed of Himself in such a way as both to raise and to answer the primary questions of God, man, and the cosmos. He reveals Himself as being in pursuit of fallen man. Man, who otherwise would never know anything for certain, has been given absolute truth in the Bible. This is why, for a Biblical Christian, the Bible is not a book, but The Book.

Indeed, Biblical Christians believe they have a tremendous God to celebrate. First of all, they celebrate God as God, as *Alpha* and *Omega*, a celebration that never ends because God is inexhaustible. They celebrate God as Creator. They celebrate God as Acknowledger or Revealor, who lets man know. They celebrate God as Redeemer who restores man to God through the finished work of God-in-Christ. They celebrate God as Guide along the way and, also, as Coming Lord and King.

Thus, they have the privilege of bowing and worshiping God in the totality of life. They bow and worship God ontologically as Creator, epistemologically as Acknowledger or Revealor, axiologically as Redeemer, and teleologically as Guide and Coming Lord and King. This is tremendous! They must, of course, strive in an imperfect age for balance in this celebration, not overemphasizing, for example, the celebration of God as Redeemer at the expense of celebrating Him as Creator or Revealor.

Intellectuals in the post-Christian West, no longer holding to the Biblical view of man as prophet, are necessarily left in a world of epistemological relativity. Accordingly, whereas Biblical Christians are never caught by surprise, knowing what has happened, is happening, and will happen and why on the basis of the Bible (truly though not exhaustively), the modern intellectual is left, in contrast, with nothing but surprise.

This is evident in all disciplines. It was impressed upon me when I was completing my doctoral work in history. At that time, I was troubled that so few people appeared to be interested in history. Finally, I realized that people are not interested in history because history does not appear to mean anything to them. Then it registered with me that history does not *appear* to mean anything to people because, indeed, it does not mean anything to them.

I then became aware that the reason for this is that the history to which recent generations have been exposed has been written, for the most part, by naturalist historians who, given their presuppositions, necessarily begin in the middle of nowhere and, therefore, end up in the middle of nowhere. Time can have no ultimate meaning.

Worse yet, because they presuppose that what exists now has always been, presumably what exists now must be **normal**. Unhappily, however, the more closely they examine presupposed normality, the more normality is discovered to be abnormal. This, again, is the case in any field: history, anthropology, sociology, psychology, and so on.

This poses a terrible dilemma because if what now exists is normal, how is it possible to explain such abnormalities as poverty, disease, ignorance, and war? To address this problem in history, it becomes incumbent upon naturalist historians to abnormalize the normal, that is, to construct some scheme to help man overcome the abnormal normal. Given a relativistic starting point, history is inescapably confusing and meaningless.

On the other hand, the Biblical Christian does not find himself caught in this dilemma. He knows that in order to understand anything—in this case, history or time—it is necessary to understand that which preceded that which now exists—in this case, pre-history or pre-time. He knows that time has not always existed. *"In the beginning God created..."* (Genesis 1:1) Before time began there was God—who was, and is, and will ever be, God plus zero. God is from everlasting to everlasting.

Thus, there is pre-history; we do not start in the middle of nowhere. God created something from nothing. God created the space-time continuum. Time is the created economy of God. Moreover, God's creation was good, even perfect. For the Biblical Christian, time or history—as well as the slice of life represented by every academic discipline—has meaning as a part of God's creation. Apart from God, however, can there be any ultimate meaning to time? Or to any other subject?

The Biblical Christian knows, moreover, that subsequent to Creation there was an event within the framework of time which was so definite that, if any one of us had been present, we could have observed it. It is described in the third chapter of Genesis and has come to be known as the Fall. Thus, on this side of the Fall there is a totally different state of affairs; that which now exists is not normality; it is, indeed, abnormality.

Therefore, the Biblical Christian is not caught in a flux of perpetual abnormality. He knows that what currently exists has not always been and will not always be. He knows that God-in-Christ has conquered Satan, sin, and death, and has ascended, and will return to consummate history—to put an end to poverty, disease, ignorance, war, and death—and to implement the perfect Kingdom of God in full power and glory in direct control over all that exists. Hence, he looks forward in hope to the Second Advent even as he looks back in faith to the First Advent.

The Biblical view of man is a high view: every man is a prophet; every man is a priest; and every man, under a sovereign God, is a king. As prophet, man can possess the truth, knowing what has happened and why, what is happening and why, and what will happen and why—on the basis of God's disclosure of Himself to man in verbal, propositional form in the Bible. As priest, man has direct access to God on the basis of the finished work of God-in-Christ. As king, man is called upon by God to take dominion over all that God has created, making godly exploration, knowledge and usage of Creation.

There Is No Institutional Interposition Between God and Man

For the Biblical Christian, God is over all of life. Institutionally, as we will be discussing, there is a holy commonwealth in which every institution (each of which is significant, having been established by God) is directly responsible to God. Every institution relates primarily to God and, therefore, the third presupposition of Biblical Christianity is, very simply and yet profoundly, that there is to be no institutional interposition between God and man. That is, for the Biblical Christian nothing, in this case, no institution, should be interposed or should interpose itself between God and man. This, again, was restated emphatically during the

Reformation in response to the heresy of ecclesiastical absolutism. There is only **one** mediator between God and fallen man—God-in-Christ—therefore, any attempted institutional intervention between God and man is a pretension to deity and is thereby inadmissible.

The Institutional Arrangement: A Holy Commonwealth and Covenantal Order

The Biblical Christian view of life or, as you prefer, of the institutions, is that of a *holy commonwealth* and a *covenantal* arrangement or order. God is over all of life and is reaching down to relate with man in all of his affairs, individual and institutional.

The term **holy commonwealth** (which could be spelled holy or wholly) flows from the Reformation period and was used extensively in Puritan America. It signifies, simply, the recognition that God is over all of life, no area excepted. It is the sovereignty of God institutionalized.

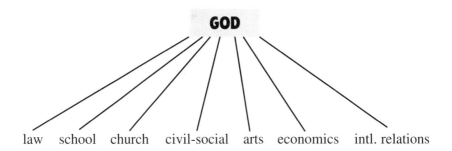

GOD

law   school   church   civil-social   arts   economics   intl. relations

Also, to read the Bible is to understand that God has provided a **covenantal order**. Because we no longer think theologically, we find this difficult to understand. To recognize that there is a covenantal order is simply to acknowledge that God has not left man alone. It refers to the reality that God has reached down to man—whom He made in His own image with an ability to respond to Him—and propositioned him. The Bible, in the final analysis, is simply propositional truth—God reaching down to man.

Today in the post-Christian West, it is difficult to grasp the concept of a covenant because we no longer think theologically, but anthropologically.

Our thoughts rarely rise above what I call the line of anthropology. We need, however, to think theologically and recognize the difference between a covenantal and a contractual relationship. Otherwise, if only inadvertently, we render a covenant into a contract, failing to distinguish the profound difference between the two.

A **contractual order** is one in which there are relations between and among men. It involves horizontal relationships. There is nothing wrong with a contract, as such, but a contract is not a covenant. A contractual order is one which is limited, God having been abandoned, to horizontal contracts.

A **covenantal order**, on the other hand, is one in which the basic relationship is with God. It is a vertical arrangement, and a particular kind of vertical arrangement which **begins with God**, who is reaching down to man. This is tremendous! God has literally propositioned man, reaching down to man covenantally in the whole of life.

This is the nature of the Bible. We call the Bible the Old Testament and the New Testament, but it is much, much more. It is the *Old Covenant* and the *New Covenant*. The New Covenant proposes, not to destroy but, rather, to fulfill the Old Covenant. Thus, they are interlocked; one cannot exist without the other.

We would not need the Bible were it not for the Fall, for our relationship with God would be perfect. Because of the Fall, however, we need the Bible. God is pursuing man in verbal, propositional form in covenantal arrangement in the Bible.

Indeed, we need to read the Bible, not merely devotionally, jumping here, there, and everywhere in smorgasbord fashion (which is good as far as it goes, God having said that His Word will not return to him void), but propositionally—as God in pursuit of fallen man in verbal, propositional form. Through the Bible God is propositioning man in a form that can be clearly understood, communicated, and lived.

Of course, the Bible is a unity and a person should not expect to be able to understand it unless it is read as such. Anyone who has not yet sat down and read from Genesis 1:1 through Revelation 22:21 in as short a time as possible will be amazed by the understanding gained by doing so. It is a very straightforward statement. Indeed, I believe that any two people (Christian or non-Christian) who will read the Bible through together, allowing it simply to say what it says (without forcing it to fit into their own view of things or the view or any other person or group) will find that they will end up instantly agreeing on, say, ninety (90) percent of what is read. [That is, not that they are in personal agreement with such, but that the message has been stated clearly enough that they will agree with respect to what has been stated.]

Unhappily, by the way, those who read the Bible too often fail to recognize that they agree on ninety percent and fail to focus on that ninety percent and exercise charity relative to the ten percent of disagreement. Instead, they attempt to cause others to line up with their view of the ten percent, which becomes their focus. That, however, is a rationalistic exercise; it is not Biblical at all.

Have you ever read the Bible as God covenanting with man? In the propositional language of His Word, God is making very clear who He is and what He has done, and what He will do if we respond to Him and His Work in His prescribed manner. Based on who He is and what He has done, He declares to us, "If you will do thus and so, I will do thus and so."

We could study at length, identifying and discussing the propositions in the Bible. Following are several illustrations:

"In all thy ways acknowledge him, and he shall direct thy paths." (Proverbs 3:6 KJV) If God is who He says He is, and I acknowledge Him in all my ways, He is obligated to direct my paths.

"But seek ye first the kingdom of God and his righteousness, and all these things shall be added unto you." (Matthew 6:33 KJV) This is a proposition. If I seek God and His Kingdom and righteousness, I will receive all that I need. I will not necessarily receive all that I want, for I often want what I do not need, but all that I need will be added to me.

"If God be for us, who can be against us? (Romans 8:31b KJV)

"I can do all things through Christ which strengtheneth me. (Philippians 4:13 KJV)

We could go on and on. God is in pursuit of man in verbal, propositional form.

The significance of the covenantal order often escapes us, living as we do in an age characterized by relativity.

When I was a lad, I used to ask many questions. I later realized that most of them were, if you will permit me, inane, asinine, or banal. Not all of them, however, were such; several were very profound, even fundamental. One such question was, "What is the difference between Christianity and all other religions?" Perhaps the reader has been asked this question or has asked this question. It is a very fair question, indeed, a very basic question.

The answer I usually received from Christians went like this: "The difference between Christianity and all other religions is that the Christians serve a God who is alive, whereas practitioners of other religions serve gods who are dead or will be dead." This response is good as far as it goes, but the more complete answer to the question, particularly for the culture in which we live, is the difference between the subjective and the objective.

Religion, by its very nature, beginning and ending with man, is subjective, and can never be otherwise. It is man reaching up and out to the ultimate. Whether we are talking about a theological religion in which man believes the ultimate to be above, beyond, outside of, and larger than himself or an anthropological religion in which man believes himself to be the ultimate, we are beginning and ending with man. Both are subjective. In all religions, man is reaching up and out to God, starting from himself and therefrom self-generating God. Through religion, man—in all sincerity and most often well-meaning—tries to find the answers to the basic questions beginning with himself.

I do not know about you, but I would not practice religion. I would not be willing to wallow in subjectivity without knowing the truth, and there would be no way to know the truth. Asking the basic questions could not be permitted in such a system. I would end up in absurdity and despair.

Biblical Christianity is not, in that sense, a religion. It is not a subjective effort which begins and ends with man reaching out to God. It begins and ends with God, who alone is objective. It is not a theological religion nor an anthropological religion. It begins and ends with God. Therefore, it is objective. This is the difference between Biblical Christianity and any and all religion(s). Biblical Christianity is God reaching down to and propositioning man and, then, man responding, whether positively or negatively. When man responds positively to God, man is thereby liberated to begin and end with God. This is tremendous!

In Biblical Christianity, the living God is reaching down into creation to man, raising and answering the basic questions, penetrating history in flesh form, living, dying, being raised again, ascending, and sitting at the right hand of the Father, interceding for each one of us. Christianity has to do with God: who He is and what He has done, is doing, and will do. Because God has propositioned man in all of life, to be a Biblical Christian is to be God-centered in both personal and corporate life, consciously and deliberately beginning and ending with God, not with man, in all of life.

Therefore, if I take a course entitled Comparative Religions, in which we have, theoretically, studied Christianity, I will not have studied Christianity because Christianity, being objective, cannot ultimately be understood as a religion—that is, as man reaching out to God. Biblical Christianity can only be understood as truth, as a covenantal order which begins and ends with God—who is reaching down to man.

Accordingly, in the final analysis, my question as a lad was not a correct question. The question is not, "What is the difference between Christianity and all other religions?" The question is, "What is the difference between Biblical Christianity and religion?" We do not need religion; we need God. What, again, is the difference? It is the difference between the subjective and the objective.

THE COVENANTAL ORDER:
PERSONAL AND CORPORATE COVENANTS

Thus, there is a covenantal arrangement or order. This is very significant and could be studied at length very profitably. There are many examples of covenants within the covenantal order, three of which are the personal covenant, the ecclesiastical covenant, and the civil-social covenant. Let us examine these.

First, there is the **personal covenant**. That is, God is propositioning every person. No person has lived in this age or will live in this age without being propositioned by God. How do we know this? We are told Biblically that the Spirit of God strives with all people. What does God propose? God proposes that every person be reconciled to Himself on the basis of the finished work of God-in-Christ, for the Lamb of God was slain from the foundation of the world.

Thus, the personal covenant, God's propositioning man in his personal life, is often referred to as the "covenant of grace," as it is by grace that man is saved and made a covenant-keeper with God-in-Christ. Man, accepting God's propositioning, receives God's provisions for him—including the finished Work of the perfect sacrifice of God-in-Christ—and agrees, on the basis of this Work and by the moment-by-moment grace of God, to be about the business of implementing the full will of God in his or her personal life. Thus, it is possible for every individual, on the basis of the finished Work of God-in-Christ, to be reconciled to God, to know God, and to accomplish God's way and will [not to ultimate perfection in a fallen world, but truly] in his or her life.

God is also propositioning man in corporate relationship. The **ecclesiastical covenant**, for example, is the recognition that the church, that is, every grouping comprising the body of believers, can know God and agree to do the full will of God—following His propositions—in their ecclesiastical affairs. The **civil-social covenant** is the recognition that man can know God and respond to God's provisions, agreeing to do the full will of God—following His propositions—in all civil-social relationships. Civil-social covenants include the marriage covenant, the family covenant, and the covenant of calling, among others. God is propositioning man in the totality of existence.

By the way, the Biblical Christian is not primarily interested in knowing the will of God. I often ask my students, many of whom appear to be involved in courtship, "How many of you are primarily interested in knowing the will of your prospective spouse?" Are you not, rather, much more interested in knowing your prospective spouse? For if you know that person, you will know the will and way of that person! If we know God, we will know His way and His will, personally and corporately.

THE TWIN CONSTANTS:
SOVEREIGNTY OF GOD AND DEPRAVITY OF MAN

The Biblical Christian subscribes to the **twin constants** of the sovereignty of God and the depravity of man. The sovereignty of God is the positive and the depravity of man is the negative.

The sovereignty of God is simply the recognition that God is the ultimate. There is nothing higher than God, nothing beyond God, nothing behind God. He is the final authority. God is sovereign, not because He has been so declared by any person or group, but because of who He is.

Similarly, man is depraved, not because He has been declared such by any person or group, but because of his fallen condition. The depravity of man requires some clarification. By the depravity of man, the Biblical Christian does not mean that man is insignificant, inconsequential, or irresponsible. Nor does he mean that man is programmed, determined, predetermined, or predestined.[7] No, that is not what is meant by depravity, Biblically. Rather, what is meant is that man, beginning and ending with himself, by taking thought and/or action, individually or corporately, cannot deliver or remove himself from the dilemma into which he was born. He is, rather, wholly dependent upon divine grace, the work and the will of God, for his deliverance.

A Biblical Rule of Thumb for Assessing Things Biblically:
–Is it based on the reality of the Sovereignty of God?
–Is it based on the recognition of the Depravity of Man?

Accordingly, the Biblical Christian is simultaneously pessimistic and optimistic.

Beginning and ending with man, there is pessimism. Why? Because man is fallen. He is in rebellion against God, refusing to bow to God and purporting even to be God. Thus, beginning and ending with man, there can only be a compounding of evil, and matters can only wax ever worse. That leads us, ultimately, to pessimism and despair. Ah, but the Biblical Christian is highly and eternally optimistic, in the best sense of that term. Why? Because the Biblical Christian has good news.

STARTING WITH THE BAD NEWS

Of course, apart from the bad news, the good news has no meaning. We need to understand the bad news thoroughly, not only in terms of its existence, but in terms of its contemporary manifestations. What is occurring today and why is it occurring? It is bad news, my friends.

The bad news is this: that the ultimate reality of this age absolutized is death. We all know this, and some of us painfully so because we have lost loved ones in very recent days. Short of the return of God-in-Christ or a miracle, every one of us is going to die. From Satan comes sin and from sin comes death. Indeed, if you know of any worse news, please bring it to my attention.

The bad news, however, gets worse. As a consequence of having abandoned the supernatural and, if only inadvertently, absolutizing this age, my friends, what we will witness is death on a wholesale basis as a way of so-called "life." That is what we have witnessed during the past century. We are so immunized against death that we have come to accept it with no comment, though millions and millions and millions and millions and millions (and we could continue to enumerate for many pages) of people have been and are being put to death in the name of applied social science. We have had holocausts and they continue.

ENDING WITH THE GOOD NEWS

Ah, but we do not stop with the reality of the bad news because we have the good news. The **good news** is that the ultimate reality of all that exists is not death; the ultimate reality of what-is is God, whom to know aright in Christ is **life eternal**. God, in Christ, has given us His Kingdom, and the Kingdom of God is a perfect rule, **a perfect kingdom**. The Kingdom of God, being spiritual, includes a present as well as a future reality. It is eternal, perfect, triumphant, and coming.

Indeed, God, in Christ, has conquered Satan, sin, and death. Thus, on the basis of the power of the resurrection of the dead available to all people, we can be reconciled to God, in Christ. If there is greater power than the resurrection of the dead, I would like to know of it. It is a limitless power, my friends. Moreover, as reconciled to God in Christ, we can be transformed and, as transformed, we can become citizens of God's Kingdom, coming to reign with God. The Biblical Christian has an accomplished victory to proclaim. God has already conquered Satan, sin, and death. The Kingdom of God has already triumphed. Christ, as it were, has been elected and we await His inauguration, when the Kingdom of God will come to reign in full, complete power, and Satan, sin, and death will be completely destroyed. This is the good news.

The good news, however, is even greater. Every person who has lived, is living, or will live can enjoy the power of the resurrection of the dead even in **this** age. Redeemed men and women, as reconciled to God in Christ on the basis of God's finished work in Christ and led and empowered by God-the-Spirit, become transformed. It is not only that they are reconciled to God in Christ; it is that God possesses them and flows through their lives moment by moment in His limitless reforming and redeeming power. Death has no dominion over them!

Unlike religion, which must be conjured up, there is among them the power of the resurrection of the dead, which flows out of them like an artesian well.

As transformed, as part of the Body of Christ on earth, they become reforming powers and influences implementing the way and will of God in all of life. Their lives serve as a means to the end of bringing that which God has created into captivity unto Himself so that it may serve its God-created and God-intended function. This is tremendous!

Of course, as any study of life past or present reveals, this does not produce perfection, for there is no perfection in this age, but it does make for a substantial difference: that which we are calling **reformation**, including relative order, harmony or community, liberty, justice, charity, and productive activity.

For this reason, unlike practitioners of religion, Biblical Christians are not preoccupied with the future. They anticipate, but are not preoccupied with the return of God-in-Christ. Rather, they are preoccupied with God who has conquered Satan, sin, and death and made available to all of us, even within the framework of this age, the power of the resurrection of the dead.

By the way, have you ever stopped to consider the significance of God's declaration that redeemed individuals are salt and light in this age? Without salt, there is no preservation of life; without light, there is only darkness and there can be no life.

We also realize that, just as the First Advent has occurred and God-in-Christ has conquered Satan, sin, and death, so there will be a Second Advent. God-in-Christ will return and institute the age which is to come. He will ultimately destroy Satan, sin, and death and institute God's Kingdom in its full power and glory over the totality of what-is.

Biblical Christians, then, are eternally optimistic, recognizing that there is good news.

ANSWERS TO THE SUBSIDIARY
PHILOSOPHICAL QUESTIONS SUMMARIZED

A Biblical Christian, then, believes in a **Biblical supernatural ontology**, that the God of the Bible created everything that exists including man; a **Biblical revelation epistemology**, that man knows on the basis of God's disclosure of the truth of Himself and all that exists to man in verbal, propositional form, which we call the Bible; a **Biblical theistic axiology**, that the Biblical God is the ultimate value, but that man created in the image of God is of infinite, eternal value; and a **Kingdom of God teleology**, that God and His rule are in ultimate control and are determinative of direction in time.

NOTES

1. Green, V.H.H., <u>Renaissance & Reformation</u>, London: Edward Arnold (Publishers) Ltd., 1952, p. 169.
2. Biographical Notes on the Reformers: <u>Martin Luther</u> (1483-1546), German reformer, Augustinian friar, professor of Biblical exegesis at the university of Wittenberg 1511-46, excommunicated 1520, Bible translator and commentator; <u>John Calvin</u> (1509-1564), French theologian and reformer, author, provided base for Biblical Christian government in Geneva, the center of reformed theology and education; <u>Ulrich Zwingli</u> (1484-1531), Swiss reformer, chaplain and reformed pastor/teacher in Zurich 1519-31, killed in battle; <u>Guillaume Farel</u> (1489-1565), Frenchman who convinced the town of Geneva to embrace reformation in 1535, persuaded Calvin to settle there in 1536, and thereafter pastored at Neuchatel 1538-65; <u>John Knox</u> (1505-1572), Scottish reformer, writer, statesman, went to Geneva 1554 and 1556-58, opposed ecclesiastical absolutism and established protestantism in Scotland.
3. Biographical Note: *John Wycliffe* (1320?-1384) was born in Yorkshire, England, and studied at Oxford (ca1372) as a doctor of theology. He taught and wrote at Oxford until 1382 when he was forbidden to teach. Wycliffe initiated the first complete translation of the Bible into English, completed by a colleague in 1388, four years after his death (by stroke). About thirty years after his death, he was condemned at the Council of Constance (1415); his body was disinterred, burned, and thrown into the River Swift. To gain an appreciation for the oppressiveness of ecclesiasticism and for Wycliffe's full-orbed presuppositional opposition to it, the compiler recommends George Macaulay Trevelyan's (1876-1962) <u>England in the Age of Wycliffe</u>, c. 1899 (London: Longman, 1972).

4. Biographical Note: *John Huss* (1369?-1415) was born in Husinetz of Czech parents and educated in Prague where he became a lecturer (1398) and finally rector (1402-03). His preaching was widely appreciated by the people and his writings were influential, especially De Ecclesia (On the Church). He was tried for heresy in 1415, condemned, and burned at the stake on July 6, 1415. [The compiler recommends John Hus: A Biography by Matthew Spinka (Princeton: Princeton University Press, 1968).]

5. Bibliographical Note: Dr. Martin Luther's three famous treatises were published in 1520 and won powerful support for reformation endeavor. The treatises are titled, "An Open Letter to the Christian Nobility of the German Nation Concerning the Reform of the Christian Estate," "The Babylonian Captivity of the Church," and "On the Freedom of the Christian." One source for them in English is Three Treatises by Martin Luther (rev. ed., Philadelphia: Fortress Press, 1970). Additionally, an excellent biography of Martin Luther is the very readable Here I Stand: A Life of Martin Luther by Roland Bainton, c.1950, available in paperback (Nashville: Abingdon Press, 1978).

6. Author's bibliographical note: For the best treatment of the Kingdom of God of which I am aware, see The Gospel of the Kingdom by George Eldon Ladd (Eerdmans, 1971).

7. By mentioning the word "predestined" here, Dr. Martin is not, I believe, seeking to stir up controversy with his reformed friends who take a so-called Calvinist position on the matter. Rather, he is attempting to remain faithful to a focus on the 90 percent of essential Biblical teaching about which epistemologically sound Biblical scholars agree, striving to give depravity its most basic Biblical meaning.

3 THE BIBLICAL CHRISTIAN WORLDVIEW: INSTITUTIONAL STRUCTURE & PROCEDURE

On Martin Luther's view of law and government:

...Luther, in fact, totally rejected the natural law concept... The Reformation everywhere plays down natural law and replaces the proofs derived therefrom with arguments that are taken from Christian morality. For just this reason, because Luther derives the state, not from below, but exclusively from above, from God's plan of salvation, he insists on its distinct character as a state whose essence is authority.[1]

W e are now positioned to examine the specific areas of the institutional structure and procedure of the Biblical Christian worldview. How should we then live? This, as we know, is the third component of a worldview. Here, we will discuss education cursorily, then look at law, the civil-social area, (government), and economics. International politics will be discussed in a later chapter.

As we have said, in a holy commonwealth, no priority is to be supposed in the arrangement of the institutions, each area being directly responsible to and of vital significance under God.

EDUCATION

In the area of education, the Biblical Christian begins with an assumption of a mastery of the rudiments (reading, writing, and ciphering or mathematics). If man knows on the basis of the Bible, people must know how to read, write, and cipher well.

Beyond this are three objectives, the first of which is to know God as applicable to all of life (that is, the Biblical Christian worldview).

The second objective is to know all other worldviews fully and fairly. It is not possible to know what one believes and why without simultaneously knowing what one does not believe and why, for nothing is knowable in a vacuum. To think Biblically is to think antithetically. Moreover, we must not structure other systems as straw men, merely to be able to knock them down; rather we must know those systems fairly, that is, on the basis of the presuppositions from which they emerge.

The third objective of Biblical Christian education is to reinterpret everything on the basis of Biblical presuppositions and a Biblical worldview. This is extraordinarily rigorous enterprise, particularly in the increasingly post-Christian West and world in which we find ourselves. We must virtually reinterpret with every breath we draw, or we will be manipulated by conclusions which are flowing from the prevailing presuppositions which are antithetical to the truth of what-is.

THE LAW

In the area of law, the Biblical Christian raises a basic question, "What is law?"

How do we as Biblical Christians answer a fundamental question like this? How do we determine the nature of any good we find evidenced in creation? Whenever we ask, "What is [____]?" —as, for example, What is <u>love</u>? What is <u>truth</u>? What is <u>beauty</u>? What is <u>justice</u>? What is <u>law</u>?, etc.—we always answer with an inversion. That inversion is always: **God** is [_____]! Thus, **God** is love. **God** is truth. **God** is beauty. **God** is justice. **God** is law.

Thus, God is Law. "For in him we *live and move and have our being.*"[2] God is the cement that holds all things together. Hence, there is a law order woven into the fabric of creation, holding it together. Moreover, we are told that the law of God is written on our hearts, which is true. Thus, on the basis of Creation alone, all people know that God exists and that there is a God-given law order to which they are responsible.

Most significantly, because God has graciously come to our epistemological rescue, we know that law is *objective*; all the objective law which is necessary for man appears in the Bible, which is God, knowable in verbal, propositional form. That is, God has articulated the law order for us in the Bible, a legal framework which is applicable to all people at all times. Therefore, Biblical Christians strive to base all law on the Bible or, indeed, on the presuppositions and principles derived therefrom. All law ultimately comes from God. There is a cement, a law order holding everything together, inhering in God.

CIVIL-SOCIAL AREA

In the civil-social area, the Biblical Christian believes that government is a gift of God for the orderly procedure of man in a fallen world. Biblical Christians recognize that man would not need government as it exists today if there had been no Fall. Given such, however, if there were no government, we would degenerate into anarchy.

The above Biblical definition of government is worth pondering because it is so fundamental.

> What is government? Government is a gift of God for the orderly procedure of man in a fallen world.

However, under the impact of successive worldviews antithetical to Biblical Christianity, many Christians have come to accept a dichotomy of sacred and secular. That is, they have come to view God as over part of life, but man (or, indeed, something or someone else) as over the rest of life. Let us stop to consider this.

For the Biblical Christian, God is sovereign. In the final analysis, God is either sovereign or He is not. Is it possible for God to be partially sovereign? This is like asking, if you will permit the comparison, "Is it possible for a woman to be partially pregnant?" If God is sovereign, He is over all of life, including government. If God is over all of life, everything is under Him and, in that sense, **everything** is sacred and nothing is secular.

For the Biblical Christian, then, there is and there can be no dichotomy. A dichotomy, Biblically understood, is a **false division**. Accordingly, as we shall be discussing, there is no such thing, theologically speaking, as secular. Those who think Biblically (and, accordingly, often find it necessary to change their vocabulary to bring it in line with their presuppositions), will eliminate that word from their vocabulary. There would be a procedural use for the word secular, but not a theological use, for if God is sovereign over all of life, everything is in that sense sacred and there is nothing secular.

Therefore, if God is sovereign, and if He is over all of life, the ultimate question for Biblical Christians is whether or not they are in proper relationship with God. The ultimate question is always the question of **reverence**. Reverence does not have reference to any single institution as, for example, the church or, even more superficially, one's posture in a pew. Reverence has reference to one's relationship with God. One is, in the totality of one's existence, either reverent or irreverent. Am I reverent? Is it reverent? Am I in a proper or an improper relationship with God? One can be just as irreverent in one's civil-social life or in one's aesthetics or one's politics as in one's ecclesiastical affairs.

Moreover, if we deny the sovereignty of God, and this applies to every area of life, including the civil-social, we will necessarily substitute something for God as sovereign. Consequently, the ultimate question will not be the question of reverence. The reality will be that whatever is substituted for God as sovereign cannot and will not be absolute. What one person has substituted for God as sovereign, another person will not accept as absolute, and vice versa. Accordingly, we end up with a world of relativity and, in a world of relativity, the ultimate question can never be one of reverence. The ultimate question can only be the question of **relevance**.

We hear this over and over again in our universities, and logically so, given the presuppositions undergirding the modern university: "Is it relevant?" Almost never is the question of reverence raised; thus, we cannot rise above the relativistic mentality or procedure.

The Biblical Christian believes in a separation of institutions—as for example, church and state—but not, as we shall see, a dichotomistic separation thereof, which is the view that God is over **part** of life but not over **all** of life. In other words, God, who is over all of life, is the author and creator of all institutions, church, state, and otherwise and, accordingly, the inter-relationship between and among the institutions is ultimately spiritual, not legal. Having been created by God for different purposes and having separate functions, the institutions are coordinated under God in a spiritual relationship toward the achievement of those objectives.

Thus, there is not a co-mingling and confusion between and among the different spheres. We do not confuse, for example, the ministry and the magistracy. The church and state are separate and have different functions and purposes under God as created by God; however, as we have said, they are not dichotomistically separate because both are under God. Both begin and end with God, and they interrelate one with the other under God and His sovereignty, His ownership. The nature of the relationship and inter-relationship is not, ultimately, legal. Nor is it hierarchical; it is, again, a spiritual relationship, for they all begin and end with God. This is the view we come to as we consider the weight of Biblical teaching, from Genesis to Revelation.

THE INSTITUTIONAL ARRANGEMENT IN THE POST-CHRISTIAN WEST

Western civilization, under the impact of the successive worldviews antithetical to Biblical Christianity, has shifted significantly away from this view. We have abandoned the sovereignty of God. There is no longer a holy commonwealth. What, then, has been done with the institutions? This is a very basic question.

First, we would note that, if there is no sovereign God, there are only two alternatives with respect to the institutions. We will have either, on the one hand, **anarchy** as the institutions become as laws of and unto themselves, or we will end up with **hierarchy** as one institution comes to lord it over the others. Neither of these is Biblical. Nevertheless, without a sovereign God, we are obviously going to have to have one or the other and, ultimately, it will be the latter if we are to have order.

By the way, the thinking of many Christians has also been profoundly affected by this shift. Many have abandoned the view that God is sovereign over all institutions, accepting instead a dichotomy of presupposed sacred vs. secular. Part of life, they hold, is under God (as, for example, the church) and is therefore sacred, but other parts of life (as, for example, the state) are presumably not under God and are thereby secular.

Let us, then, follow where this shift has taken the post-Christian West. As we have said, if we deny the sovereignty of God, we will ultimately end up with either anarchy or authoritarianism. Ultimately, however, there is no difference between the two because anarchy begets authoritarianism.

Why? Because if we deny the sovereignty of God, we have a vacuum and something must fill that vacuum.

What, then, has modern man substituted for God as sovereign? Again, very logically, man has substituted that which Western man first believed himself to have created, institutionally speaking. What are we taught about this institution, so much so that we know it by rote? We are not taught the holy commonwealth view, that it is of God, by God, for man [to the glory of God]. Rather, we are taught that it is of, for, and by man. Man is the creator of government!

First, of course, government is of, for, and by the people. Then, government is of, for, and by the state. Having presupposed that man created government, it is easy to slip government into the vacuum and subsume all of life under the state. The state becomes sovereign. Indeed, we live today in a time in which this is accepted as a given—even, unhappily, by most Christians. My friends, the state is not sovereign, God is, and the sovereignization of anything other than God is not only idolatry (substituting a created thing for God), it is blasphemy (a created thing usurping the place of God).

When, if only inadvertently, God is no longer acknowledged as sovereign over all institutions and the state, if only inadvertently, is substituted for God, people will come to one of two logical conclusions about the state.

First, if I presuppose that the state is sovereign and I am in power, I will survey the realm and discover that there are issues which we identify as **problems** demanding a solution. Having no god to look to for a solution, and having no reason to limit the role of the state, it will be easy to conclude that there is an obvious answer for those problems: more power to the state.

I myself was once part of this flow! Why was I so committed? Because, if we presuppose that the state is sovereign and we are troubled by problems such as poverty, disease, ignorance and war, the answer to these problems can only be more power to the state. Indeed, people who hold that presupposition cannot reach any other conclusion. Having abandoned the Biblical view of the depravity of man, we presuppose that autonomous man will be able to identify his own problems and find his own solutions for them. Something must be done to ameliorate or alleviate—if not eliminate—these problems! We must give the state more power to deal with them. That is the faith and that is the hope. That, indeed, is the religion. This faith is pervasive today and it is profoundly held.

Some Christians, failing to understand that the authoritarian state is a logical consequence of the prevailing worldview, become frustrated with the authoritarian state. It is, however, a logical imperative, my friends! If I subscribed to the prevailing presuppositions, I, too, would be advocating an authoritarian state as the only answer!

Ultimately, if we follow this presupposition to its logical expression (and it is the presupposition we are talking about, not the principle and not the procedure), we will end up, not only with the authoritarian state but, finally, with the so-called totalitarian state, as the state not only becomes the redemptive agency (and necessarily so), but it literally becomes God.

Secondly, on the other hand, let us hypothecate that I presuppose the state to be sovereign but I am **not** in power and I despair of ever coming to power. The temptation becomes all but overpowering to conclude that the state and government are themselves evil and, ultimately, then, to call for the abolition of the state, or anarchy.

At first, I will say, "Well, it is the people who are running the government who are evil. If we only had the right people in office..." Finally, however, if I despair of ever coming to power, the temptation will become too much, and I will conclude that the problem is not the people but government itself. Government will be viewed as evil and, therefore, I will come to despise and even deny the state, calling for its abolition. This, however, is not Biblical. Indeed, it is a form of blasphemy, for if I argue that government is evil and call for its abolition, I am saying that God is the author of evil, that He did not know what He was doing.

Finally, we would observe that to despise and deny government leads, first, to anarchy, but ultimately, back to tyranny. Out of anarchy must necessarily come authoritarianism, because anarchy produces nothing but a vacuum, and a vacuum must and will be filled.

The Biblical Christian does not fall into either of these dilemmas. There is no need, on the one hand, to worship and absolutize the state nor, on the other hand, to despise and deny the state. Rather, the Biblical Christian reverences government as a gift of God for the orderly procedure of man in a fallen world. This is tremendous! Today, however, sadly, under the impact of successive worldviews, Christians have lost sight of the concept of the holy commonwealth, that God is over all of life, including the civil-social area.

AREA OF ECONOMICS

Finally, in the area of economics, the Biblical Christian believes in and practices private property and freedom of enterprise with two very important Biblical qualifications.

That private property is Biblical is evident in the Eighth Commandment, "Thou shalt not steal," (Exodus 20:15 KJV) the presupposition being that one cannot steal that which is not possessable. Thus, the Biblical Christian believes that God has ordained private property or private ownership. The Biblical view of private property, however, is not in the sense of individualism, that "what is mine is absolutely mine."

Rather, the Biblical Christian believes in private property in the sense of the stewardship of private possessions under God. In other words, every person is a steward of God in terms of the totality of what exists. Each person is responsible to God and will give an account for every decision made relative to the use of his or her time, energy, gifts or talents, and possessions.

Secondly, the Biblical Christian believes in freedom of enterprise, with an important Biblical qualification. The Biblical Christian recognizes that the market is created by God and, as such, is the primary mechanism for establishing prices and wages. Being based on voluntary exchanges between parties, from which both parties benefit, the market produces prices and wages which are, for the most part, just. The market, however, like everything else apart from God, must never be absolutized. Therefore, every person retains the responsibility, when necessary, to temper the market with justice in prices and wages. This is the important Biblical qualification: justice in prices and wages.

The logical question is raised: "What is a just price? What is a just wage?" A just price is a price asked by a seller and paid by a buyer in clear conscience with a quiet heart before God. This is simply to recognize, once again that, Biblically, every person is responsible to God in all of his or her relationships, including market relationships. When I enter the market, whether as a seller or as a buyer, I do not leave God behind. I am responsible, not to the market, but to God for the price which I ask as a seller and the price that I pay as a buyer!

We recognize, moreover, that there are two sides to each of these coins. We often think of justice only in relationship to the seller, but the buyer is equally responsible. The seller must **ask** a just price, not necessarily all the market will allow in a given situation, but the buyer also must **pay** a just price, not always the minimum the market will allow in any given situation. There is nothing wrong with a bargain; God wants us to be frugal, but there is everything wrong with injustice.

That we often fail to recognize the buyer's responsibility is evidenced by our language. We will find a tremendous bargain and call it "a steal" or report that we "stole" someone blind meaning, not that we literally stole something but that we paid less than a just or fair price. Whenever we offend justice in a transaction, however, we will certainly give an account to God one day for theft. This is fundamental. Indeed, justice is highly signficant in the application of the Biblical Christian worldview to every area of life. The God of the Bible is a God of love and justice and, accordingly, there is no love without justice and no justice without love.

While lecturing years ago in Europe, I overheard a young man commenting favorably on a recent windfall profit a friend of his had gained in California. It turned out that this friend, who was a Christian, had purchased an antique automobile from an elderly lady for a fraction of its true value. I did not learn why the elderly lady was selling the automobile, but to her the automobile was simply an old car and she priced it accordingly. The young man, however, recognized that the automobile she was selling was not merely an old automobile; it was an antique, worth several thousands of dollars. Thus, he purchased it from the elderly lady for a fraction of its true worth because she did not realize that it was an antique.

I felt like interrupting the conversation to suggest that one day his friend would stand before Almighty God and give an account for theft. What did not happen was significant; what did not happen was justice. What did not take place was that the young man did not inform the elderly lady, "Ma'am, you need to understand that your automobile is an antique and is worth several thousands of dollars." If the elderly lady had said, "Look, young man, I appreciate your honesty, but I would have sold that automobile to anyone else for the price I'm asking, and I'm going to honor the price for you," that would have been a bargain! That is not, however, what took place. Although God created the market, He does not expect us to absolutize it.

The same is true relative to wages. An employer who practices Biblical Christian economics will pay a just and a fair wage, not necessarily the minimum the market requires. Conversely, an employee will ask a just and a fair wage for his or her services, not always however much the market will allow, or all that maximum political pressure can wring out, productivity not withstanding. All market transactions are to be tempered with justice.

Biblically speaking, it is wrong for an employee to seek, by means of collusion, to take advantage of political or other types of pressure in order to require an employer to pay wages which are far beyond the rate of productivity (a rate which, by the way, is mathematically calculable). Effecting an unjust wage, which distorts the market and drives wages up above the level that would be justified on the basis of productivity, results in systematic theft from everyone because others, usually the consumers of the product, will have to make up the difference. Thus, injustice results from unjust wages as well as unjust prices. Whenever prices or wages are artificially driven above the market level (determined, as we have said, substantially by the rate of productivity), the result is theft.

By the way, Christian enterprises which are striving to be Biblical will trust God to be able to provide just wages. We are told Biblically that "the labourer is worthy of his hire." (Luke 10:7 KJV)[3]

A Market Tempered with Justice

With respect to economics, every person should read Adam Smith's classic, <u>Wealth of Nations</u>, which has been recognized as basic since its publication in 1776. Although his starting point was not the Biblical God, Smith was highly influenced by the holdover of Biblical Christianity and was brilliant in terms of his understanding of market relationships. The genius of Adam Smith, in a nutshell, is his recognition that no two people will voluntarily make an exchange (the operative word is *voluntarily*) unless both parties believe they will benefit from that exchange. The Biblical Christian agrees with this analysis.

The Biblical Christian, however, goes beyond a profound appreciation for the voluntary nature of each exchange to an even more profound recognition that each party in any exchange is ultimately responsible to God for that exchange. This brings the love and justice of God, who is "no respecter of persons," (Acts 10:34 KJV) to bear on the market. Accordingly, the reverence in the marketplace which flows out of the Biblical Christian worldview, produces communities which operate, not only within the framework of the market, but substantially within the framework of the market plus justice. There is a clear conscience, a quiet heart before God.

When the Biblical qualification of justice under God is removed from an economy, it is not long before it is recognized that the market (now absolutized) cannot possibly produce justice and, moreover, will get us into trouble (as will anything else absolutized). The result is economic anarchy. Concerned individuals then seek to find some way to institutionally guarantee justice in prices and wages. This, however, is not possible. Who is going to determine or predetermine a just price? Only God can do that!

Consequently, whenever we have either the church or the state attempting to set prices and wages in a pursuit of justice, we have substituted that particular institution (or more, precisely, the people who run that institution) for God. That is very dangerous. We call this a **planned economy**, and we end up with injustice compelled as a way of life! This is basically where we find ourselves today in the West.

The abandonment of justice in any economic transaction—whether a consequence of economic anarchy (libertarianism) or authoritarianism (a planned economy), must, ultimately, be destructive, and the widespread abandonment of justice in the economic affairs of a nation or civilization will ultimately bring about the collapse of the economy of that nation or civilization.

Biblical Christians must remember, particularly at a time when economic determinism is prevalent and people, therefore, tend to absolutize their economics—whether a socialistic planned economy or, often in reaction against such, a naturalistic market economy that, for the Biblical Christian—the market, like everything else apart from God, is never to be absolutized and must be tempered with justice.

Work as a Form of Worship

What is the Biblical view of work? For the Biblical Christian—and I like this—work is a form of worship. The English word **work** literally derives from the word **worship**. That is, work is *worth-ship* of and unto God. Indeed, as citizens of God's Kingdom, we worship God just as much when we are in the field, behind the desk, or behind the lectern, as we do when we are sitting in the pew. We should be aware that work is a tremendous privilege.

Moreover, each person, as created by God, is unique and created for a purpose and, through the leadership of God-the-Spirit and the covenant of calling, has a work to do. Such work is, indeed, worship. This is tremendous. Once again, we refer to the basic presupposition that man is king, called upon by God to take dominion over creation. Every occupation, under God, is highly significant.

If we work of and unto God, we will be successful; we will be productive. This is true, for example, of students, who are called of God to study as a means to His end in and through their lives. You show me a Biblical Christian student, and I will show you a successful student, not necessarily a straight-A student, though perhaps that, but certainly a successful student. Why? Because a Biblical Christian student is working, not of and unto himself, not of and unto any professor, not of and unto any goal such as a major or a degree or, even, employment, but of and unto God as a form of worship, and any person who works of and unto God will be successful. As a general rule, if a student is not academically successful, that student is not worshipping God. Work is a form of worship; it is a privilege.

Indeed, there is one expression which has been widely used by Christians but for which the Biblical Christian has very little use today: full-time Christian service. This implies that there must be part-time Christian service. This, however, is nonsense. As we have noted, every person is created by God for a purpose and, therefore, is engaged in full-time work of and unto God. I can be just as worshipful if I become a medical doctor, an attorney, a professor, or a farmer, as if I become a minister of the gospel. This is highly significant, particularly because of the shift in the view of work in the general culture which has taken place as a consequence of the shift in worldviews.

A History of the View of Work in Western Civilization: A Form of Worship to a Form of Slavery

What has happened to the view of work in Western civilization? As we pursue that question briefly, we need to recognize that the economic question is, ultimately, a political question, which is, ultimately, an intellectual/philosophical question, which is, ultimately, a theological question. One's theology will, ultimately, drive one's economics as, indeed, it will drive everything else.

With the shift to Rationalism (1600s-1800s), work came to be viewed, not as a form of worship of and unto God as had largely been the case up to that time in the West under the influence of Biblical Christianity, but as a means of conforming with the so-called laws of nature. Accordingly, it was not long until it was widely assumed that a person whose work conformed with the laws of nature would thereby profit, and as one profited everyone would profit. Gradually, we began to think of work as an end in itself for individuals, first in pursuit of profitability, then for self-aggrandizement. Many libertarians today continue to claim that self-interest, that is, what benefits me, will benefit everyone. Finally, we slipped into workaholism, if only inadvertently, absolutizing work, indeed, worshipping work! This is debilitating.

Worse yet, as we moved from Rationalism through Romanticism/Transcendentalism (1770s-1860s) and on to Process Philosophy (1870s-present), we found ourselves in a world of relativity. In a world of relativity, work, like everything else, loses any ultimate meaning, purpose, or significance. We have only subjectivity, relativity, and probability. Consequently, the basic objective becomes that of doing as little work as possible for as much as one can get. We are reduced to the line of least resistance. Don't fall into that mentality, my friends! In other words, we seek to escape work because it has no ultimate meaning, purpose, or significance. Something, of course, must be substituted for work, and that is play or recreation, which becomes an end in itself. Unhappily, all of this renders everyone in their thinking and ultimately in their practice parasitic. No nation or civilization can long survive given such a procedure.

Once again, we must always be reminded that the economic issue is ultimately a political issue which is ultimately an intellectual/philosophical issue which is always a theological issue. The reason we are in such straits economically today (not just in the United States, but globally) is that we have the wrong theology, not the wrong economics. Yes, we have the wrong economics, but it flows from the wrong theology. In the final analysis, if we do not begin and end with God, we will simply not be able to work sufficiently to make productive use of creation to the extent of sustaining our existing standard of living, let alone achieve a rising standard of living.

Wealth or Poverty?

The Bible, as we noted earlier, is made up of interlocking propositions. We are told by God (paraphrased): ***Seek first God and His kingdom and everything that is needed will be added unto you.***[4] He promises to provide, not all that is wanted, but all that is needed. That is a proposition. If we fulfill the first part of the proposition, God will fulfill the last. Therefore, it follows that a person who works as a form of worship of and unto God will be a productive and successful person, someone whose services are in demand. One of my professors used to say, "Be careful what you want; you may get it," a warning worth heeding.

Accordingly, I do not believe that it is possible for a Biblical Christian to be in a state of perpetual poverty—it matters not when the Biblical Christian lived, or where. We are speaking here of perpetual poverty, not momentary need, because God may ask us to give away everything we have. Or, He may take us through circumstances to make us aware that we are totally dependent upon Him and that we should be grateful to Him. He may allow economic persecution. In general, however, Biblical Christianity produces wealth, not poverty. This, indeed, is evidenced in the history of individuals, nations, and civilizations. If we work as a form of worship of and unto God—it matters not when we live or where we live—we will be productive and our services will be in demand.

Caring for Those Who are Unable to Work

What about those people who cannot work, that is, those who are not gainfully employable? Please note that we are not talking about people who can work but refuse to work. In fact, in the holy commonwealth established by the Puritans, a significant distinction was made between these two groups.

In Puritan America one of the most severe punishments was the punishment meted out to people who could work but would not do so. Of course, the naturalist historians, sociologists, economists, and psychologists, given their presuppositions, do not understand such punishment. They surmise that the Puritans must have been trying to make up for a shortage of labor! Not so. The Puritans were attempting to be Biblical and, for them, work was a form of worship of and unto God. *"Six days shalt thou labor..."* (Exodus 20:9 KJV)[5] Therefore, a person who could work but would not do so was engaged in blasphemy and if blasphemy were to be permitted, it would not be possible to have Biblical Christian order and society. One of the diversity of punishments used by the Puritans in such a case was to make very widely known that here was a person who was lazy, who would not work. Severe punishment was considered imperative.

Punishment, by the way, was not viewed by the Puritans as an end in itself, as the naturalist historians would have us believe. They were not perfect for, of course, there is no perfection in this age, but they viewed punishment as being of God and as being a means to the end of the repentance [changing direction] of the person. If the person repented genuinely, then everyone was to accept such and proceed as if the person had never erred. In fact, the Puritans enjoyed significant success with this procedure.

Today, of course, we do not believe in repentance, so all we do is gossip about a person. Instead of accepting someone's repentance and forgetting a repented wrong, we continue to gossip about the fault as long as we think about the individual. This is horrendous! We do not actually confront people. If you hear that so and so is running out on his wife, confront him! Then, if he is repentant, forgive him! All we do, however, is talk and talk, and we never really confront sin. The Puritans confronted sin, but they also were very forgiving of the repentant person. This is a tremendous Biblical Christian procedure.

Christian Charity: The Love of God Flowing through Man

What, then, Biblically speaking, are we to do with people who cannot work: the maimed, the blind, the halt, the old, the diseased? The Biblical view is that they are the responsibility of the Christian community. This has been fundamental to any Christian society that has ever existed: those who cannot work are the responsibility of the Christian community. Other people, given their depravity, are often wallowing in themselves, whereas many Christians are able to be genuinely concerned for others, including those who are not gainfully employable.

We should understand, of course, that there are disadvantaged people who, nevertheless, not only can work but want to work. Thus, one of the first objectives of Biblical Christian charitable endeavor is to assist handicapped people in being able to obtain gainful employment. Indeed, some of the most productive people who have ever lived have been handicapped people, often because they are grateful for the opportunity to work and are willing to persist in overcoming obstacles. These individuals can make a tremendous contribution to productivity if they are permitted to do so. We do not want to deny them the privilege of worshipping God.

What, however, do we do with those people who simply are not gainfully employable, people who cannot work because of their condition? They are the responsibility, Biblically speaking, of the Christian community in a procedure which was once known as Biblical Christian *charity*. We still have the terminology deriving from this, though we have largely lost sight of the intellectual content. That terminology is **tithes and offerings**.

Everything belongs to God, but we evidence that by giving to Him the tithe, the first fruits, the first ten percent of our productivity. This, indeed, belongs to God. There should never need to be a sermon on tithing for the Biblical Christian. I have even heard such ridiculous statements as, "It pays to tithe," which is like Benjamin Franklin's, "Honesty is the best policy." It pays to tithe? Perhaps in a sense it pays to tithe, which is to say that it does not pay to steal and, particularly, it does not pay to steal from God (and all stealing is stealing from God in any case). It is true that we have known people who began to prosper tremendously once they began to tithe. We do not tithe, however, to gain wealth, but to honor God our Creator. We owe God everything, but we demonstrate our gratitude to Him, our Landlord and King, by joyously giving Him the first fruits of our labors, the ten percent.

The Biblical Christian procedure, then, has been to go beyond the tithe and give offerings. Traditionally, in the West, these offerings have largely been used to care for those who could not work. Thus, we have had

Biblical Christian charity. This has often been provided through the institutional church, though we recognize that the church, as the invisible body of Christ, is not necessarily the visible church, though, hopefully, there will be overlapping.

Where is Biblical Christian charity today? Sadly, we have substituted the welfare state for Biblical Christian charity and we have substituted confiscatory taxes for offerings. There is nothing wrong with taxes, that is, revenue raising taxes for the purpose of maintaining government for the orderly procedure of man in a fallen world, but there is everything wrong with confiscatory taxation which is designed for the redistribution of wealth. God-in-Christ indicated that taxes are of God when he stated: "Render to Caeser the things that are Caesar's" (Mark 12:17 KJV)[6] He did not, however, say, Render unto Caesar everything.

What we have done is to have substituted confiscatory taxation for offerings—to the extent that by the time one pays one's tithe (the ten percent) and one's confiscatory taxes, it takes a great deal of faith to give an offering in the modern Western world.

Much more significant, however, than the substitution of confiscatory taxation for offerings is our substitution of the welfare state system for Biblical Christian charity. Many people have argued against the welfare state on purely utilitarian grounds or purely economic grounds, arguing that the welfare state does not work well. They conclude that it becomes something of an ill-fare state and, indeed, it is poverty feeding upon itself.

The Biblical Christian recognizes that, although such may be true (which is without question the case because wealth is sucked out of the private sector and placed under government control where it is used less productively, non-productively or even anti-productively), it is ultimately beside the point. The economic issue is a political issue, which is an intellectual/philosophical issue, which is a theological issue. The Biblical Christian is unalterably opposed to the welfare state system because it is by its very nature diabolical.

Why so? Let us examine the welfare system. The person who is the recipient of that which comes from the welfare state system is not drawn to God but is drawn towards the state as his or her source of sustainment. From a Biblical perspective, this is idolatry, the substitution of any created thing for God. Indeed, it goes beyond idolatry to blasphemy as the state deliberately interposes itself between God and man. This is diabolical because people are compelled to worship the state as their sovereign, as their Lord. Consequently, as we have said, an ever-larger percentage of the wealth is sucked up by the absolutized state. Thus, the Biblical Christian opposes the welfare state system.

Let us also take a look at the other side of the coin. That person who is the recipient of that which comes through Biblical Christian charity is not drawn to any individual, or any group of individuals, or even to the institution, usually the church, through which charity flows, but is, rather, drawn to God as his or her source or sustainer. Why? The reason for this is that, knowing ourselves, we know that man is by nature selfish, and we know that people will not voluntarily share of their possessions unless they are moved upon by a higher power. Thus, the recipient of Biblical Christian charity is drawn to the love of God and, therefore, to God as his or her source and sustainer.

The word **charity**, by the way, is a very good word. We no longer understand that word because it has been redefined as a result of the presuppositions antithetical to Biblical Christianity which have come to prevail. Charity simply means "the love of God flowing through man."

There is another good reason why charity should be administered through the church rather than through the state. The church, and here we are talking about the institutional church, is theoretically made up of those who are redeemed and who recognize their responsibility under God for those who cannot work. Therefore, charity is much less likely to be corrupted if administered through the church rather than the state, because the state is made up of both the redeemed and the non-redeemed. Thus, indeed, there is a much greater likelihood of corruption should charity be administered through the state. Even in the case of church administered charity, of course, there must be constant vigilance toward avoiding corruption, as there is no perfection in this age.

A good friend of mine, the Biblical Christian economist, Professor Tom Rose[7], who taught for years at Grove City College (PA), made a telling point a few years ago while lecturing a second time for our division-sponsored lecture series at Indiana Wesleyan University. He noted, using the United States as an example, that if all professing Christians in the United States would simply pay their tithes, the church would have far more than enough to care for all those in need of charity in this country! We would not need the welfare state system! This is so significant. It is true many times over and again. This does not even mention offerings! As we move away from Biblical Christianity, however, we have a downward spiral of productive endeavor and an exacerbation of the whole issue of poverty.

There is, my friends, a Biblical Christian view of economics. The answer is not the state, nor is it the market. The answer is the recovery of a Biblical view and practice of economics under a sovereign God.

CONSEQUENCES OF THE INSTITUTIONALIZATION OF THE BIBLICAL CHRISTIAN WORLDVIEW

What were the consequences of the Reformation, that is, the most recent reaffirmation, restatement, and reapplication of the Biblical Christian worldview? They cannot be overstated. Certainly, Western civilization would not exist as it exists today were it not for the work of God through what we are here calling the Reformation.

First, we would reiterate that the Reformation, as it labored to restore a Christocentric church, broke the back of ecclesiastical absolutism, returning the institutionalized church, both Catholic and Protestant, toward the pattern of divided authority and diffused power which, as we have discussed, is characteristic of the Biblical Christian view of the institutions.

Additionally, as a consequence of the Reformation, the restated and reapplied Biblical Christianity would become intellectually dominant in

Europe, particularly in northern Europe, temporarily derailing rationalistic Renaissance Humanism. It virtually obliterated Renaissance Humanism in the north of Europe, and it temporarily derailed Renaissance Humanism in central and southern Europe. Renaissance Humanism would reappear a little more than a century later in the form of Enlightenment Rationalism.

The timing of this was highly significant. In 1492, only twenty-five years earlier (as a consequence of a Biblically revitalized Christianity which had swept across the Iberian peninsula in antithesis to the religion of Mohammed), the Western Hemisphere had been discovered by the West. Consequently, the restatement and reapplication of Biblical Christianity which came to dominate, first, the north of Europe and, then, North America, would subsequently come to dominate the Western Hemisphere, and the Western Hemisphere would become the dominant global force.

Biblical Christianity became the dominant global influence, and has continued to have significant influence through the last half millennium. Indeed, it would not be possible to imagine what the world would have been like during the last five hundred years had it not been for this reality: the relative order, community, liberty, justice, charity, and productive activity which has resulted from the grace of God flowing through Western/American civilization. To the extent we live and function effectively in the West today, we do so on the basis of that which God established through the Reformation.

The Reformation of the sixteenth century is the most recent restatement and reapplication of Biblical Christianity and the Biblical Christian Worldview. It was not the first statement thereof nor, as our Lord tarries, will it be the final statement thereof. It was, however, the most recent restatement.

To be more explicit, in North America, the Reformation provided the **basis** for an entire civilization: American civilization, which later came to be the United States of America. The reason for this was that North America was largely settled by Biblical Christian groups (some of whom were fleeing from persecution). The foremost of these, in terms of Biblical Christian leadership, were the Puritans. The Puritans were Biblical Christians. They were seeking to implement the way and will of God in all of life. Indeed, in my analysis, while they were not perfect, the Puritans in North America went further in implementing the way and will of God than any other group of people before or since to date.

There is good reason for this. Wherever Biblical Christianity has come to flourish, it has necessarily been forced to admix with what was already present. The Puritans in North America, however, had a relatively free hand to implement the way and will of God in all of life. There were only a relatively few natives or aborigines as they were called—not even 100,000 of them—east of the Mississippi River. Some of them were converted to Biblical Christianity. Others, unhappily, were exterminated by the ravages of European disease or in fighting one another. Still others went West. Excepting for this relatively small handful of aborigines, the Puritans were relatively free to implement the way and will of God in what they called New England, and they did so more extensively and more intensively than any other group of which we are aware.

Of course, in addition to the Puritans, a number of other groups came to the English colonies in North America in the seventeenth century (1600s). Most came as Biblical Christians in order to have a relatively free hand to implement the way and will of God in all of life. This was true, not only of the Pilgrims, but also of the Dutch Reformed, the Presbyterians, the French Huguenots and even, to a lesser degree, the Anglicans and the Quakers. This is very significant.

Accordingly, Biblical Christianity, which prevailed in the English colonies for several generations, would supply the base for an entire civilization or nation: American civilization and American government. This had never occurred in all of history, and the world has been blessed as a result of this Biblical base. Again, it did not issue in perfection for, as we have said, there never has been and never will be perfection in this age and, moreover, it came to be compromised by rationalism, but it did issue in a substantial difference. It accounts for the blessings which have flowed from American civilization, including relative order, community, liberty, justice, charity, and productive activity.[8]

It needs to be recognizd that the Puritans of North America have been given a very bad "press" by the naturalist historians. Indeed, we would be surprised were it otherwise because, given their presuppositions, it is not possible for the naturalists to understand the Puritans, let alone represent them justly in their histories. Presupposing as they do that Biblical Christianity is based on a mere superstition, they cannot, obviously, credit the Puritans for having produced the blessings which have flowed from American civilization.

Unhappily, to the extent that they have understood them, they have often falsified their depiction of the Puritans in North America. It is always a temptation, if one cannot win one's argument "on the level," finally to resort to deception to make one's point. Thus, we have had a misrepresentation, disinformation, and falsification of the Puritans.

Of course, in our zeal to reinterpret, we must be careful not to swing from one extreme to the other. We must ever recognize that there is not perfection and there never has been. Nevertheless, a restated and reapplied Biblical Christianity, as was significantly the case in the English colonies in North America and, particularly, in Puritan New England, makes a profound difference, as it did with respect to American civilization.

NOTES

1. Holl, Karl, <u>The Cultural Significance of the Reformation</u>, Meridian Books, Cleveland, OH; The World Publishing Company, 1959, p. 50-51.
2. Bible Reference, *Acts 17:24-28* (KJV): The God who made the world and everything in it… made every nation of men, that they should inhabit the whole earth; and he determined the times set for them and the exact places where they should live. God did this so that men would seek him and perhaps reach out for him and find him, though he is not far from each one of us. **"For in him we live and move and have our being."** As some of your own poets have said, 'We are his offspring.' [emphasis added]
3. Biblical Reference: *Luke 10:7 (KJV)*: "And in the same house remain, eating and drinking such things as they give: **for the laborer is worthy of his hire**." Paul, writing to Timothy (*1 Timothy 5:17-18*), says, "The elders who direct the affairs of the church well are worthy of double honor, especially those whose work is preaching and teaching." For the Scripture says, 'Do not muzzle the ox while it

is treading out the grain,' and 'The worker deserves his wages.'"

4. Bible Reference: *Matthew 6:31-33* (KJV): "Therefore take no thought, saying, What shall we eat? or, What shall we drink? or, Wherewithal shall we be clothed? (For after all these things do the Gentiles seek:) for your heavenly Father knoweth that ye have need of all these things. **But seek ye first the kingdom of God**, and his righteousness; **and all these things shall be added unto you.**" [emphasis added]

5. Bible Reference: See Exodus 20:9 (KJV)

6. Bible Reference: This account is related in three of the gospels, in *Matthew 22, Mark 12, and Luke 20.* "Then Jesus said to them, 'Give to Caesar what is Caesar's and to God what is God's.' And they were amazed at him." (*Mark 12:17*)

7. Bibliographical Note: Professor Tom Rose, who has taught economics for years at Grove City College, has written excellent books on Biblical Christian economics, including a textbook: <u>Economics: Principles and Policy from a Christian Perspective</u>, Mercer, PA: American Enterprise Publications, c1986 [www.biblicaleconomics.com].

8. <u>Author's Bibliographical Note</u>: Alexis de Tocqueville (1805-1859) bears witness to the dynamic Christian base of American civilization and the ordered liberty of the society in his classic <u>Democracy in America</u>, 2 volumes (1835, 1840). Other books on this topic recommended by Dr. Martin include Russell Kirk's <u>The Roots of American Order</u> (Malibu, CA: Pepperdine Univ. Press, 1974) and Allen Carden's excellent <u>Puritan Christianity in America: Religion and Life in Seventeenth Century Massachusetts</u> (Grand Rapids, MI: Baker Book House, 1990).

4 THE RATIONALIST WORLDVIEW (ENLIGHTENMENT FORMULATION 1600–1800)

On John Locke:

"How does knowledge arise? Have we, as some good people suppose, innate ideas as, for example, of right and wrong, and God—ideas inherent in the mind from birth, prior to all experience?...

But Locke, good Christian though he was... could not accept these suppositions; he announced, quietly, that all our knowledge comes from appearance and through our senses—that 'there is nothing in the mind except what was first in the senses.'"[1]

The Rationalist worldview, which emerged out of the so-called Enlightenment, is the second prevailing worldview which we will discuss. As a part of the intellectual tradition which begins and ends with man, it stands in contrast to and in conflict with the Biblical Christian worldview and Biblical Christianity.

The Enlightenment is dated variously. Most scholars would agree that it was most certainly under way by 1650 and that it continued in its intensity through the following century. A wider expanse of 1600 to 1800 is preferred here but, admittedly, those dates are arbitrary.

EMERGENCE OF THE RATIONALIST WORLDVIEW

The Enlightenment had roots in Greek "rationalism," scholasticism, and Renaissance-Humanism. Those who subscribed to this worldview were called Rationalists. They believed that God is rational and that God created man to be rationalistic.

The Rationalists of the seventeenth and early eighteenth centuries (1600s-1750s) energetically promoted a significant epistemological shift. They believed that the unrestricted exercise of reason in the search of truth would lead to a better world, and that no authority or religion should be allowed to impose a limit on it. Accordingly, they attempted to use the many scientific and technological advancements produced at that time to discredit faith in Biblical revelation.

Faith vs. Reason

The Rationalists, of course—as do those who propagate their views today—heralded this epistemological shift from faith to reason as an incontestably beneficial one. In their view, a person lives either 1) on the basis of faith, in which case one is not thereby exercising any reason, or 2) on the basis of reason, in which case one is not thereby exercising any faith. Given these two alternatives, any thoughtful person, obviously, would opt to live on the basis of reason.

The Biblical Christian, however, understands that this view of faith versus reason is mythological. It is a dichotomy (once again, a false division) because the epistemological question is never *faith versus reason* but, rather, it is always faith-in-<u>A</u> versus faith-in-<u>B</u>. Therefore, we understand that the shift brought about by the Enlightenment was an epistemological shift from faith-in-Biblical revelation to faith-in-reason (that is, the human intellect) which, when absolutized, brings us to Rational*ism*.

Parenthetically, although not many struggle with this today, it is important to note that, when we speak epistemologically of faith-in-Biblical revelation, we do not mean that the Bible is the final screen—God is. We do not absolutize the Bible [in the sense of viewing it in isolation as sufficient apart from the Trinitarian God]; we absolutize God.

Additionally, we need to reaffirm that faith in Biblical revelation does not diminish man's intellectual activity relative to this age, but rather establishes and encourages, even mandates it. The Biblical view is that God created the heavens and the earth and gave man dominion over creation, calling upon man to exercise godly exploration, knowledge, and usage thereof.

Copernicus (1473-1543): Discrediting Faith in Revelation

The Rationalists used scientific and technological accomplishments to discredit faith in Biblical revelation. In this regard, they leaned particularly hard on the conclusions of Copernicus[2] (1473-1543) who, as we know, was the astronomer whose work had shifted the Western mind from a geo- to a helio-centric astronomic view. His views had been published in 1543. For the Rationalists, this shift from the view that the earth is the center of the universe (geocentricity) to the view that the sun is the center of the universe (heliocentricity), suggested that what happened on earth could no longer have direct supernatural causation and explanation but was simply a byproduct of the motions of the heavenly bodies.

We should pause before pursuing this to ask the logical question, "Was Copernicus correct? Is the center of the universe at a point within or near the sun?" The Biblical response is immediate, "Absolutely not." Nobody can declare anything to be the center without seeing the whole and, obviously, Copernicus did not see the totality of what is and, therefore, he was not absolutely right. Just as there was a pre-Copernican astronomy, followed by a Copernican astronomy, so there will most certainly be, as our Lord tarries, a post-Copernican astronomy. Only God, who sees everything, could definitively declare what is the center of things. Therefore, we will always have modifications to any hypothesis which is spun from the human intellect.

Reckoning with Infinity and Eternity

Indeed, we can recognize that, Biblically, the system is not one in which the sun is the center. Rather, the Biblical system is one in which the center is everywhere present and the circumference is non-existent. Two realities are illustrative of that truth. They are known as **eternity** and **infinity**. Eternity is the reality that I can begin, as it were, at any given point and go "outering" and never get there. Infinity is the recognition that I can begin at a given point and go "innering," as it were, and never get there.

The scientific community is up against both of these realities. Telescopically, we peel back galaxy after galaxy after galaxy, only to recognize that there are even more galaxies to be discovered. Microscopically, we penetrate world after world after world, only to recognize that there are within those worlds additional worlds. Thus, we move from the molecular to the atomic to the sub-atomic and so on. In fact, given infinity, one can play philosophical games, "proving" philosophically, for example, that, given infinity, it is impossible to get a spoonful of ice-cream into one's mouth, all space being infinitely divisible. My only observation has consistently been, "Thank God we do not live philosophically!" In other words, beginning and ending with the human intellect, there are limitations.

It is necessary to add one final comment concerning Copernicus, whose <u>On the Revolutions of the Heavenly Spheres</u> was published in 1543, the year of his death. It used to be thought that Copernicus did not want his views published until after he died because he was fearful of being prosecuted and persecuted by the church. It turned out that nothing could have been further from the truth. There is always intense pressure to conform, and I submit that the most intense pressure to conform is that which takes place within the so-called intellectual community. We are suggesting that he had been intimidated, not by ecclesiastical absolutism, but by Renaissance-Humanism.

Sir Isaac Newton (1642-1727) and the Potential of the Human Intellect

The brilliant observations of Sir Isaac Newton[3] (1642-1727) concerning the motions of the heavenly bodies convinced many that the universe could be explained ultimately on the basis of the human intellect.

When Newton came along a century and a quarter after Copernicus and made penetrating observations about the motions of the heavenly bodies, the Rationalists, building on Newton absolutized, concluded that, just as Newton had discovered the so-called laws of nature governing the motions of the heavenly bodies, so man, by exercising his reason rightly, could discover the laws of nature governing all of life including human relationships.

The Rationalists, however, failed to understand something which Newton understood very well. Newton was, without question, one of the most gifted intellects to have lived and one of the most outstanding (if not the most outstanding) of the mathematicians. He would never, however, have absolutized any of his observations, including the so-called law of gravity. In fact, Newton, on the basis of his penetrating observations, was so impressed with creation, indeed, the wonder of creation, that he concluded how much greater the Creator must be. Accordingly, he spent the last twenty years of his life—an entire generation—studying the Bible and theology to learn more about God. The Rationalist community has long since observed, in effect, "What a waste! Think how much closer Newton could have brought us to an understanding and mastery of the universe if he had continued to employ his brilliant intellect in contemplation of the motions of the heavenly bodies."

John Locke (1632-1704): Right Reason and Natural Law

John Locke[4] was a Rationalist. He made sociological application of Newton absolutized and held that, just as Copernicus and Newton had presumably discovered the laws of nature governing the heavenly bodies, so man, by exercising his reason rightly (and these are the very words of John Locke: *right reason*), could discover the **laws of nature** governing all of life including human relationships. With others of his day, he was fired by the hope that, if those laws could be discovered and observed, the result would be increasing order and harmony, if not perfection—certainly a worthy objective toward which to direct human endeavor.

I have often been asked by students to evaluate the claim made by a number of well-meaning contemporary Christian groups that nature's God as referred to by the Rationalists is, for all intents and purposes, the same as the God of the Bible, or that nature is the same, in effect, as Creation. If such individuals would read for themselves Locke's <u>An Essay Concerning Human Understanding</u> (1690), they would readily see that his source of knowledge and truth was the human intellect, not divine revelation. Of course, unlike the later Rationalists such as Rousseau, Locke was functioning in a setting in which Biblical Christianity still had significant influence, which is reflected in his thinking and vocabulary. Yet, the difference between Locke and the later Rationalists is a difference in degree, not in kind.

Focus on This Age: Right Reason, Not Revelation

For the Rationalist, then, God had started everything but then had gone wandering off. Inasmuch as God's creation was complete, He no longer had any need to be involved in His creation, including man; therefore, He has no relationship with His creation, including man. If God, after creating man, has no further interest in man, man should have no further interest in God. Man should abandon his needless preoccupation with God, his other-worldly fixation, and apply his God-given abilities to discovering and learning about this present existence. Thus, the focus should be "right reason," not divine revelation. The focus should be on the human intellect, not on a presupposed revelation.

Ontological Shift: Natural Theism to Deism

The Rationalist worldview is based, first of all, on a new epistemology, a shift from the utilization of reason grounded in a (presumably) rational divine revelation to a use of reason grounded in the (presumably) rational human intellect. Given this *epistemological* shift, the Rationalists slip *ontologically* into a deism. Deism is the view that God started everything but then went wandering off like the old Swiss watchmaker, never to have further relationship with His creation, including man. Thus, for the Rationalists, God is *Alpha* but he is **not** *Omega*.

If we stop to consider this, however, we can see immediately where rationalism will ultimately end up. If God is not Alpha and Omega, He cannot, ultimately, be Alpha. We see that, inherent in deism is non-theism. Deism is simply a way station from Biblical theism to non-theism.

What, then, is the Rationalist view of the Bible? For the Rationalist, the Bible is useful instruction in the moral laws of nature. It is not to be considered as divine revelation; there is no such thing. Such a view would be irrational. The Bible was a noble attempt, albeit an incomplete attempt, to discover the laws of nature which should govern human conduct.

Who, then, was Christ? Christ, for the Rationalist, was the great, if not the greatest, moral teacher, a brilliant intellect who was able to discover a great deal about the laws of Nature which should govern human conduct. Christ was not, however (as He and others such as Luke, John, and Paul had contended), God-in-Christ. That, once again, would be irrational.

Several observations from a Biblical Christian perspective may be made at this point. First of all, it is from Rationalism that we gained the concept of **morality**. The Biblical Christian does not believe in morality. Someone will suggest, "Wait a minute. Does that imply that a Biblical Christian believes in immorality?" No. The Biblical Christian believes in **truth**. Morality is man-made or man-ascertained truth. It derives from the Enlightenment, not from Biblical Christianity, and by its very nature morality is relative!

Therefore, it is a matter, not of morality, but of *truth* versus *error* (or the lie), *righteousness* (or godliness) versus *unrighteousness* (or ungodliness).

A second observation, which saddens me, is a heavy charge which requires explanation. It is that the Rationalists of the eighteenth century

(1700s) took the Bible more seriously and attempted to live the Bible more consistently than most Bible-believing Christians—including Evangelical Christians—do today. How is this possible? Although the Rationalists rejected the Bible as divine revelation because, as we have said, for them the idea of revelation was irrational, yet they believed that the Bible should be universally applied. To them the Bible was morality. It was man-ascertained truth. To the extent that morality had become known, it should be universally applied. Accordingly, they studied the Bible. They took the Bible seriously, and they attempted to live on the basis of the morals found in the Bible.

Many individuals exemplified this, one of whom was Benjamin Franklin (1706-1790), a very well known Rationalist. Indeed, he was the best known person alive in the West during his lifetime with the exception of Voltaire. Franklin was The Philosopher, Dr. Benjamin Franklin.

The reason that the eighteenth century Rationalists took the Bible more seriously than Evangelicals do today is that although Evangelicals retain the belief that the Bible is divine revelation, they fail, if only inadvertently, to recognize that God applies to all of life. Of course, over time, following the human intellect, the Rationalists will be carried beyond the Bible, and the conclusions they add to the Bible will ultimately come to take precedence over the Bible.

For the Rationalist, man no longer needed the way of salvation described in the Bible. Man was no longer viewed as incapable of his own salvation or dependent upon divine grace. Rather, salvation is of this age and takes place when men discover and are willing to live by the laws of nature. If everyone would recognize and live thereby, there would be, accordingly, perfection. Their deistic God played only an indirect role in the Rationalists' view of salvation. God had given man reason, and not the Word.

The final observation to be made is that the Rationalists were half right. They argued that this age is significant. They were interested in applying their world and life view to every area and to every institution of this age. The unity of truth and the determination to find and apply truth to all of life is Biblical. The only problem was that the Rationalists, if only inadvertently, absolutized this age. Because they had confined themselves to a rationalistic epistemology, they had slipped into a deistic ontology and had cut God away from this age, even as they had cut Him away from the totality of what-is. They had, as it were, absolutized the dominion mandate. Indeed, as we have said, the Biblical view of man includes the view of man as king under God, charged by God with the so-called *dominion mandate*. This age is significant under God, though it is never to be absolutized: God is.

PRESUPPOSITIONS OF THE RATIONALIST WORLDVIEW

The rationalists' triune presuppositions were and are as follows:

- the inherent goodness of man
- the perfectibility of man
- the inevitability of progress.

We will look at each more closely. Recognizing that nothing can be understood in a vacuum in a fallen world, we understand that it is not possible to know what we believe and why without simultaneously knowing what we do not believe and why. Consequently, it is not possible to understand Rationalism without understanding Biblical Christianity and vice versa. The same is true today with respect to the religion of non-theism. The religion of non-theism prevails, but very few of the practitioners understand their own position.

We recall that the starting point for the Biblical Christian worldview is God. The primary presupposition is that God and His Kingdom are spiritual, that God and His rule involve the totality of what is, that God and His Kingdom are triumphant over Satan, sin, and death on the basis of God's finished work in Christ, and that God and His Kingdom are coming to reign in full power and glory over the totality of what-is. God is Alpha and Omega. The beginning and the terminal point is God.

We also recall that, Biblically speaking, man is depraved which, again, does not mean that man is insignificant, inconsequential, or irresponsible or that he is programmed, determined, predetermined, or predestined but, rather, that man by taking thought or action (individually or corporately) cannot deliver himself from the dilemma into which he was born. He is dependent upon the work and will of God for his deliverance.

Now, in contrast and in conflict with Biblical Christianity, the Rationalist begins and ends with man. He does not begin and end with God, but with man because the Rationalist's God is at best deistic, at best Alpha, never Omega. Man, accordingly, is left to his own devices and, thus, the primary presupposition is the inherent goodness of man.

We need to clarify, however, what is meant by **the inherent goodness of man**, because the Rationalists did not mean that man was automatically, inevitably, or irresistably good, that is, that man could do no evil. What was meant by the inherent goodness of man was that man, starting from himself alone (autonomously), had the cognitive ability, by taking thought, to come to a knowledge of the truth.

If, then, man would take thought and exercise his intellect rightly, he could know, and as he learned knowledge and truth and acted on the basis thereof (and, presumably, as he learned knowledge and truth, he would act in accordance therewith), he would perfect himself and, ultimately, there would be human perfection.

Hence, the **perfectibility of man** flows logically from the inherent goodness of man; and the perfectibility of man will ultimately produce the **inevitability of progress**. These, then, are the triune presuppositions of the Rationalist's faith.

Thus, for the Rationalist, men are not depraved. *Adam's race* is not divided into the redeemed and the non-redeemed (those who have been reconciled to God in Christ and those who have not). Rather, man is inherently good and people are divided into the enlightened and the unenlightened (those who recognize that man is inherently good as defined above and those who have failed to recognize such).

This is where the term Enlightenment emerges. In fact, out of the Rationalist faith came the expression, "Let me enlighten you." (If I ever use that expression, please command what is closest to you and send it in my direction with considerable force that I might be awakened, rudely if necessary, from my intellectual stupor.) From the Biblical perspective, we can be enlightened only by the One who alone is Light. The Rationalists, on the other hand, presuppose a naturalistic enlightenment. Man, as created by a deistic God, can achieve enlightenment autonomously.

RATIONALIST ANSWERS TO THE PHILOSOPHICAL QUESTIONS, SUMMARIZED

Thus, the rationalists subscribed to a **deistic supernatural ontology**, that God theoretically started everything but then went wandering off never to have further relationship with His creation including man; a **rationalistic epistemology**, that man knows on the basis of his own intellect, his own cognitive ability; that by taking thought he can come to a knowledge of the truth; a **humanistic axiology**, that man and particularly the awesome potential of his intellect is the ultimate value; and a **Kingdom of Earth teleology**, that some yet-to-be-discovered *natural* force is in ultimate control and determinative of direction in time.

NOTES

1. Durant, Will, The Story of Philosophy, NY: New York, Pocket Books, Inc., 1926, p. 256.
2. Biographical Note: Nicholas Copernicus (1473-1543) was born in Prussian Poland and educated at Krakow, Poland, and Bologna, Italy. He became the *canon* (from *canonicus*, "one living under a rule," the name for a clergyman belonging to the chapter or the staff of a cathedral or collegiate church) of the cathedral at Frauenburg, where he served many years. His great work, On the Revolutions of the Heavenly Spheres was completed about 1530, but was published in 1543.

3. Biographical Note: Sir Isaac Newton (1642-1727), English philosopher and mathematician, wrote <u>Principia</u> in 1687, proposing the idea of universal gravitation. Newton served as Lucasian professor of mathematics at Cambridge University 1669-1727 and as president of the Royal Society from 1703 until his death in 1727. The full title of his work is <u>Mathematical Principles of Natural Philosophy</u>.

4. Author's Note: John Locke did not believe that the Bible is the epistemological authority and the basis of understanding. Although he was *dichotomistic*, he was in terms of the weight of his work in light of the prevailing views of his day a rationalist. He is not as *consistently* rationalist as Rousseau 1712-1778 or as Marx 1818-1883, but he was nevertheless rationalistic. The dilema is that we are all prone (and we must continuously work hard to avoid this) to read back into history that which we believe, attempting to identify those people who imbibed such, and then, if only inadvertently, absolutizing those people. We must be careful not to do that with any person. In terms of the perspective presented in this book, for example, one might be inclined to absolutize an Augustine or a Luther. However, these men were not perfect; nor was their work. Augustine and Luther were clearly Biblical (unlike Locke) in that they believed the Bible to be the authority, not the human intellect. Moreover, they were very rational, but they were not rationalistic. However, they were not perfect.

5 THE RATIONALIST WORLDVIEW: INSTITUTIONAL STRUCTURE AND PROCEDURE

On Voltaire:

"The Deists' attacks on revelation... had been calm and moderate in England, but in France they were bitter and impassioned...[Voltaire] was [w]itty, erudite, and irascible, he ridiculed Christianity, attacking it as a system of absurdities. In his estimation, Christ was a religious fanatic, the Bible was the work of ignorant men, and miracles should be dismissed as simple falsehoods."[1]

For the Rationalists, whose hope was in enlightenment, which institution would we expect to be primary in terms of the institutional structure and procedure? Education. Indeed, there is ultimately nothing higher than education. The worst "sin," then, is ignorance. Accordingly, those who are the most highly committed to Rationalism, the Rationalist "missionaries" so to speak, take upon themselves the task of delivering people from ignorance. Here, however, we omit discussion of education to focus on the areas with which we are concerned in this book.

AREA OF LAW

The Rationalists, with presupposed nature as their starting point, shifted to the view of a presupposed natural law and concluded that all law is to be based upon the **laws of nature** or principles drawn therefrom. If, again, everyone would observe and practice the laws of nature in the whole of life, there would be, not only increasing order and harmony but, ultimately, perfection.

At the time of the early Rationalists, these natural laws, comprising a mechanistic system, were deemed, like Biblical law, to be immutable and indestructible. They were absolute. Therefore, the view of law in the West under the impact of the Enlightenment continued to presuppose immutable, indestructible law as it had under Biblical Christianity, but it was natural law, not the law of God.

It is worthy of note, however, that, although we do not yet shift from presupposed absolute law to presupposed relative law, we do have the relativization of law because natural law, as the product of the human imagination, is by its very nature relative. With Rationalism began the natural law jurisprudential procedure, which has a long history in Western civilization.

By the way, sadly, it is natural law, not Biblical law, which has been the American national legal foundation. American Christians who plan to serve in the legal profession need to reinterpret their way, not only out of sociological law back to natural law, but even out of Natural law to formulate a Biblical understanding of law. This is fundamental to enabling Christian lawyers to be reforming powers and influences in the legal profession. We do not, in other words, need Christians in law; we need Biblical Christian law.

CIVIL-SOCIAL AREA

In the area of civil society or government, the Rationalists believed that, just as every individual can and should learn and practice the so-called laws of nature in personal living and relationships, so man can and should contract to observe collectively the laws of nature in corporate or social relationship If this were done, it was believed, there would be ever increasing order, community, liberty, justice, charity, and productive activity, issuing ultimately, perhaps, in perfection.

A Social Contract (Democracy) Replaces the Holy Commonwealth

Thus came into being the **social contract** idea and what we call **democracy**. One of the most well known of the Rationalist civil-social theorists was John Locke (1632-1704). He believed that government was a creation of man who voluntarily exchanged his natural state for a civil state; this, of course, is a page right out of Enlightenment Rationalism.

This idea of democracy, and this needs to be repeated until it registers, does not flow from Biblical Christianity. That which flows from Biblical Christianity is, rather, the democratic procedure, characterized by divided authority, diffused power, and limited, responsible leadership in every area of life.

Nor, as those who have re-written history to fit their presuppositions have suggested, did democracy, as philosophically defined today, emerge from the ancient, Classical world. This is often taught today, but it is a reading back into history. Attempts to practice democracy and, even, the very idea thereof, are a derivative of the Enlightenment. Democracy never existed—even in theory—prior thereto. In fact, democracy was an imperative of the Enlightenment, because something had to be found to replace the holy commonwealth, which was not able to survive the cutting away of God from life. The idea of democracy would not have been possible had not Biblical Christianity intervened between the Classical period and the birth of the modern idea of democracy.

Once, when sharing this conclusion while teaching at Wheaton College, a student could no longer contain himself and all but interrupted his professor with the following observation: "There are three forms of government: government by one, a monarchy; government by a few, a plutocracy or an aristocracy; and government by the many, the people, the *demos*, a democracy." When he had finished, he was asked to repeat what he had said. Thinking his professor was a bit hard of hearing, he repeated himself. Finally, it was pointed out that all he had accomplished was an exercise in the art of counting which, however, does not succeed in addressing the nature of government, only its form.

However, even if we accept the superficial definition of democracy as government by the many rather than by a few or by one with respect to its form, we discover that, contrary to what we are often taught, democracy did not exist in the so-called Classical world, even in the most "enlightened" of the Greek city-states—the Athenian, even in its so-called Golden Age (461-429 B.C.). A person must take flight from rationality to reach such a conclusion. Neither so-called democracy nor the democratic procedure were followed.

As evidence, consider that the following groups were excluded from the civil-social process in ancient Athens, even during the Golden Age: first of all, the slaves (more than fifty percent of the population of ancient Athens, according to some estimates, were slaves). Secondly, the aliens or non-citizens, of whom there were many in the ancient city-states. Thirdly, the women. At least half of us will agree (and no invidious comparison is intended here) that if one excludes slaves, aliens, and women, one certainly does not have "government by the many." It is a myth.

Nature of Democracy: Government a Creation of Man, Not a Gift of God

This, however, is beside the point because democracy must be philosophically understood and defined. It does not have to do so much with the form of government as it does with the nature of government. That is, with democracy as derived from the Enlightenment, we shift from the holy commonwealth view of Biblical Christianity—that government is by God, of God, for man—to the view that government is of, for, and by man, or the people as it is usually expressed. In other words, instead of government being a gift of God for the orderly procedure of man in a fallen world, government comes to be viewed as a creation of man for the working out of his own happiness, in this case, on the basis of so-called indestructible, immutable, natural laws. Man ought to socially contract to observe collectively those laws in corporate relationship.

It is important to recognize that the view of the civil-social area which began with the Rationalists has far reaching implications for every area of life and every institution. Why? Because man is actually viewed as the author of government! This is a highly significant shift. If we presuppose that man is the creator of government, what will we ultimately and logically end up concluding? That man is the author and creator of every other institution, including, even, the church. Thus, the idea of democracy flowing out of rationalism comes to affect every institution. Indeed, the Biblical Christian, John Cotton (1584-1652), a Puritan clergyman, clearly recognized the nature of presupposed democracy. Once, while contending that God never meant for man to have democracy, he raised the penetrating question, "If the people be governors, who shall be governed?"[2]

The destructive influence of the myth of democracy which flowed out of the Rationalist worldview can readily be seen today on any institution we would like to trace. Let us take, for example, the foundational institution of marriage. Under the influence of the myth of democracy, even Evangelical Christians have largely abandoned the Biblical understanding of marriage.

The Biblical Christian to Rationalist View of Marriage

For the Biblical Christian, marriage is **holy matrimony**. Although we still use the term, we have largely lost sight of its content. Holy matrimony involves three parties: God, a man, and a woman within the framework of marriage. The holy commonwealth arrangement, which is applicable to every institution, is here applied to marriage. Thus, for the Biblical Christian, marriage is a vertical, triangular, covenantal, spiritual relationship beginning and ending with God. Therefore, it is a form of **communion**.

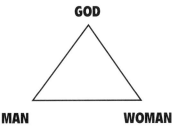

GOD

MAN   WOMAN

Communion is very significant and has implications for every area of life. The term, by definition, involves more than two parties; union can be achieved, theoretically, with two parties, but communion involves three or more. Without communion there can be no community. Too often, communion is defined very superficially today in Christian circles in reference to the Lord's Supper. Biblically speaking, however, communion has to do with relationship with God in the large sense, both as gaining a reconciled relationship with him on the basis of His finished work in Christ, and in beginning and ending with God in the totality of life. God-in-Christ is not only Savior, He is, indeed, Lord, and God is intimately involved in every area of life. Therefore, marriage from a Biblical perspective is holy matrimony.

What happens to the institution of marriage as a result of the Enlightenment? God is cut away from the institution of marriage, as He is cut away from all of life and, thus, marriage can no longer be a vertical, triangular, covenantal, spiritual relationship. Rather, it becomes a linear, horizontal, contractual, legal relationship. It is, theoretically, a binding legal contract between a man and a woman. But stop and consider this with me for a moment: on whose terms is such a contract established? If God is not there as the absolute basis and foundation of the arrangement, what else can serve as an absolute foundation?

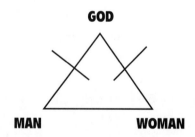

If God is not a party to this arrangement, we no longer have the possibility of **communion** from which we can derive community, without which there can be no enduring civilization. The best that can be said of a linear institution of marriage is that it is, theoretically, a **union**.

The Biblical arrangement is, as has been said, holy matrimony, beginning and ending with God. It is not an arrangement in which the wife is hierarchically subordinate to the husband or the husband is subordinate to the wife. It is an arrangement in which each and both are subordinate to God.

What, then, has happened to the institution of marriage?

Under the influence of Rationalism it was first viewed as a **binding contract** (within the natural law order) between a man and a woman. This is the strongest bond possible given a presupposed union. Being bereft of the glue of communion, however, this view gradually declines, until marriage becomes a **conditional** or **experiential contract**; in which either party, for whatever reason or reasons, can opt out of the contract with increasing ease.

Ultimately, the institution of marriage ceases even to be a contractual relationship and becomes simply an **experiential relationship**; any two parties desiring to live together simply move in together. What happens when such a relationship disintegrates, as it almost inevitably will? Who gets what—not to mention children who may have been born into the relationship? Some may assume, "Oh, that can be resolved in the courts." On what basis, however, will such be resolved in the courts, for there is no legal ground or basis for the relationship!

Courts necessarily become cluttered with such cases. The most celebrated such case in the United States to date was the 1976 Lee Marvin case in which the California Supreme Court ruled relative to Marvin and his seven-year cohort, if one can follow this tortured logic, that the relationship could be construed as a marital relationship provided it could be established that it was not primarily based on sex. If that does not epitomize anarchy, I do not understand the meaning of the term.

The reason that the family is disintegrating today is that we have gravitated so far from Biblical Christianity that we no longer understand the nature of the family. Indeed, the whole marital structure is disintegrating and what remains of it is being very seriously challenged.

The basic unit of government is the family, and where government disintegrates, there can be no order.

"Democracy" (Majoritarianism) Institutionalized in the West

Democracy, then, flowing out of Enlightenment Rationalism, came to be institutionalized in Western civilization. It was an arrangement in which it was held that man was the author of government, in which presupposed sovereign individuals would live together and work out their own happiness in their relationships one with the other in corporate relationship under the *laws of nature*. The will of man in majoritarian relationship replaces the will of God. The ruler is no longer held responsible to God but, presumably, to the people in majoritarian relationship, and law is no longer that of God but of man in majoritarian relationship, that is, of the majority which is deemed to be sovereign.

The Rationalist worldview effected a shift in the approach to man. The focus at first was individualistic, but it soon shifted, as we will see, to a focus on collective or social man, a shift which is finally absolutized, becoming collectivism.

ECONOMICS

In the area of economics, the Rationalists believed that, just as individuals can learn and practice the laws of nature in all other areas, so it is possible to discover and practice the laws of nature governing market relationships. They conclude, logically, that whatever benefits an individual, being consistent with natural law, will benefit the society as a whole. Therefore, to encourage individuals to engage in market activity with a view to their individual benefit is a worthy objective toward which to direct society.

What has taken place in the Western view of economics under the influence of the Rationalist worldview is that, once again, God has been cut away, and what remains—in this case the market—will come to be, if only inadvertently, absolutized. This is in line with the general shift from theocentrism to anthropocentrism.

Just as the Rationalists had earlier absolutized the brilliant observations of Isaac Newton (Principia, 1687) rendering them into unchangeable laws of nature, so they now absolutized the brilliant observations of Adam Smith (1723-1790) (who, however, unlike Newton, was a deist). As we noted in our discussion of the Biblical Christian view of economics, Adam Smith's monumental The Wealth of Nations, published in 1776 is perhaps the most penetrating analysis of economics ever written.

Smith's observations relative to the workings of the market were pressed into natural laws—as, for example, the so-called, presupposed "law" of supply and demand. It was presupposed that, as each individual discovered the laws of nature and practiced those laws governing market relationships, so that every individual would prosper, and as every individual prospered, so the whole of society would prosper. Thus, we have the absolutizing of the market, if only inadvertently, because God has been left out.

Consequently, the concept of justice is ignored. We no longer have a market tempered with justice in prices and wages on the basis of individuals beginning and ending with God in all of their relationships including market transactions. Buyers and sellers are no longer expected and no longer see themselves as responsible under God to maintain a clear conscience and a quiet heart before God. Rather, it is presupposed that enlightened self-interest alone, given the inherent goodness of man, will suffice to enable man to learn and practice the natural laws of market relationships.

The Biblical Christian, of course, knowing what is in fallen man, recognizes that, in the final analysis, what we have here is the enthronement of selfishness. Do whatever you will within the framework of the market absolutized—anything that benefits you, and whatever benefits you will benefit everyone else. We have, if only inadvertently, an absolutized market economics which, being derived from natural law will not, finally, be able to counteract man's fallenness sufficiently to sustain economic liberty. We have lost, once again, the communion which sustains a holy commonwealth. This is a fundamental shift.

I would hasten to add that an absolutized market economy, though by no means Biblical, is most certainly closer to a Biblical view of economics than a planned, state-controlled economy (which we will later discuss). It needs to be recognized, however, that a planned, state-controlled economy logically emerges out of the absolutized market. Why? If the market is absolute—that is, if there is no absolute justice [Biblical God] behind the market—then when people observe the injustices persisting in or resulting from an absolutized market economy, the obvious response will be that someone must do something to remedy the injustice, and to whom will we look? The absolutized state! Those who have, under the influence of Rationalism, cut God and His Word away from economics have, perhaps unwittingly but nevertheless inevitably, set the stage for a planned economy.

NOTES

1. Snyder, Louis L., <u>The Making of Modern Man</u>, NY: New York, D. Van Nostrand Company, Inc., 1967, p. 238.
2. Citation: Thomas Hutchinson, <u>History of the Massachusetts Bay Colony</u> (Boston, 1764), vol. 1, appendix 3 [per <u>http://www.swarthmore.edu/</u>SocSci/bdorsey1/41docs/21-cot.html].

6 CONSEQUENCES OF THE ENLIGHTENMENT AND THE RATIONALIST WORLDVIEW

"As to Jesus of Nazareth, my Opinion of whom you particularly desire, I think the System of Morals and his Religion, as he left them to us, the best the World ever saw or is likely to see; but I apprehend it has received various corrupting changes, and I have... some Doubts as to his Divinity... I see no harm, however, in its being believed, if that belief has the good consequence of making his doctrines more respected and better observed."

Benjamin Franklin, 1790[1]

How would we summarize the consequences of the Rationalist worldview which flowed out of the Enlightenment in terms of its impact on Western/American civilization? We will briefly mention its major expressions in the West generally, then shift our attention to its impact in America, particularly with respect to American government.

Three Major Expressions in the West and World

Three major expressions of the Enlightenment in the West and world are readily apparent.

The first is the French Revolution (1789-1794). From the Rationalists' standpoint, the French Revolution was both a positive and a negative effort. It was positive in that the revolutionaries were attempting to implement the rationalists' faith and vision. However, obviously, it would not become possible to implement Rationalism, which stands in antithesis to Biblical Christianity, as long as Biblical Christian influence and Biblical institutions, structures and procedures remained in place. Therefore, the French Revolution was negative in that it deliberately sought to exterminate that which remained of Biblical Christianity.

A Declaration of the Rights of Man was voted by the French Constituent Assembly on August 27, 1789, and a determined effort was made to reinstitutionalize France, Europe, and the West on the basis of the Rationalist worldview. The effort finally disintegrated, however, into the Reign of Terror (1793-1794) and, ultimately, into the emergence of the military dictatorship of Napoleon Bonaparte in 1799. Napoleon, himself a child of the Enlightenment, then sought to export the gospel of reason by force of arms to all other nations.

Why was the French Revolution largely abortive in Europe? Thanks largely to the work of God through John Wesley (1703-1791), it was Biblical Christianity, not Humanism/Rationalism, which had come to prevail in late eighteenth century England. (We often think of the Wesleyan influence only in terms of the Wesley revivals, tending to overlook the tremendous reformation that came out of the Wesleyan movement.) Biblical Christian statesmen such as Edmund Burke (1729-1797), a member of the English parliament from 1765-94, were able to capitalize on this revitalized Christianity in their efforts to counter the revolutionary tide sweeping across Europe. In his Reflections on the Revolution in France (published in 1790) Burke warned the English, making very clear what was at stake in the struggle, stating that either the French Revolution would be defeated or Christian Europe would cease to exist.

Thus, England arose as an entire nation to resist the effort being made by the revolutionaries in control of France to overrun Europe and the rest of the world in order to implement the Rationalist faith and vision. Indeed, their resistance was implacable, culminating in the defeat of

Napoleon and revolutionary France in the Battle of Waterloo in 1815.

However, although revolutionary and Napoleonic France was defeated militarily and politically, the French Revolution resulted, intellectually, in what I call "the advent of the revolutionary West." Ever since that period, the intellectual community of the West has in one measure or another been caught up in the enterprise of completing of the work begun in 1789, striving to remake the world in keeping with the presuppositions of Rationalism and its derivatives.

The second major expression of the Enlightenment is the Darwinian Hypothesis (1850s-Present) and the so-called evolutionary faith. <u>On the Origin of Species by Means of Natural Selection</u>, written by Charles Darwin in 1844 and published in 1859, was immediately controversial. Those of a revolutionary mentality hailed his work and, although there was significant opposition from what remained of the Biblical Christian tradition in the intellectual and scientific communities, the revolutionary tradition ultimately carried the day, and the Darwinian hypothesis and evolutionary faith became the new prevailing dogma of the intellectual and scientific communities.

The third expression is the Marxist analysis of history (1847-Present), which will be discussed in a later chapter. Karl Marx (1818-1883) formulated an analysis and interpretation of history which, like the Darwinian hypothesis, was first met with significant opposition, but finally came to be adopted by nearly all intellectuals in the world. It became a significant component of the post-Christian worldview, and carried the legacy of the Enlightenment into the twentieth century and beyond. In fact, if you go to most of the leading universities today—Yale, Princeton, Harvard—you will find that it is still largely the Marxist analysis of history and a call for revolution, whether soft or hard, which is being taught.

Four Consequences of the Rationalist Worldview in America

What were the consequences of the Rationalist worldview and the Enlightenment in American civilization? Without question, Biblical Christianity had been the dominant worldview in the English colonies in

North America during the 1600s, providing the foundation for American civilization. Therefore, we would ask, if Biblical Christianity produced the significant order, community, liberty, justice, charity, and productive activity for which American civilization came to be known during the seventeenth century, what happened to it during the eighteenth century (1720s-1780s)?

For our purposes in this book, we will mention the first two consequences only briefly and focus on the last two: the impact of the Rationalist worldview on the American Revolution of 1776 and the American Constitutional Order and System.

The Christian-Rationalist Conglomerate

The first consequence was the shift in the intellectual community from a firm and highly rational Biblical epistemology to a rational but dualistic epistemology with a gradual shift in focus from the Bible to the human intellect as authoritative. This produced in American civilization a conglomerating of Christianity and Rationalism which could be called Rationalist Christianity or Christian Rationalism but which, for want of a better term, we call the Christian-Rationalist conglomerate. As a result, Americans lost sight of the sovereignty of God and the depravity of man and came to consider themselves in a different light. The eighteenth-century thought-leaders began to de-emphasize or even deny the doctrine of original sin and the view that man is dependent upon God for his salvation.

Most thinkers became Christian-Rationalists, demonstrating an admixture of Christianity and Rationalism. Two obvious examples of this were Thomas Jefferson (1743-1826) and Benjamin Franklin (1706-1790). Jefferson appears to have leaned very much towards Rationalism, as evidenced by his effort to re-write the entire Bible to excise anything that had to do with the supernatural. Nothing could be more Rationalistic! One must be highly committed to expend such effort which, of course, cannot be done in a day.

How would we expect this shift from Biblical Christianity to a Christian-Rationalist conglomerate to affect the general institutional structure and procedure? We would have, of course, the abandonment of the holy commonwealth, the view that God is over all of life. In its place, the intellectual community came to accept the dichotomy of sacred and secular. The first sphere to be cut away from God or secularized would be the civil-social area, as the Christian-rationalists would come to accept the conclusion of the rationalists that government is a creation of man. Under the influence of such Rationalists as John Locke (1632-1704), government comes to be viewed as of, for, and by man. We cut God away from the state and the state is rendered secular.

Biblical to Evangelical Christianity

The second consequence of the compromise with Rationalism was among those Christians who refused to give up the Bible as their epistemological authority. The state came to be looked upon as secular and profane, and it was argued that the church should have nothing to do with the state. This, in turn, would give rise to the notion that all politics and all politicians are evil. Increasingly, the Body of believers withdrew from the various areas of life, from the arts, from the media, from politics. Consequently, the opposition simply proceeded to completely control politics and, indeed, run the civilization and nation, moving it ever further away from what remained of Biblical Christianity. Today, all that remains is a Christianity which, emptied of its intellectual content, can no longer be recognized as a worldview, as universally applicable.

Of course, the Great Awakening and the Evangelical Christianity it produced was good as far as it went. Indeed, the author considers himself to be an Evangelical Christian. The term evangelical is a very good term. Biblically it is a good term because a person who is evangelical is a person who is an evangel, a bearer of good news or glad tidings. Christians are, indeed, bearers of good news: the good news of God's finished work in Christ and His Saviorhood and Lordship on the basis thereof! Thus, Christians should be evangelical; indeed, a Biblical Christian must be evangelical.

However, I would propose the careful use of another term: Biblical Christian for a person who, while being evangelical in the large sense, goes one step further than most Evangelicals today in the recognition that Christianity is a worldview, that there is a holy commonwealth and, therefore, that Biblical Christians can serve as salt and light in every area of life.

THE AMERICAN "REVOLUTION" OF 1776

The American Revolution (1776), was simultaneously two things: a counter-revolution to preserve and perpetuate Christian Rationalism and a successful rebellion to achieve *de jure* independence.

By this time, a significant shift from thinking theologically to thinking anthropologically had taken place. When the thinking had been theological, the church had been a highly significant institution, but with the shift to the anthropological, the state became the institutional focus. Consequently, by the time of the rebellion in 1776 and the Constitutional conventions which followed, the basic question had become the political question, "What is the nature of the state?"

It has been accurately observed that the American Revolution was a "revolution prevented, not a revolution made." Indeed, it had by nature virtually nothing in common with the French Revolution of 1789 which, as we noted earlier, was occurring at nearly the same time in Europe. Rather, it was **a counter-revolution** to preserve and perpetuate Christian Rationalism.

It was not, on the one hand, an effort to preserve and perpetuate Christianity or, more specifically, Biblical Christianity, which had provided the basis for American civilization but from which American civilization had already shifted; nor was it an effort to revolutionize on the basis of the Rationalist worldview; rather, it was an effort to preserve and perpetuate the Christian-Rationalist faith, conglomerate, and order as it had come to obtain in American civilization.

Scholars can argue which component was more influential as the day is long, but the point is, however you cut it, we are not talking about Christianity or Rationalism, but about the Christian-Rationalist conglomerate. The effort was being made to protect the Christian-

Rationalist conglomerate from further onslaughts of rationalism flowing from the Continent. Many feared, indeed, that Parliament was coming further under the influence of Rationalism.

The American Revolution was, politically, **a successful rebellion** to achieve a *de jure* independence. *De jure* means "with regard to the law," that is, a legal independence. To understand this we need to recognize that by the mid-point of the eighteenth century (1750s) the English colonies in America were already independent as a matter of practice.

The reason for this *de facto* independence was twofold. From the planting of the first colonies in North America in 1607 (technically, in reality, from 1620 or 1628 until 1680) until the expulsion of the French by the English in 1763 more than a century and a half later, the English colonies in North America had been virtually independent. One reason for this was that because of Biblical Christian influence in England, the English colonies in America were, from the beginning, less tightly regulated by intent than were the Spanish and the French colonies. The English, for example, permitted those who were religious dissenters to settle in their colonies; even those who were not British subjects.

The second reason for the *de facto* independence of the colonies, however, was that the the English colonies in North America were largely neglected by their mother country, England being preoccupied with both international and domestic political issues.

The domestic struggle between the Puritans and the Anglicans and between the Parliamentarians and the Monarchists began about 1640 and finally issued, as we know, in the indictment, trial, and execution (1649) of Charles I. Charles I had made a deliberate attempt to exterminate Biblical Christianity and was responsible, along with Archbishop William Laud (1573-1645), for terrible persecutions and deaths among the Puritans. There followed the Cromwellian Protectorate (1649-53), then the restoration of the Crown in 1660.

Under James II (r. 1685-88), a Catholic and a pensioner of Louis XIV of France, there was, once again, a move to exterminate Biblical Christianity.

At this, the English, having finally had enough, rose up. Whigs and Tories united to remove James II from the throne and to effect the so-called "Bill of Rights" stipulating what the Crown thereafter could not do. It could not raise an army; it could not tax. These powers belonged henceforth to Parliament. This was the so-called Glorious or Bloodless revolution of 1688. It flowed in substantial measure from the Reformation and made possible an ordered liberty in England.

Indeed, no people were more independent than the English colonists in North America by the second half of the eighteenth century. The Americans, then, were not rebelling to achieve a new freedom and independence. They were rebelling to preserve and perpetuate the freedom and independence which they had long since enjoyed.

This became an issue because, after the expulsion of the French from North America in 1763, the English king's party came to control Parliament and Parliament began to give closer attention to her colonies in North America. Moves were made to "tidy up the empire," and it was suggested that Parliament might, indeed, begin to regulate the colonies more tightly. In addition, the mother country was beginning to discuss, and not without some justification, the need to force the colonists to pay for services rendered, which the colonists had hitherto successfully avoided, given the English international and domestic preoccupations. The proposed regulations, though they would never have become cruelly oppressive as many historians of the period would have it, threatened to set aside the institutions, customs, and traditions which were more than a century and a half old.

Thus, it was the threat of regulation to which the colonists reacted. Determined to preserve and perpetuate the liberty and independence they enjoyed, they rebelled in 1776, declaring *de jure* independence which, with the aid of the French, they achieved in 1783.

The rebel government was not revolutionary; it made no effort to smash existing Christian-Rationalist institutions. (Several individuals who fomented rebellion were, as would be expected, of a revolutionary ilk, but the government in place opposed revolution and revolutionaries.)

The American Revolution, then, was not a revolution. It was, intellectually, a counter-revolution to preserve and perpetuate Christian Rationalism and, politically, a successful rebellion to achieve a *de jure* independence.

THE AMERICAN CONSTITUTIONAL ORDER AND SYSTEM 1789

Much more significant than the so-called American Revolution (1776) in a discussion of the Enlightenment in America is the American Constitutional Order and System.

What was the nature of the American Constitutional Order? It was an effort to preserve and perpetuate Christian Rationalism or the Christian-Rationalist conglomerate. Therefore, it was, by nature, dualistic. Accordingly, as we examine the American Constitutional Order and System, we must discuss the two components of that dualism, the one flowing from Biblical Christianity and the Biblical Christian worldview and the other flowing from the Enlightenment and the Rationalist worldview. The American Constitutional Order and System was influenced by both the remnants of the holy commonwealth concept and the Lockean natural rights thesis.

Within the Christian-Rationalist conglomerate there was a substantial "hangover" of the idea of a society under the God of the Bible, which the forefathers had called a holy commonwealth. This idea is derived, as we know, from the conviction that God is sovereign, that man is depraved (in the Biblical sense of being unable to deliver himself from the dilemma into which he is born), and that government is a gift of God for the orderly procedure of man in a fallen world.

Without question, a number of those present at the Constitutional Convention were strongly influenced by the Christian component of the Christian-Rationalist view. A number of them were Biblical Christians. They subscribed to a measure of Biblical Christianity, including the view that God is over all of life. They recognized the reality of the sovereignty of God and the depravity of man. They knew that ultimate power is never in government, but in the Biblical God. They recognized a need for limited government.

The Rationalist component of the American Constitutional Order and System was John Locke's natural rights thesis, to which many of the framers subscribed.

How, Locke (1632-1704) asked rationalistically, are life, liberty, and property to be preserved in the presupposed anarchistic state of Nature, in which man finds himself, a state which is not able to preserve and perpetuate or guarantee man these so-called natural rights? He proposed an answer to this dilemma, arguing that man voluntarily exchanges his natural state for a civil state.

Locke then addressed the question: What is to take place if government becomes destructive of the end for which it was created, that is, if government should begin to destroy life, liberty, or property? Locke argued that precautions should be taken from the start by limiting the power of government. If government goes beyond its limitations, overstepping its bounds, it is then the right or the duty of the people to alter or abolish that government so as to force government to comply with its man-created and intended function: to preserve life, liberty, and property. Locke asserted, on this rationalistic basis, the right of revolution.

Declaration of Independence: A Classic Restatement of Locke's Natural Rights Thesis

The classic restatement of John Locke's *natural rights thesis* is found in the American Declaration of Independence, which Thomas Jefferson (1743-1826) penned, as it were, "with his dog at his side." Jefferson was quite intoxicated with Rationalism, which is evidenced by his conversion (or, as one may prefer, perversion) of Locke's "life, liberty, and property" into "life, liberty, and the pursuit of happiness." Government would become the great engine which would release man theoretically into a pursuit of happiness!

If one believes, by the way, that the American Revolution was all but thoroughly Christian, consider the following. First of all, who wrote the Declaration of Independence? Thomas Jefferson. The framers did not call upon a Biblical Christian to write the Declaration; they called upon the man among them who was probably farther removed from Biblical Christianity than anyone else they could have selected!

Secondly, we should re-read the Declaration and ask ourselves, to what did Jefferson appeal as the framers' authority for what they were about to do? The Holy Scriptures? No. The case for the American rebellion was not based on the Bible; it was based on the natural rights thesis of the rationalist, John Locke! Therefore, there are no grounds for stating that the American Revolution was a Biblical movement. Indeed, any credible scholar would laugh one out of the room for taking such a position. Christians must not fail to recognize and understand the dualism.

On the other hand, of course, most scholars today, given their presuppositions, take the opposite and equally untenable position, heaping scorn on anyone who refuses to accept the argument that the American Revolution was a revolution, a derivative of Rationalism and akin to the French Revolution. Once again, nothing could be further from the truth. The nature of both the American Rebellion and the Declaration of Independence was dualistic.

If one is being honest, or scholarly, or both, one will not go to either extreme because, in the end, while the appeal is to Locke's natural rights thesis, there is still an evident "hangover" of Biblical Christianity which holds that government must be limited in power because God is sovereign.

A Biblical Christian who reads the Declaration of Independence readily recognizes that it is not Christian for yet another reason: it is full of lies and misrepresentations. The long list of grievances against the King listed in the Declaration makes it appear that the colonists were the most oppressed people who ever lived, when the truth is just the reverse. The colonists enjoyed great liberty and were virtually independent. Their independence was being threatened, but not to the extent implied in the document; many lies are stated. Of course, most who teach the Declaration of Independence today refer to the list of grievances (how Americans love grievances!) as "propaganda." What is propaganda? It is taking one's position and one's preference and absolutizing it—which, of course, is not Biblical. We should not hesitate to call propaganda by its real name: a lie.

To return, then, to the American Constitutional Order and System itself, we recognize that its two components had a touching point. Both the proponents of Locke's natural rights thesis and those who perpetuated that which remained of the holy commonwealth idea believed that government should be limited in power. That was their point of agreement.

> **The American Constitutional Order and System:**
> *Locke's Natural Rights Thesis* ➜ *LIMITED GOVERNMENT*
> *Holy (Biblical) Commonwealth* ➜ *LIMITED GOVERNMENT*

A System of Divided Authority and Diffused Power

How, then, did the framers propose to effect a system which would perpetually limit the power of government? As we know, theory is one thing and translation of theory into workable machinery is something altogether different. They began by devising a system of divided authority and diffused power which they sought to implement mechanically in two dimensions: horizontal and vertical.

The horizontal diffusion of power was known as "separation of powers," as the powers of the general government were divided among three branches of government: **the legislative**, **the executive**, and **the judicial**. The legislative was to draw up the laws, the executive was to execute those laws, and the judiciary was to resolve conflicts relative to law, clarifying what the law says. These three branches were intended to check and balance one another and, thereby, perpetuate limited government

Only a mere fourteen years after the ratification of the Constitution, one of the three branches arrogated to itself the final authority and was positioned to dominate the other two branches. This occurred in 1803. This authority, by giving the judiciary power to nullify the actions of the legislative branch if, in its judgment, the legislators drew up a non-Constitutional law, destroyed the horizontal diffusion of power.

To understand this, we need to ask the question, "What is the function of the court system which, in the American Constitutional system, culminates in the Supreme Court?" It is a very basic function. The courts are to determine **what the law says** and, thus, to resolve conflict relative to law.

To illustrate, let us hypothecate that a given law is legislated and executed. One person believes that the law says "thus and so" and acts in concert therewith, and another person believes the law says "thus and so" and acts in concert therewith, and the two come into conflict. Who is right? There must be some way of adjudicating that question, and that is the function of the courts. Perhaps the first person was right; perhaps the second was right; perhaps neither is right. This is the function of the courts.

This function, however, was abandoned when, under the Chief Justiceship of John Marshall (1735-1835), who served in that capacity from 1801 until his death in 1835, the Supreme Court assumed the extra-Constitutional (even, I would submit, *anti*-Constitutional) power of *judicial review.*

What was the intent of the framers relative to the legality or constitutionality of a law? This is a legitimate question, the answer to which is obvious, even blatantly manifest, I would submit, in the Constitution—certainly implicitly, if not explicitly. The intent was that the final court of appeal relative to such an issue would be the states and the people respectively. How do we know this? It was stipulated that every two years, that is, every other year—which is a very short time, the **entire membership** of the lower chamber of Congress (the House of Representatives) would be up for election, and **one-third of the membership** of the upper chamber (the Senate) would be up for election. Thus, if a certain law were legislated and executed but then was deemed not to be constitutional by the states and/or the people, every two years the states and the people would have the opportunity to change the membership of the Congress sufficiently so as to be able to modify or even repeal such a law or statute! That is very significant.

Thus, the intent of the framers was that the people and the States would be the final court of appeal in determining the legality or constitutionality of a law. It was not intended that the court would do such. The Supreme Court, however, arrogated this power to itself. Chief Justice John Marshall—who, by the way, was a Nationalist, even an ardent Nationalist, assumed for the Supreme Court, beginning with *Marbury v. Madison* in 1803, the power to determine whether or not a law is legal or constitutional. This assumption of power, known as judicial review, contained within itself the seeds of tyranny because it sovereignized the Supreme Court, rendering it, in effect, into God.

At first, the ability of the absolutized Supreme Court to cause mischief in this regard did not appear because, basically, the Court used this power to strike down statutes which proposed to expand government beyond its constitutional bounds—justices still being of a mentality to promote limited government.

In the late 1930s, however, as a consequence of the second American revolution or New Deal, which we will later discuss, we had the advent of the Franklin Roosevelt Court, which began to use the power of judicial review to effect revolutionizing legislation. The Roosevelt Court began, not only to sanction legislation that proposed to expand the power of government beyond Constitutional bounds but, simultaneously, to use the power of judicial review to investigate any and every issue. The court now simultaneously adjudicates, legislates, and executes for, indeed, the latest decision of the Supreme Court becomes the highest law of the land.

That the Supreme Court has become the highest law of the land becomes glaringly apparent when we examine a decision such as Roe vs. Wade (1973), when the U.S. Supreme Court, which had every prerogative to do so given judicial review, found the premeditated taking of a life to be constitutional. By the way, I would like to go on record that no civilization which mandates first degree murder as a way of life, or should we say death, is going to survive for long. It should be apparent to any rational person, even if God were mythological, that this reclassification of a group of people as non-persons, followed to its logical conclusion, will ultimately result in our own destruction. Recognizing this, Francis Schaeffer very accurately titled a film series on this topic, "Whatever Happened to the Human Race?"[2] The films are an excellent tool for making others aware of these realities.

The power of judicial review has no beginning and no end and, accordingly, the separation of powers has been destroyed. This is so fundamental. If we have a Biblical reformation, the courts will be de-sovereignized and the separation of powers restored.

Vertical Diffusion of Power: Federal and State Levels

We will now examine the vertical diffusion of power, the "division of power" between the federal and state levels of government. That limited government was the objective of this division of power is clearly evident in the Constitution, culminating in the first ten amendments and, in particular, culminating in the 9th and 10th Amendments.

We need to recognize that, although the first ten amendments to the Constitution were technically "amendments," in reality they were a part of the original document. Why is this? The states of Massachusetts, New York, and Virginia agreed to ratify the Constitution only with the understanding that the first order of business of the new government would be to pass what became the first ten amendments. If the amendments had not been proposed, Massachusetts, New York, and Virginia would have withdrawn from the so-called union, and without those states we never would have had a Constitutional order and system. Thus, although they are technically amendments, they are actually part of the original document.

These first ten amendments have become known, erroneously, as a Bill of Rights. The framers were not interested in rights, but in liberties. There is no right named anywhere in the Constitution! (Of course, everything is a right today. We have proceeded to absolutize presupposed rights, even—to demonstrate the absurdity of our position—going so far as to absolutize, in the case of Roe v. Wade, a presupposed right to privacy, then giving this presupposed right to privacy preference over the presupposed right to life!)

The first ten amendments, instead of being called a Bill of Rights, should be called a Bill of Prohibitions, because the gun is, as it were, being pointed against the general or central government, and the first ten amendments stipulate what privileges that central government cannot abridge [cut off or diminish]. It cannot abridge the privileges of worshipping freely, speaking freely, assembling freely, bearing arms freely. All of this culminates in the 9th and 10th amendments, which state that all powers not expressly granted by the Constitution to the federal level of government, or denied thereby to the states, are left to the states or to the people respectively.

The American Constitutional Order and System is a system of federalism, which is derived from what is generally called feudalism (which, as we discuss elsewhere in our analysis of the so-called Middle Ages, was largely a working out of Biblical Christianity in the civil-social area). In fact, we can trace directly the lines which lead from feudalism to federalism. Like feudalism, federalism is a system of divided authority and diffused power, the presupposition being that God is sovereign, the final power, and man is depraved. The use of the term federal indicates the measure of Christianity that remained during the Christian-Rationalist period in the early republic.

Nomenclature

What should the American Constitutional Order and System be called? It is erroneously called a democracy. Democracy, which we discussed earlier, is a theoretical construct flowing out of Rationalism which has never existed in practice, only in theory. In any country which has been called a democracy, whether ancient or modern, it has, in fact, been not the people, but special interest groups, which have ruled. The nature of the idea of democracy, as it was hammered out by Western intellectuals during the Enlightenment, is that government is a creation, not of God, but of man.

If it was not a democracy, what was the American system as intended by the framers? It was a republic in contrast to the prevailing form of government in that day, a monarchy. The framers were deliberately instituting a republic and, moreover, a particular kind of republic: a republic with a written constitution. The American people were not the first to have a constitution. The Romans had a constitution. The British had a constitution. The Americans, however, were the first to have a written constitution. This does not mean that the Roman or English constitutions did not appear in writing. It means that they accumulated gradually over time, whereas the framers of the American constitution sat down at a given point in time and proposed to reduce to writing a system of government that would forever limit the power of government.

Thus, the American system was a republic with a written constitution or, as it is often called, a **constitutional republic**. This was unprecedented historically. Indeed, those who opposed establishing a constitutional republic did so on the grounds that such would be insufficient to limit government, given that it would rest upon a written document, rather than, as was the case in England, a more substantial unwritten constitution based on "common law" which had come about gradually over a period of time and was deeply woven into the thought and character of the society.

WHERE DOES THE FINAL AUTHORITY RESIDE

What was the intent of the framers relative to final authority? When I was in high school, my classmates and I would debate this question. I discovered later that we were generating far more heat than light, but we would go after one another as to whether the state level of government or the federal level was to be the final authority.

Upon analysis, it is apparent that the framers did not intend final authority to reside anywhere in government! Presumably, then, there was a final authority higher than government. Let us spell that out. On the one hand, those drawing from the "hangover" of Biblical Christianity would reserve the final authority for the Biblical God. For the Rationalists, natural law would be the final authority. Therefore, both proposed to effect a system of **perpetual tensions**, both horizontally and vertically. With these tensions perpetually in place, government, which was not viewed as the final authority, would be **limited** in power.

Why did this effort to establish enduring horizontal and vertical separations of powers designed to be in perpetual tension fail? Why did the American Constitutional Order and System last such a short time (1789-1860s), and what happened to bring about the demise of the system? The answer, I believe, is found in the nature of the system. The system was, by nature, dualistic. For that reason, therefore, it did not last very long and could not last very long. Not being in line with the Judeo-Christian tradition beginning and ending with God, it was only a question of how long it would last. The Christianity which remained at the time of the formulation of the American Constitutional Order and System was too greatly compromised by Rationalism.

What would have been the case had the system not been dualistic? If it had been fully Biblical Christian, the framers would have presupposed and explicitly stated that God is sovereign and that government is a gift of God for the orderly procedure of man in a fallen world. Thus, people would have been much more likely to reverence government as a gift from God and, therefore, to maintain limited government, never allowing any branch or part thereof to usurp the place of God.

As it was, the Christian-Rationalist framers believed what about the nature of government? They held that government is a creation of man. Obviously, if I believe something to be a creation of man, I might admire it, I might respect it, I might even venerate it, but I most certainly will not reverence it. If one does not reverence something, the temptation becomes all but overpowering to tinker or to tamper with it, particularly in a fallen world, as we who know ourselves recognize.

As we will discuss more thoroughly in the next chaper, interest groups would emerge from the next prevailing worldview—Transcendentalism—who, given their presuppositions, no longer saw any need to preserve and perpetuate limited government. Indeed, they would require that more power be focused in government in order to achieve their ideological and opportunistic objectives.

Thus, in the mid-nineteenth century (1855-1877), we had a shift from a federal to a national government, from a federal union to a national union. We were nationalized. The central government was, in effect, rendered sovereign, and we were shifted from a federal state with its divided authority and diffused power to a national state with its sovereignized power. This, the first revolution in American civilization, is called the Civil War and Reconstruction.

The Civil War and Reconstruction was, in reality, I submit, a revolution. The federal union would be revolutionized by bayonets. This is not, of course, the interpretation we have all imbibed under the tutelage of the naturalist historians. It is evidenced, however, by two realities.

First, consider the change in nomenclature. The change from the plural to the singular gives it away. Prior to the Civil War it was always referred to as "**These** United States are (or were)." Subsequent thereto it became known as "**The** United States is (or was)."

Secondly, consider the telling loss of liberty in the Biblical or Lockean sense. I tell my students that, if they can fill in the following blanks, I will place an A+ beside their other scores in the score book because no one has ever completed the statement:

> With the first American revolution, we will shift
> from a _____ system to a _____ system.[3]

The next question became, "Where within the central government will the absolute authority reside?" That question would be answered by the second American revolution, which emerged as a consequence of the intellectual shift to **process philosophy** (1870s-Present). This revolution, called the New Deal (1930s), resulted in a sovereignized national executive.

In many nations, to have a reformation would require a change in the **form** as well as the substance of government. A reformation in the United States, however, would not yet require such. We could simply breathe new life back into the federalistic form which remains. Indeed, the result would be even greater life than was originally the case because, presumably, the dualism would be recognized and dealt with and the government would be more firmly established as Biblical.

NOTES

1. Lemisch, L. Jesse, ed., Benjamin Franklin: The Autobiography and Other Writings, New York, NY: The New American Library, Inc., p. 337.
2. Bibliographical Note: The thoughtful Biblical Christian 3-part film series, *Whatever Happened to the Human Race*, is available from Gospel Communications International (P.O. Box 455, Muskegon, MI 49443-0455; 1-800-467-7353; gospelcom.net). Dr. Martin suggests that the fourth chapter: "The Basis for Human Dignity" in the accompanying book of the same title (coauthored by Francis A. Schaeffer and former U.S. Surgeon General C. Everett Koop, Revell, 1979) is the most profound, succinct summary of the history, nature, and consequences of the current thinking in the West of which he is aware.
3. Answer: The answer is that we shift from a voluntary system, wherein the states enter into the union voluntarily and remain in the union voluntarily, to a compulsory system. Whenever anything is compulsory one smells a rat because somebody is attempting to play God!

7 ROMANTICISM-TRANSCENDENTALISM (1800s–1860s)

Standing on the bare ground—my head bathed in the blithe air and uplifted into infinite space—all mean egotism vanishes. I become a transparent eyeball; I am nothing; I see all; the currents of the Universal Being circulate through me; I am part or parcel of God.[1]

Ralph Waldo Emerson

A s we discuss the intellectual flow during the first part of the nineteenth century (1800-1860s) and the impact of shift in prevailing worldviews, we recognize that we are tracing two conflicting intellectual traditions.

First, we have the tradition which begins and ends with man. This includes the revolutionaries and the revolutionizing movements which flowed out of the advent of the revolutionary West (1789); it has been the prevailing tradition since that time. In England, it was introduced by Jeremy Bentham and others who promoted what became known as Utilitarianism (1820s-Present). On the continent of Europe, we had Romanticism. In America, Romanticism admixed with Christian-Rationalism, becoming known as Transcendentalism.

Secondly, we have what remains of the tradition beginning and ending with the Biblical God, which continues to have significant influence. This, during the period under discussion, became known as Neo-Evangelicalism.

We include here an introduction to Utilitarianism with its impact on law and government, followed by a discussion of Romanticism-Transcendentalism and its impact, particularly on American civilization.

REVOLUTION FROM WITHOUT OR FROM WITHIN?

Before we discuss Jeremy Bentham and then Romanticism-Transcendentalism, it is necessary to note that revolutionaries take one of two approaches. Some believe that the revolution can and will occur by working from within the existing establishment or system. Others conclude that the revolution cannot succeed gradually from the inside but must come from the outside, that the current system must be completely smashed and obliterated in order for a revolutionized society to appear.

This, indeed, was the significance of Karl Marx. Marx theorized that revolution and the better order which would issue therefrom were historically predetermined and inevitable, but would only come about by the destruction of the present order. Force, violence, and bloodshed would be inescapable as the method by which history would effect the change. Marx believed that man could only recognize the process, applaud the process, and fall in step with the process, accepting force, violence, and bloodshed as the only means to the next stage. But some of his disciples, including Lenin, believed that man can, should, and must take a more active role in smashing the established order to bring in the new age. Marxists believe that it is possible to manipulate from within, but that the purpose of such manipulation must ultimately be to bring about a complete destruction of the established order and system.

If we do not understand these methodologies, we can fail to recognize that we are dealing with revolutionaries. Perhaps it was because there was a greater residue of Biblical Christianity in England, and this is conjecture on the author's part, that the intellectuals in England who were moving away from Biblical Christianity took the posture that the revolution could be effected from the inside. Jeremy Bentham was such a person, as were the playwrights Beatrice (1858-1943) and Sidney (1859-1947) Webb and George Bernard Shaw (1856-1950), the leading members of the Fabian Socialist society. These accepted a Marxist analysis of the flow of history, but rejected the idea that force, violence, and bloodshed would be required.

Those who have been committed to working from within have been much more influential than may at first appear. Without them, the Marxists could not have gained control during the twentieth century. The Marxists are always dependent on the inside work, taking advantage of that work to, in effect, move into the resulting vacuum. Indeed, it would appear that the Marxists would not have been able to accomplish much at all from the outside were it not for the work that had been and is being done on the inside.

UTILITARIANSIM: THE PLEASURABLE SOCIETY (1820S-PRESENT)

The Englishman, Jeremy Bentham (1748-1832), believed in revolution from within.[2] John Stuart Mill (1806-1873) wrote of him, "The father of English innovation (better translated 'revolution') both in doctrine and in institutions was Bentham."[3] This is true, to a large degree, of revolution in America as well as in England. As a child of the Enlightenment, Bentham (who was either a deist or an atheist) believed that the human intellect was capable of producing a better, if not perfect society. He also believed that the whole was nothing more than a sum of its parts. Thus man, taking thought, could discover the parts and, eventually, having discovered all of the parts, come to an understanding of the whole. Therefore, as men would act on the basis of an understanding of the whole—being nothing more than the sum of its parts—there would be progress, if not ultimately perfection.

For one beginning with such a faith, the question becomes, "On what basis do we begin to address the obvious problems?" Bentham came up with a calculus suggesting that there was a **pleasure-pain equation** which, when recognized and applied, would yield the **pleasurable society**. Radiating an absolute confidence in the human intellect, he presupposed that men have only to be shown that it is possible to solve the pleasure-pain equation and they will act accordingly. Obviously, neither the Fall nor sin had a place in Bentham's conception of the universe.

The objective, in Bentham's schematic, is to increase pleasure and avoid pain—which, by the way, are not to be defined superficially, but philosophically. How, then, do we do so? He proposed a utilitarianistic procedure. As we allow people to be free to solve the pleasure-pain equation, deciding voluntarily that which is pleasurable from the largest possible perspective, they will do so, and we will ultimately achieve **the greatest good for the greatest number**. The proper procedure, then, is a majoritarianism, sometimes called an *absolute democracy*. Alexis de Tocqueville, (1805-1859), author of Democracy in America (1835-1840), referred to such as democratic despotism. The obvious procedure which results from this theoretical construct is that, in order to have the pleasurable society, we need to pursue by **majority vote** that which will produce the greatest good for the greatest number.

This procedure of the majority vote has profoundly impacted the West. Indeed, it is now characteristic of the Western mind. You want what is pleasurable and I want what is pleasurable, so we will vote and the majority will win; therefore, we will have the greatest good for the greatest number and we will move, thus, more rapidly toward the pleasurable or, as you prefer, the painless society.

Of course, in analyzing Bentham's thesis, we notice a glaring difficulty, which is at the heart of the very idea of pleasure and pain. In this regard, by the way, C.S. Lewis (1898-1963) has written an instructive book entitled The Problem of Pain.[4] First of all, we have the question of the **nature** of pleasure and pain. We also have the problem of a **definition** of pleasure and pain, which is a very serious problem beginning and ending with man because, having no possibility of absolutivity, what is, theoretically, pleasurable for one person may, given the relativity, be painful for another!

Is there any value in pain? If we operate on the basis of the presupposition that we live in a fallen world, a presupposition which Bentham was not acknowledging (being at best a deist), we recognize immediately that it most definitely does. We read, *"For whom the Lord loveth he chasteneth."* (Hebrews 12:6 KJV)[5] I have often used the following example, which is a bit exaggerated but, I believe, is a fair one.

Those of us who have had the privilege of raising children—which is a privilege, though it is, by the way, a painful process—understand that we do not want our little child to crawl into the hot oven. Therefore, we may touch the child's hand briefly to the hot oven. The little child gets the message and thereafter will not crawl into the hot oven. A father who truly loves a child does not want that loved one, if only inadvertently, to find himself or herself in a situation that would be very dangerous, so he prepares that child. The point is that, beginning and ending with man, we have a serious problem in attempting to define pleasure and pain.

The next question, for Bentham, was methodological. If we may simplify and generalize Bentham's thought, I would suggest that it was a five-pronged program toward achieving the so-called "pleasurable society." By following strictly rationalistic lines, something of a social checkerboard, we can gradually achieve an egalitarian reconstruction of society through the following procedures.

Universal Male Suffrage

As we know, over time, Western civilization had devised procedures relative to suffrage designed to limit suffrage to the most responsible and informed members of society. Bentham, in contrast, promoted universal male suffrage. Later social reconstructionists, of course, would suggest that, though he was well on his way, Bentham was not fully enlightened because his proposal did not include women.

Parliamentary (or Congressional) Revolutionizing Reform

It is not necessary to use the word "revolutionizing" in intellectual discourse today. Indeed, revolution is generally discussed as "reform." For example, the movement in the United States from the 1830s-1860s is generally discussed as reform, not revolution (as in such books as Freedom's Ferment[6]). What is being discussed, however, is revolutionizing reform; reform for the purpose of revolution. Bentham proposed that we accomplish reform through the legislative body, that is, from *within* the system, through Parliament or Congress.

A Powerful Executive

Recognizing the need for an "engine" to drive the process, Bentham urged people to accept the need for powerful executive leadership. In other words, again, what is needed is an executive who has a vision for and commitment to revolution, though they astutely refrain from calling it by that name. This is not to suggest that Bentham was promoting or was involved in anything clandestine or sinister or conspiratorial. He was simply operating on the belief that the revolution could take place **within** the system.

Popular Mass Education

Bentham proposed popular mass education or compulsory public school education as it became known once institutionalized. The school will become an agent of the state. This renders it, in effect, an agent of the revolutionaries. This was a cardinal doctrine of revolutionary thought. To remake the world, it would be necessary to take the schools away from the family and the influence of the church, the Body of believers. Biblically, we are told: *"Train up a child in the way he should go and when he is old, he will not depart from it."* (Proverbs 22:6 KJV)[7] Bentham's view is antithetical to the Biblical view that parents are responsible for the education of their children and that schools, an outgrowth of such, are not under the state, nor under the church, but under God.

Relative Law—No Absolutes

Finally, Bentham sought to have the idea of relative law adopted. Obviously, if we are to have revolution, which is not possible if anything is fixed, everything must ultimately be plasticized, including law. Law is, at it were, rendered into a tool of convenience to be treated like mathematics or physics. We lose the need for checking and balancing; it has been replaced by what we are calling majoritarianism.

Given the above realities, we recognize that Bentham (1748-1832), with his emphasis on economics anticipated Marx (1818-1883), and with his emphasis on the so-called **democratic process** anticipated John Dewey (1859-1952) and Dewey's formulation known as Pragmatism. In fact, quite frankly, people who are intellectuals who do not begin and end with God, necessarily take what others have already proposed and simply re-package it. Thus, it is possible to follow the thread of ideas right down through history.

ROMANTICISM–TRANSCENDENTALISM

The major intellectual current in the world during the first half of the nineteenth century (1800-1850) became known on the Continent as Romanticism. In the United States, admixing with what remained of Christianity, it became known as Transcendentalism, with Ralph Waldo Emerson (1803-1882) and Henry David Thoreau (1817-1862) as its leading spokesmen. As an extension of the tradition beginning and ending with man, of which Rationalism had been the latest expression, it was, simultaneously, an extension of Rationalism, yet at the same time a revolt against Rationalism.

Rationalism (1600-1800), of course, in the minds of thoughtful people, had run its intellectual tether very quickly. Such philosophers as the Scotsman, David Hume (1711-1776), for example, concluded that it is not possible to know anything for certain beginning and ending with the human intellect in contemplation of so-called Nature. Thus, the pendulum swings from Rationalism to Romanticism, a swing to the irrational side. This is to take another step away from what remains of theocentrism toward anthropocentrism, toward reaffirming, rearticulating, and reapplying the oldest religion in the world, which began in Genesis 3:5 and has been most thoroughly institutionalized, as we have suggested, in Eastern Hinduism.

By the end of the eighteenth century (by 1790s), relatively little remained of the Biblical Christian tradition on the Continent. The French *philosophers* had done a devastating job, followed by the German philosophers Immanuel Kant (1724-1804) and G. W. F. Hegel (1770-1831), and thus when the Rationalist intellectual community began to swing to Romanticism, embracing a theological shift from deism to pantheism, there was not much resistance left against this additional step in the direction away from Biblical Christianity.

[Individuals associated with Romanticism on the Continent would include Jean Jacques Rousseau (1712-1778) [who, in his book Emile introduced a revolutionizing approach to elementary education], the Englishmen: William Wordsworth (1770-1850), George Gordon Byron (1788-1824), and Samuel Taylor Coleridge; the Frenchman Francois Chateaubriand (1768-1848); and the Germans: Johann Gottfried von Herder (1744-1803), Johann Wolfgang Goethe (1749-1832), Johann Friedrich von Schiller (1759-1805), a poet/playwright; and Friedrich Schleirermacher (1768-1834), an influential theologian in Berlin.]

There was, however, a substantial measure of resistance to Romanticism in the United States, primarily in the form of Evangelical Christianity (1720s-Present). Additionally, there was an admixture of what remained of the Christian tradition with Romanticism as it flowed through the Christian-Rationalist conglomerate. This produced the unique American variant of Romanticism called Transcendentalism. Transcendentalism is, in a certain sense, an admixture of Christianity and Romanticism, something of a "Christianized" Romanticism.

One can build a very strong case that, by this time, Christian Rationalism had come to be in a very serious epistemological bind. The Christian-Rationalists had rejected Biblical revelation on the basis of right reason, yet had not rejected all the conclusions knowable only on the basis of Biblical revelation, including the conclusion that there is life after death and that there is a place called heaven.

Transcendentalism was, then, like Romanticism, a revolt against the Enlightenment of the eighteenth century in its extreme form and the slavish devotion of that era to Rationalism and, simultaneously, a revolt against the remaining vestiges of Biblical Christianity. It was a revolt against "Christian" Rationalism.

A "New" Ontology and a "New" Epistemology

The Transcendentalists sought a new ontology and a new epistemology which would recognize man as an absolutely free being. Thus, man would be liberated both from the slavery to reason and mechanistic nature to which the Rationalists had subjected him and from the slavery to the sovereign supernatural to which Biblical Christianity had subjected him.

In effect, however, the Transcendentalists merely reinterpreted the Rationalist tradition. Like the Rationalists, they also looked to Nature, but they redefined Nature. Instead of Nature being mechanistic or static, operating on the basis of immutable, indestructible law, Nature became organological. It was alive, the permanent abode of an immanent, all-pervasive cosmic mind.

This was best expressed in Emerson's famous essay entitled "The Oversoul." Following are excerpts from <u>Nature</u> and *The Oversoul*:

Standing on the bare ground—my head bathed in the blithe air and uplifted into infinite space—all mean egotism vanishes. I become a transparent eyeball; I am nothing; I see all; the currents of the Universal Being circulate through me; I am part or parcel of God.[8] . . . [W]ithin man is the soul of the whole; the wise silence; the universal beauty, to which every part and particle is equally related; the eternal ONE.[9] [That is, all men are different, but each in his own peculiar way expresses the Oversoul within him.]

Man and Nature and God are one and the same. With this new view of Nature, deism is thrown out and we have the advent of a new ontology: pantheism. Francis Schaeffer uses a good term for this theological posture: pan-everythingism. Thus, the Romanticists-Transcendentalists presupposed a pantheistic ontology.

Holding a pantheistic ontology logically leads to an intuitional epistemology. If man is God or part and parcel of God, then man knows, not on the basis of outside or divine disclosure, nor by taking thought, but simply because he is; he intuits. Thus, we have an intuitionalism. Emerson held that there is a universal mind which is the common property of all men, and that each person is, as it were, an incarnation of that mind. Thus, for human knowledge, there is no revelational or logical basis, but only an intuitive one.

Sovereign Man Has Unlimited Potential

Romanticism, then, is, in essence, a religion of man. Rationalism was, in essence, a religion of Nature, but Romanticism renders man into a god. With the Renaissance, we shifted in focus from God to man as central, and then as sovereign. More precisely, with the Enlightenment, the focus had shifted to the human intellect, but the human intellect in contemplation of nature, not God. With Romanticism, we shift to man himself as the focus. Thus, we have completed the process of deifying man even as we have humanized God—until they have become one and the same. Therefore, again, Romanticism-Transcendentalism was, in reality, a religion of man. This, of course, led to the conclusion that man is sovereign.

This was, in the beginning, a very optimistic outlook. Man's imperfection is no longer viewed as being a consequence of a presupposed Fall. Nor is it a failure to be enlightened. Rather, it is the failure on the part of man to recognize his true nature, his true godness. There is no limit to what we can be and what we can do! Man has unlimited potential, bearing the spark of deity within his soul. Indeed, man is capable of conducting himself in his liberty in such a manner that his spiritual nature will evolve into something heretofore unimaginable.

Emerson caught the essence of Romanticism-Transcendentalism in the following words: Let **man stand erect, go alone, and possess the universe**.[10] Let **man**—man is our starting point, for he is god. Let man **stand erect**—this anticipates the evolutionary hypothesis because, heretofore, man has been, as it were, down on all fours. Let man . . . **go alone**—he does not need anyone else, being god—**and possess the universe**—get it all together, perfect that which exists. That is the ultimate revolutionary's statement.

The Twin Imperatives: Liberty and Equality, Libertarianism and Egalitarianism

If, then, Man is god he must be simultaneously absolutely free and absolutely equal. God cannot have any restrictions; he must enjoy absolute liberty, which brings us to libertarianism. Nor can god have any superior; he must in every part be equal, which brings us to egalitarianism. Thus, the twin imperatives of Romanticism-Transcendentalism were libertarianism and egalitarianism.

As we abandon God as the starting and terminal point, the result is ever greater intellectual fragmentation. This cannot be emphasized enough.

Impact on Evangelical Christianity: Man as a "Free Moral Agent"

As we would expect, Evangelical Christianity, now on the defensive, was heavily affected by Romanticism–Transcendentalism, accepting the idea that that man is a free moral agent. The Biblical Christian does not believe that man is a free moral agent.

To trace the derivation of the notion of Man as a free moral agent, we must recollect the Enlightenment shift from righteousness to morality which, being man-ascertained and, hence, man-made "truth," is, by its very nature, relative. Now, in reaction against morality, man is viewed as a free moral agent, the captain of his own ship; the determiner of his own destiny. Biblically, however, man is not the captain of his own ship nor the determiner of his own destiny. He did not create himself nor will he sit in judgment of himself.

Biblical Christian man is responsible man. Indeed, there is one choice which man cannot make: the choice not to respond to God. We are individually who we are because of our response to God, whether positive or negative, and we are who we are as a nation, civilization and, indeed, the entire race because of our response to God.

Because of this reality we are enjoined by God to "keep thy heart with all diligence; for out of it are the issues of life" (Proverbs 4:23 KJV)[11] (and death). Why the heart? Because the heart is the seat of our responsibility. "God sees not as man sees, for man looks at the outward appearance" (you and I can deceive one another), "but God looks at the heart." (I Samuel 16:7 NASB)[12] God is not deceived or deceivable.

Therefore, Biblical Christian man is not autonomous nor an automaton. The man of Romanticism-Transcendentalism, however, is autonomous. As we would expect, in response to this there will be, after Romanticism-Transcendentalism is spent, another pendulum swing. The man of process philosophy becomes an automaton.

ESSENCE OF THE LAST THREE CENTURIES: HAPPINESS, FREEDOM, AND EQUALITY

We would also observe that the essence of each of the last three centuries can be captured in one word for each century. The eighteenth century (1700s) can be captured in essence in the word "happiness." Happiness was the great objective. The Rationalists concluded, as in Jefferson's improvement on Locke, that man can be released into the "pursuit of happiness" on the basis of the framework of the state. The essence of the nineteenth century (1800s) can be captured in the word "freedom," and it will be agreed with Hegel that freedom can only be realized within the framework of the state. Finally, the essence of the twentieth century (1900s) can be captured in the word "equality," and it will be agreed with Marx that the egalitarian society can be achieved only as compelled by the state. In the case of freedom (1800s) as the great objective, which we are now discussing, you would have a very obvious torque if you would propose that it is possible to compel freedom— a matter, however, about which there will be much more to say below.

To understand the terminology, we would contrast transcendental with transcendent. On the basis of the Bible, we recognize that God is transcendent, simultaneously separate from and sovereign over all creation, including man. On the other hand, the god of Romanticism is not transcendent but transcendental, commingled and confused with everything else that exists. There being no transcendence, the transcendental is, if only inadvertently, absolutized. Hence, the term for the view is Transcendental*ism*.

The influence of the East is apparent here as we trace the pantheistic transcendental view of Romanticism ultimately back to the ancient world with its city-state arrangement, particularly as it culminated in Greece, which was a transcendental arrangement. Divinity and humanity were commingled and confused within the Greek state, in an essentially Eastern arrangement known as the *polis*.

THE IMPLEMENTATION OF TRANSCENDENTALISM: REFORMISM (1830s-1860s)

American intellectuals influenced by Transcendentalism, having become convinced of the desirability of the libertarian and egalitarian society, began to face the next question: "How do we go about effecting such?" To do so it would be necessary to revolutionize, after having gained sufficient power and influence to be able to do so. Concurrently, it would be necessary to eliminate that which remained of Biblical Christianity.

Indeed, the period between the 1830s and the 1860s was one of the major reformist periods in American civilization, in which an attempt was made to reinstitutionalize all American institutions in keeping with the presuppositions and objectives of Romanticism-Transcendentalism.

As a result of the reformism of the 1830s-60s, very few institutions were left unchallenged in American civilization, and the result was a social upheaval of a magnitude which earlier would have been inconceivable. This involved chattel slavery, education, legal systems and practices, the issue of war and peace, the role of women in society, marriage, the family, the relations of the sexes, and even personal habits. An intensive effort was made to restructure all of these institutions in line with the imperative of absolute liberty and equality toward achieving a more perfect order.

How, more precisely, was this attempted? Revolutionaries, because their first priority is to gain sufficient power to make a difference, are not primarily concerned with individuals. However, as a means to the end of implementing their faith and vision, in this case, the presupposed libertarian and egalitarian society, they need a **pretext** (or issue) for coming to power.

Which disadvantaged people did the American Transcendentalists exploit in order to come to power in the United States, a nation where the democratic procedure was most certainly in place? To answer this question, we need only ask, "Who were the most disadvantaged people during the 1830s in the United States?" The answer is obvious. Chattel slaves were the most conspicuously unfree and unequal people.

By the way, chattel slavery, a system in which one person, theoretically, legally owns another, was already a deep concern among committed Christians during this period. John Wesley and others had been advocating for years that slavery be abolished, both in Europe and America. Finally, in 1833, slavery was abolished in England; slaves were purchased and set free. The "manumission" movement was likewise at work in America. A person who owned a slave would legally free that slave, whether during his or her lifetime or in his or her will upon death.

George Washington, for example, had done this. Indeed, it is my thesis—and I studied this at length in graduate school—that slavery would have been eliminated voluntarily from American society by 1860 had it not been for the activist revolutionaries.

What took place, however, was that a host of activists emerged, fired by the revolutionary contagion of Romanticism-Transcendentalism. They took up the slavery issue, became abolitionists and, thus, were politically activized in an effort to bring about the libertarian and egalitarian society. Exploiting the slavery issue, they succeeded in stirring up the nation, coming to power, and effecting a revolution. If Biblical Christians had led the effort, slavery would have been dealt with on the basis of reformation, not revolution. In the direction that it took, however, sadly, the movement came to be dominated and fired by the revolutionaries flowing from Romanticism-Transcendentalism. The result was incalculable destruction and death.

CONSEQUENCES OF THE INSTITUTIONALIZATION OF TRANSCENDENTALISM 1830S-1860S

In the United States, roughly from the 1830s to the 1860s, Romanticism-Transcendentalism made its inroads, primarily in the North, centered in New England and the Yankee zone of settlement. At the same time, a neo-Evangelicalism spread through the South and into the Midwest, which was largely settled by southerners. Ultimately, the United States divided into two antithetical cultures. The result was a cultural dualism.

Gradually, the Northern Yankee-dominated culture transcendentalized, abolitionized, and politically activized. Finally, it began to clash with the Southern neo-Evangelicalized culture. The southern culture sought to perpetuate limited government and governmental institutions. The northern culture adopted the cause of abolition and finally fell in step behind the revolutionaries who, as we have said, were seeking to consolidate their power in the state in order to coerce liberty and equality.

In the United States they would need to effect a revolution in government to shift the government from a **federal** state or union with divided authority and diffused power to a **national** state or union with sovereignized power.

Ultimately, the cultural dualism was so complete that the only thread holding the two cultures together was a political thread, that of the Democrat Party. Nearly all the other institutions had been broken over the rock of cultural dualism. (We trace these realities in detail in my lectures on American history.)

The Three Stages of Revolution

Like many revolutionizing movements, that which flowed from Romanticism-Transcendentalism went through three stages on its way to implementation. The first stage was the **educational or voluntary stage**, in which it was presupposed that all that would be necessary to effect the libertarian and egalitarian society would be to educate man to his true nature—his true "godness." If man came to realize who he was—part and parcel of God—he would act in concert therewith, and the result would be gradual progress toward ever greater liberty and equality. This, however, did not work, for the more man imagined himself to be free in the "autonomous" sense, the more he used his imagined liberty to "get one up" on his fellows, and the less equality there appeared to be!

Thus, we entered the second stage, in which it was concluded that to have an egalitarian and libertarian society, it would be necessary to coerce the society by force of law—**the political stage**. It would be necessary to legislate liberty and equality. Neither, however, did this meet with success.

Finally, we entered the third stage in which it was concluded that if we are to have the egalitarian and libertarian society, it will have to be coerced, by force of arms if necessary, bringing us to **the military stage**. This was the stage implemented in Europe in the Revolution of 1848. In the United States it brought about the first large-scale attempt to implement revolutionary ideology in what is known as the Civil War and Reconstruction (1855-1877).

The Revolutionary Nature of the Civil War and Reconstruction

The so-called American Civil War and Reconstruction was, as we have said, the first revolution fired by the revolutionary faith and vision in American civilization. The Union was revolutionized with bayonets, successfully shifting the United States from a federal union or state to a national union or state by force of arms. It was not, then, in the final analysis, fought over chattel slavery, but resulted from a clash of worldviews.

Chattel slavery was the pretext. The injustices apparent in the institution of slavery were used to drum up support for the revolutionaries' effort, which had a much larger objective than the elimination of slavery. The issue was the nature of the state. Shall the state be that of a federal union, that is, a Constitutional union, or shall it be that of a national union? Shall we continue with a system of divided authority and diffused power, or shall we proceed to a system in which government is given the final authority and, thereby, is rendered sovereign? Will we move away from federalism derived from feudalism to embrace nationalism? That was the question. In this regard, we would note that the United States was the last of the Western nations to go nationalistic.

That the aggressors were motivated, not primarily by concern that slaves were being unjustly treated but by an ideology which necessitated a centralization of power, is supported by the following two statistics.

First, we are told that the primary concern of the anti-slavery people whose efforts triggered the conflict was the expansion of slavery into the territories. Yet, in 1860 there were a total of sixty-three (63) chattel slaves in all of the seven United States' territories combined. Slavery in the territories was not a significant factor and was not likely to become such. What person in his or her right mind would possibly suggest that the Americans should fight a war costing more than a million lives (military and civilian) because sixty-three persons in the territories were slaves?

Secondly, in 1860 there were, in all of the so-called "slave states" (that is, states in which chattel slavery was legal) 2,500,000-3,000,000 African

Americans. Of these 500,000-1,000,000 were not chattel slaves, but were actually free persons. Why? This was a consequence of the significant manumission movement which was gaining momentum.

The manumission movement, however, was stopped dead in its tracks by an event which occurred in 1831 in southeast Virginia. A brilliant chattel slave by the name of Nat Turner (1800-1831) obtained and read some inflamingly revolutionizing abolitionist literature and was incited to violence. He raised a band of followers who, before they were stopped, put to death more than eighty (80) persons in southeastern Virginia. This became known as the Nat Turner rebellion, and it sent shock waves throughout the southern states. Tragically, it all but eliminated the manumission movement and generated fear in the hearts and minds of Southerners, inducing some Southerners to take positions which were not Biblical as, for example, that slavery is a positive good and all the rest that the revolutionaries who have written the histories like to focus on. How much better it would have been if the institution of slavery had been eliminated voluntarily.

A further tragedy is that ideological warfare, unlike warfare undertaken in the context of the tradition beginning and ending with God, results, and logically so, in widespread unmitigated violence. When one goes to war for purely ideological reasons, one really does not know when to begin and when to end that war. Therefore, fired by revolutionary zeal, one can slip into the mentality that the good (ideological) end justifies any and every means. The result is **total war** and **unconditional surrender**.

In the post-Classical West, warfare had essentially been, with respect to its procedure, a clash between military forces. Following the engagement, both sides, victor and vanquished, would sit down and work out a new arrangement in light of the new power realities. Modern war, however, has a new target: the defenseless civilian population made up of older men, women, and children. It also brandishes a new weapon: fire. Both were evident in, for example, the 1864 activities of Sheridan and in Sherman's march to the sea.

Indeed, the latest expression of modern warfare to date is terrorism, in which innocent bystanders, whether in an airport, restaurant, or wherever, can suddenly be blown into smithereens for ideological reasons. Of course, terrorism is not the ultimate expression of modern warfare; we see germ warfare and biological warfare on the horizon today, with their unimaginable horrors.

Elsewhere we chronicle the events and attempt to come to grips with the unprecedented revolutionary destruction and devastation which took place during the American Civil War. Suffice it here to note that when General Robert E. Lee surrendered at Appomattox courthouse, it was not as a consequence of having been driven from the field of battle. It was because, as a Biblical Christian, Lee had reached the conclusion that there was no Biblical justification for further loss of life.

By the way, examining chattel slavery on the basis of the weight of the entire Bible (because, of course, if we only pick and choose isolated bits and pieces we can come up with anything we wish) we find that it is not Biblical to declare unequivocably that slavery is inherently evil. We find in the Bible, for example, a case in which a chattel slave is being instructed by God through the Apostle Paul to return to his master. Therefore, if chattel slavery were inherently evil, God would be the author of evil, as He commanded evil through the Apostle Paul.

Nevertheless, slavery, wherever it appears (chattel or otherwise), is a consequence of evil and the sludge of the Fall coming down so heavily to each of us and, accordingly, Christians must always lean hard against slavery in whatever form it takes (chattel or otherwise). Accordingly, it is Biblical to pray and work toward the abolishment of slavery; the stance during the 1800s would have been pro-abolition.

Moreoever, two wrongs have never made a right, nor will they ever make a right. Chattel slavery was legally recognized by the United States Constitution; slaves were legal property. Biblically speaking, therefore, those who induced their slaves to leave their masters were guilty of theft and will one day stand before God and give an account. Obviously, the Constitution needed to be changed, and the democratic processes should have been used to render chattel slavery illegal and bring about the legal abolition of slavery.

If the abolitionists had been sincere, they could have passed the hat among themselves and, with the proceeds, they could have purchased the liberty of chattel slave after chattel slave after chattel slave. There is a saying in the United States that if one really believes in something, one is willing "to put one's money where one's mouth is." The Englishman John Wesley (1703-1791), as a Biblical Christian, was strongly opposed to slavery; he was pro-abolition. One of his Biblical Christian followers, William Wilberforce (1759-1833), came to oppose chattel slavery to the extent that he devoted his service as a member of Parliament to the struggle against slavery; these efforts were strenuously opposed because of the wealth associated with slavery. He worked tirelessly in Parliament, indeed, with incredible persistence against seemingly insurmountable odds, to bring about the legal abolition of chattel slavery.

The efforts of Wilberforce first began to realize success when Parliament passed A Bill for the Abolition of the Slave Trade in 1807. Finally in 1833, the year he lay dying, Parliament legislated the abolition of chattel slavery throughout the whole of the British empire. The methodology which was used to liberate the slaves was Biblical and included a very important, Biblical Christian proviso: the liberty of every chattel slave would be purchased at a just market price.

With respect to the Civil War and Reconstruction, before it was all over (as late as the 1920s), the general U.S. government paid out "bonuses" (political handouts) to the veterans of the Union armies totaling more than twenty billion dollars ($20,000,000,000). It would have cost, however, less than twenty billion dollars in 1860 to have purchased the liberty of every chattel slave in the nation at the going market price! This is not even to mention the cost of the war, and we cannot put a price on one single life, yet there were more than 1,000,000 lives lost in the Civil War and Reconstruction, military and civilian combined.

As an aside, it is sobering to realize that the worst form of slavery the world has known to date has been the slavery we have witnessed during the twentieth century. Chattel slavery was a system in which one person could theoretically own another, but we have witnessed in the twentieth century a system of slavery in which it is presupposed that the state can legally possess all the people who live within its framework and can arbitrarily do with those people whatever it chooses!

The tragic stories of people who have lived in communist-controlled nations exemplify this form of slavery—people in Poland, people in former Soviet Russia, people in Cambodia, North Vietnam, North Korea, China. If the state deems that everyone would be better off without you, you have no hope. On the whim of the sovereign state, you could be sent to a slave labor camp or a mental institution or subjected to humiliations or death. If it is true that Biblical Christians must lean hard against slavery in whatever form it appears, what are we proposing to do about this?

There is a Biblical Christian methodology, my friends. The end does not justify, and never will, any and every means. Certainly, during this turbulent period of our history, a Biblical Christian would have resisted slavery, but would have done so Biblically. In the United States, a number of Biblical Christians, such as Charles Finney (1792-1875) and others, were engaged in abolition for what we might call the "right" reasons; however, they were outnumbered and, in many cases, their efforts were bent and blent into the grand schemes and designs of revolutionary abolitionism.

NOTES

1. Citation: From Ralph Waldo Emerson's first book, <u>Nature</u> (Chapter 1), first published in 1836, found in <u>The Complete Essays and Other Writings of Ralph Waldo Emerson</u>, New York: The Modern Library, 1940, p. 6.
2. Compiler's Biographical Note: According to John Stuart Mill, whose father, James Mill, by the way, was a leading utilitarian and the primary promoter of Bentham's ideas, it was Bentham who "broke the spell" of reverence for English institutions and introduced a criticism of them which would not theretofore have been tolerated. Mill also indicates that Bentham's greatest influence was through his writings. In 1776, as a young jurist, Bentham wrote critically of [that is, revolutionarily opposed] William Blackstone's Bible-based four-volume <u>Commentaries on the Laws of England</u> (1769) charging it with being a stumbling block to reform. He also wrote <u>Introduction to the Principles of Morals and</u>

Legislation (1789) and, in 1823, helped establish *Westminster Review* to spread his [revolutionary] doctrine.

3. Citation: "The father of English innovation both in doctrines and in institutions, is Bentham: he is the great subversive, or, in the language of continental philosophers, the great critical, thinker of his age and country." Quoted from an essay on "Bentham" by John Stuart Mill, *London and Westminster Review*, Aug. 1838 (also revised and published in Mill's Dissertations and Discussions, Political, Philosophical, and Historical, vol. 1, London: Parker, 1859).

4. Bibliographical Reference: Lewis, C.S. The Problem of Pain, Macmillan, 1962.

5. Bible Reference: *Hebrews 12:6:* For whom the Lord loveth he chasteneth… (KJV) See also Deuteronomy 8:5, Job 5:17, Proverbs 3:11, Hebrews 12:5, 6, 7, 8, 11, Revelation 3:19.

6. Bibliographical Note: Freedom's Ferment: Phases of American Social History to 1860 is the classic cataloging of antebellum reform written by Alice Felt Tyler (b. 1892), Minneapolis, MN: The University of Minnesota Press, 1944 (608 pp.).

7. Citation: *Proverbs 22:6 (KJV)*

8. Citation: From Ralph Waldo Emerson's first book, Nature (Chapter 1), first published in 1836, found in The Complete Essays and Other Writings of Ralph Waldo Emerson, New York: The Modern Library, 1940, p. 6.

9. Citation: Emerson, Ralph Waldo, *The Over-Soul*, in The Complete Essays and Other Writings of Ralph Waldo Emerson, New York: The Modern Library, 1940, p. 262.

10. Compiler's Citation: I could not find the entire phrase in Emerson's writings. However, the separate phrases are well represented; examples follow. "…let the soul be erect, and all things will go well." (*The Transcendentalist* in The Complete Essays and Other Writings of Ralph Waldo Emerson. New York: The Modern Library, 1940, p. 90.) In the essay *Self Reliance*: "We must go alone…" (Essays by Ralph Waldo Emerson, Harper & Row, Publishers, 1951, p. 52.) Regarding the phrase "possess the universe:" "Historical Christianity…dwells, with noxious exaggeration about the person of Jesus. The soul knows no persons. It invites every man to expand to the full circle of the universe…" He also says of the scholar, "Let him know that the world is his, but he must possess it by putting himself into harmony with the constitution of things." (p. 173) (*Literary Ethics (1838)*, in Nature: Addresses and Lectures, published in Centenary Edition: The Complete Works of Ralph Waldo Emerson, 12 vols., Vol. 1, pp. 153-187.)

11. Bible Reference: *Proverbs. 4:23 (KJV)* (*NIV:* Above all else, guard your heart, for it is the wellspring of life.)

12. Bible Reference: *I Samuel 16:7* (*NIV:* The Lord does not look at the things man looks at. Man looks at the outward appearance, but the LORD looks at the heart.)

8 PROCESS PHILOSOPHY (1870s–PRESENT)

*Our twentieth century has turned out to be more
cruel than those preceding it. . . .
Let us not forget that violence does not and cannot
flourish by itself: it is inevitably intertwined with
lying. . . . In Russia, proverbs about truth are favorites.
They persistently express the considerable, bitter, grim
experience of the people, often astonishingly:
"One Word of Truth Outweighs the World."*

Alexander Solzhenitsyn[1]

W e will now discuss the view which has predominated during the last
century and a quarter. This view came to be known as process
philosophy. We will begin with its nature, then its presuppositions, followed
by a look at one of its major expressions, Marxism, from among the four I
usually discuss: Darwinism, Pragmatism, Marxism, and Freudianism. We
will then be in a position to examine and summarize the institutional
structure and procedure of process philosophy.

THE ABANDONMENT OF THE SUPERNATURAL

Process philosophy emerged out of the failure of Romanticism-
Transcendentalism, a failure which resulted in a very profound theological
shift. The reader will recall that with Romanticism-Transcendentalism
(1830s-1860s) there had been a restatement of pantheism—the view that

God, man, and Nature (so-called) are one and the same. Those who subscribed to Romanticism-Transcendentalism had anticipated that, as this view was implemented, given the presupposed reality that man is God or part and parcel of God, the result would be progress if not ultimately perfection.

Instead, it resulted in the Revolutions of 1848 in Europe—during which thousands of lives were lost and many people fled (emigrating, by the way, most significantly to the United States)—and in the First American Revolution, known as the Civil War and Reconstruction (1855-1877), in the United States—during which more than a million lives were lost, both military and civilian. Indeed, the loss of life and the destruction wrought during the Civil War and Reconstruction was unprecedented in the post-Classical West.

The intellectual community was devastated. Faced with the obvious failure of Romanticism-Transcendentalism, it struggled to begin to explain the nature of the flaw in Romanticism-Transcendentalism and to find a new faith and vision by which to live. Ultimately, it found itself forced to conclude that the basic problem must be the very idea of God. Viewing it as something of an all-or-nothing proposition, the prevailing view shifted from pan- (or all) theism to a- (or non) theism.

This produced the view which has prevailed for the last century and a half—which I call **the theology of non-theism** and **the religion of non-theism**. Instead of returning to the Biblical God and embracing the tradition beginning with God, the intellectuals of the world eschewed the very idea of God, necessitating an even greater repudiation of Biblical Christianity.

This shift was articulated in a very influential book by the German philosopher, Ludwig Feuerbach (1804-1872), published in 1843, titled The Essence of Christianity. In this book, Feuerbach (who had a profound influence on Marx and Engels) proved to his satisfaction the mythology of the supernatural and of Christianity. His arguments satisfied most of the leading intellectuals of that day. Indeed, Feuerbach came to be worshipped by the intellectual community, and many of the brightest young people went to Berlin to study with him.

The Migrating Intellectual Center of Western Civilization

It is helpful to keep in mind that, as we had moved out of the eighteenth century into the nineteenth century, the intellectual center of the West had shifted. Where had been the intellectual center during the eighteenth century (1700s)? In **France**, obviously. Voltaire, for example, was probably the best known person in the world during his lifetime. One could argue that the previous century, the seventeenth century (1600s), had been intellectually centered in **England**. As we move, then, into the nineteenth century (1800s), the intellectual center will shift from France to the **German states** (so called in the recognition that Germany was not united until 1871). Throughout the nineteenth century most intellectuals, including Americans, went to one or more of the German universities to complete their graduate work, including their terminal degrees. (United States institutions did not grant terminal degrees until 1876 when Johns Hopkins University, modeled after the German universities, offered a Ph.D.)

Thus, as early as 1843, we have Feuerbach arguing quite persuasively among the intellectual community the non-existence of God and the mythology of the supernatural and of Christianity. Feuerbach presaged the existence of **process philosophy.**

By the way, regarding the tradition beginning and ending with God, although his work did not become internationally known, there was a Biblical Christian in Holland by the name of Guillame Groen van Prinsterer (1801-1876) who published in 1847 a penetrating, Biblical Christian analysis of the nature of revolution and its consequences; indeed, it is the best treatment of which I am aware. The work became a Dutch classic (<u>Ongeloof en Revolutie)</u> but was not made available in English until 1989: <u>Groen Van Prinsterer's Lectures on Unbelief and Revolution</u>, edited by Harry Van Dyke (Wedge Publishing Foundation, Jordan Station: Ontario, Canada).

Abandonment of the Supernatural Yields: Naturalism, Materialism, Historicism, Socialism, Relativism

What are the intellectual consequences of concluding that there is no supernatural, no God? They are inescapable. If there is no God the only remaining possibility becomes Nature or the natural which, when absolutized brings us to **Naturalism**. If there is no supernatural, there most certainly can be no Biblical supernatural—no Biblical God—and if there is no Biblical God, there can finally be nothing spiritual and the only remaining possibility becomes the material, which when absolutized brings us to **materialism**. If there is no Biblical supernatural, there can finally be nothing eternal and the only remaining possibility becomes the temporal or the historical, which when absolutized brings us to **historicism**. If there is no Biblical supernatural there can finally be nothing personal and the only remaining possibility is the social, which when absolutized brings us to **socialism**. If there is no Biblical supernatural then there can finally be nothing absolute—permanently fixed—and the only remaining possibility is the relative which when absolutized brings us to **relativism**.

If one understands what has just been stated, one can understand the modern world; however, a failure to understand what has just been stated is a complete failure to understand the modern world because what has happened, particularly during the last century and a quarter, is a direct consequence of the abandonment of the supernatural and all that is necessitated by such in thinking and behavior. Ultimately, as we shall see, there will be efforts to implement views which are the convergence and conglomeration of naturalism, materialism, historicism, socialism, and relativism.

> **Consequences of the abandonment of the supernatural:**
> Supernatural to Natural (to naturalism)
> Spiritual to material (to materialism)
> Eternal to temporal (to historicism)
> Personal to social (to socialism)

THE PROFOUND SHIFT FROM ABSOLUTE
TO PROCESS PHILOSOPHY

The abandonment of the supernatural, then, leaves us with a process view of life and existence, including man. We shift from an absolutist view to a process view, which comes to be known as process philosophy. Prior to the abandonment of the supernatural, most intellectuals believed that reality is ultimately based on that which does not change—whether a presupposed Biblical supernatural or a presupposed immutable, indestructible natural law or, even, a presupposed organological nature with theistic characteristics. Thus, the unintelligible is unchangeable. With the abandonment of the supernatural, however, the conclusion was reached that there is nothing but change. Life and existence are but a perpetual flux, a phenomenal flow, an endless stream, a chain of events, a process of becoming. To use the metaphor popularized by Heraclitis, the Greek (500s-400s B.C.), one could never step into the same river twice.

Given this shift, we no longer, ontologically speaking, have the possibility of being, but only of becoming for, indeed, I am not at this moment what I was a moment ago and I am not now what I will be a moment hence. Nor are we; nor is anything. Everything is in the process of change.

The difference between these two views of existence—the so-called absolute and process views—is titanic. Both hold that reality is behind appearance, that that which appears to be is not, in fact, the case. The absolutist would argue that that which appears to be in a process of change can only be ultimately understood on the basis of being in relationship with that which does not change—once again, such as the Biblical God or immutable, indestructible, natural law.

Conversely, the process thinker would argue that that which appears to be fixed can only ultimately be understood as being in the process of change. For example, a chair in the room in which one is located appears to be fixed, but in reality it is in a process of change. The process philosophers would advance theories to try to document the nature of this change as, for example, the molecular, then the atomic, then the subatomic theories. Everything is in perpetual motion. Thus, the ultimate reality of what-is is **process** or change. It is not possible to understand the history of the world from the nineteenth century forward without understanding this profound shift from absolute to process philosophy.

Three Revolutions Productive of the Modern World

Indeed, to understand the modern world, including the prevailing views of government, law, economics, and international relations, we must understand the three revolutions which have been productive (or as we would prefer it—destructive) thereof.

The first of the three overpowering revolutions, which we have been laboring to summarize at some length, is the shift from theo- to anthropocentrism—from God-centeredness to a man-centeredness. The second, which we have just introduced, is the shift from a presupposed absolute to a presupposed process philosophy or view of existence. The third, which we will later introduce, is the shift from an antithetical to a synthetic mentality and way of thinking.

PRESUPPOSITIONS OF PROCESS PHILOSOPHY

Inherent in so-called process philosophy are four presuppositions:

- relativism
- environmentalism
- progressivism
- developmentalism.

These four presuppositions constitute the mentality of so-called modern and post-modern man.

Relativism: There is Ultimately Nothing Fixed

We have already noted that, if there is no Biblical supernatural then, finally, there can be nothing absolute—permanently fixed—and the only remaining possibility is the relative. This, when absolutized, brings us to relativism. We are left with nothing beyond the space-time continuum. Everything is in the process of change. Nothing is fixed. There is no truth in any fixed sense.

With the advent of process philosophy, many became concerned with the so-called moral relativity which it produced. There being no longer any possibility of truth in any absolute sense, presupposed morality based on either natural law or a presupposed organological unity disintegrated. We were left with relative opinions or life-styles and there was no basis for holding that any one was better than another. Biblical Christians recognize that what we have lost is not morality, but knowing and doing the truth, which is godliness or righteousness.

Environmentalism: Material Constituency is Determinative

The second presupposition is to acknowledge that the material constituency or environment is the ultimate. In this case, everything is determined by the material constituency. We call this an environmentalism in popular parlance.[2] It is no longer that man, made in the image of God, is to exercise dominion over creation or his "environment." Rather, it is that the eternal, ever-changing environment has itself produced man. Thus, the environment determines who man is and, accordingly, as the environment is changed, so man will be changed.

The process thinkers, however, have never agreed among themselves as to which component of the so-called material constituency is determinative. For a Darwin it was the biological component. For a Marx it was the economic component, for a Dewey the volitional component, for a Freud the presupposed psychic component, for a Crick the chemical component, for a McLuhan the media component, and on and on we could go. The point of agreement is that the environment or its constituency is determinative—environmentalism.

Progressivism: Presupposed Progress

The third presupposition is progressivism. This is the faith that the movement or flow of that which exists is progressive. This is certainly a leap of faith. Obviously, if the movement is not progressive, it is regressive, and we could not live on the basis of such. Therefore, we presuppose that the movement is from lower to higher, from simple to complex, from savagery to civilization, from primitivism to perfection. Indeed, as we listen to the way people speak, even in the face of things being to the contrary, people continue to categorize things as being "primitive," "civilized," or "progressive." We have all heard, for example, of primitive man.

Developmentalism: The "Genetic" Method

The fourth and final presupposition of process philosophy is developmentalism, which is the view that the only way to understand where we are and why we are where we are is the genetic method. Thus, we must trace everything back to its point of origin, follow it therefrom to where it now stands in all its complexity and, then, on the basis of how it has developed to date, we can project where it is trending.

So, in the case of homo sapiens [sapiens meaning wise or intelligent], which is presumably the highest form of existence to date, we trace back to the presupposed unicellular protoplasmic object from which we emerged and follow the gradual development until we reach the current apex of complexity to which we refer as *homo sapiens*. Having followed our genetic development to the present moment, we are now positioned to project where we and, indeed, all of existence, are trending. On this basis, we speculate as to the possibilities. This is developmentalism. If one does not think this mentality is pervasive, consider how often we use the term develop as in, "Let me develop this for you." I slip into that mentality myself.

The four presuppositions of process philosophy, then, which came about as the result of the abandonment of the supernatural are relativism, environmentalism, progressivism, and developmentalism.

By the way, the influence of process philosophy has been increasingly evidenced in the lives of students with whom I have worked. For example, I have noticed in my teaching that the present generation, raised almost exclusively on a diet of relativity, is all but incapable of constructive classroom discussion. The best one can expect is an exchange of opinions. God could care less, however, about my opinion—or anyone else's opinion. For this reason, even in discussion courses, I have found it necessary to minimize the time for discussion. Moreover, process philosophy is so pervasive today that there is a tremendous price to be paid for standing against it. To stand for absolute truth and for knowing and doing the truth requires incredible courage and determination. This is true in almost every field of study and endeavor.

For the last century and a half, it has been process philosophy which has been filtering down from the intellectual community into the general culture. There have been a number of influential expressions of process philosophy, all of which could be discussed profitably. I usually discuss at length the following four: Darwinism, Pragmatism, Marxism, and Freudianism. Here, however, we will discuss only Marxism, given its profound influence in international politics.

NOTES

1. Solzhenitxyn, Alexander, <u>Nobel Lecture</u>, NY: Farrar, Straus, and Giroux, 1972, p. 22, 33-34.
2. Compiler's bibliographical note: Environmentalism is treated Biblically in Francis Schaeffer's <u>Pollution and the Death of Man: the Christian View of Ecology</u>, Tyndale House, 1970.

9 THE MARXIST ANALYSIS OF HISTORY (1870s–PRESENT)

"The purpose of my writing ... is to convert people from theology to anthropology, from love of god(s) to love of their fellow human beings, from being candidates for life after death to being students of this life; to free them from religious and political servitude to heavenly or earthly monarchies and aristocracies; to make them into self-confident citizens of the Earth."

Ludwig Feuerbach[1]

It is quite obvious that, of all of the expressions of process philosophy to date, the Marxist expression has had the greatest global impact. This is certainly the case in terms of international politics, with which the twentieth and twenty-first centuries have largely been preoccupied. Indeed, it is not possible to understand what transpired during the twentieth century or what is taking place today without an understanding of the Marxist analysis of history, the Marxist-Leninist-Communist faith and vision (1870s-present), and the pervasive influence of Marxism in the intellectual community of the non-communist West and world. Please note that Karl Marx lived from 1818 to 1883 and Vladimir Lenin some fifty years later, from 1870 to 1924.

The following analysis of Marxism owes much to the life and work of the brilliant Australian, Dr. Fred Schwarz. See his excellent, brief volume, You Can Trust the Communists to Be Communists.[2]

KARL MARX (1818-1883):
HIS PRESUPPOSITIONS AND ANALYSIS OF HISTORY

Karl Marx lived and worked from 1818 to 1883. Marx subscribed to what might be called the "triune doctrines" of 1) atheism, 2) materialism, and 3) economic determinism.

In the first place, Marx, agreeing with most contemporary intellectuals, dispensed with the idea of God and, accordingly, was forced to turn elsewhere to explain the origin and nature of man. Consequently, he adopted materialism, and relative to this second basic doctrine he was equally emphatic: Man is an evolutionary animal, the highest of the animals, and yet an animal and no more; man is, as it were, matter in motion. Finally, and yet more significantly, Marx posited an economic determinism: the view that man is a victim and product of the economic component of his material constituency.

Having said this, however, we have said nothing, for the theoretical essence of Marxism is **dialectical materialism**, which Marx derived by taking the dialectic from the German philosopher, Friedrich Hegel (1770-1831), and fusing it with the materialism of the German philosopher, Ludwig Feuerbach (1804-1872). To understand Marxism and, even more significantly, to understand the third overpowering revolution in thought forms which has produced the modern world (see box below), we must first understand dialectical materialism.

> **The Three Revolutions of the Modern West and World**
> Theocentrism to Anthropocentrism
> Absolute to Process Philosophy
> Antithetical to Synthetic Mentality

To understand dialectical materialism, we must understand its first vital component: Hegelian dialecticism. This will prove well worth our effort, as it was Hegelian dialecticism which was productive of or, as I have often said, destructive of, the third of the revolutions in thought form. Therefore, it is not possible to understand the modern West and world without understanding the nature of Hegelian dialecticism.

HEGELIAN DIALECTICISM: ADVENT OF THE SYNTHETIC THOUGHT FORM

Georg Wilhelm Friedrich (G.W.F.) Hegel[3] (1770-1831) was a very complex individual. He is reputed to have said, "Only one man has understood me, and even he has not."[4] (Marx, however, came along, as we shall see, and said that he understood Hegel whereas Hegel had not understood himself!)

Hegel was simultaneously a philosopher and a historian and, as such, he was interested in the history of philosophy and the philosophy of history. Most people who have studied the history of philosophy have been rather bored. I personally enjoy the study of philosophy, but I can understand why most people do not, because the history of philosophy proceeds something as follows: a given individual will appear and suggest that the answers to the basic questions are to be found within a particular framework or circle; it is not long, however, before another individual or group of individuals will articulate flaws and suggest an alternative framework or circle; in time, yet another individual or group of individuals suggests yet another framework; and on we go *ad infinitum, ad nauseum.*

Hegel, recognizing this and attempting to solve the dilemma, suggested that the reason we have not "gotten it all together" and, indeed, are not "getting it all together" is that we have not been thinking correctly. Heretofore, we have been thinking Biblically, in so many words (though, of course, Hegel did not say that directly); instead, we need to learn to think historically. Heretofore, we have been thinking linearly, that is, in terms of thesis vs. antithesis. Thus, if "A" is true, "non-A" is false, so it is either "A" or "non-A." Hence, thinking linearly, we have been thinking absolutistically, "A" vs. "non-A," antithetically. Biblical or linear thinking is crudely illustrated in the following diagram:

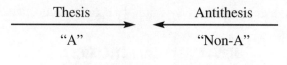

EITHER "A" <u>OR</u> "NON-A"

Hegel argued that, if we are to understand existence and the process of history, we must learn to think historically. (Hegel, by the way, is an excellent example of a person who has succumbed to historicism, one who absolutizes history). Therefore, to understand the process of history, Hegel suggested, we need to learn to shift in our thought forms. Instead of thinking linearly, absolutistically, and antithetically, we should think triangularly, relativistically, and synthetically. It is not thesis vs. antithesis; it is not "A" vs. "non-A;" it is not either "A" or "non-A." It is <u>both</u> "A" <u>and</u> "non-A."

Thus, it is **thesis, antithesis, synthesis**. "A" is true in one sense, "non-A" is true in another sense, so the two are fused into a synthesis which enables one to enjoy the best of both. In effect, it is imagined—falsely and, indeed, tragically from the Biblical perspective—that one can "have one's cake and eat it, too," as the saying goes.

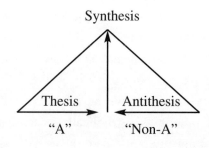

BOTH "A" <u>AND</u> "NON-A"

Hegel's suggestion effected a revolution in thought form because, prior to Hegel, most intellectuals tended to think linearly, absolutistically, antithetically. That is to say, they thought in terms of truth versus error, good versus evil, righteousness versus unrighteousness, light versus darkness. Subsequent to Hegel, and influenced thereby, intellectuals came increasingly to think in varying shades of gray, in terms of a process of ongoing relativity. They began to think triangularly, relativistically, synthetically.

This revolution in thought form swept through the intellectual community, but did not work its way into the general culture in Europe until the inter-war years between 1919 and 1939, and did not come to influence the United States with full force until after World War II (1939-1945). It became particularly apparent during the 1960s. At that time we were told that Americans were suddenly suffering from a generation gap, because children could no longer communicate with parents and parents could not communicate with children. We were not, however, suffering from a generation gap. We were experiencing and witnessing a revolution in thought form. Parents in the United States born prior to World War II were born into a time in which there was at least a hangover of the antithetical mentality, but children born to parents in the United States subsequent to World War II were born into an era increasingly possessed of a synthetic mentality.

To illustrate the profundity of this shift, this, indeed, revolution in thought form, one could, as an example, tell a young lady to "be good" and, prior to the revolution in thought form, that conveyed a certain absolute content suggesting that the young lady could do certain things but should refrain from doing certain other things. Subsequent to the revolution in thought form, however, one could, as an example, tell a young lady to "be good," and that conveyed no absolute content. All that was being suggested was "do what you will."

The **dialectical** or synthetic thought form, then, was introduced by Hegel, who attempted to understand all of life beginning with a dialectical philosophy of history.

MARX FUSES THE DIALECTIC WITH
A THOROUGH-GOING MATERIALISM

How was it that Marx thought that he understood Hegel whereas Hegel did not understand himself? Hegel was a so-called *idealist* philosopher, believing that the historical dialectical process was driven by "spiritual" forces (to which he referred variously as the World Spirit, or Destiny). Marx, on the other hand, having been liberated from idealism, had become a thorough-going *materialist*. Accordingly, Marx believed that, unlike Hegel, he had penetrated to the understanding that the dialectical process is being driven materialistically; he had arrived at materialistic determinism.

How did Marx arrive at a materialistic determinism? He did so by embracing the materialism of Ludwig Feuerbach. As a student of political science at the University of Berlin (1830s), Marx, along with Engels and many other intellectuals, came under the influence of what was known as "left-wing Hegelianism," which was another name for Feuerbachian Hegelianism. This materialistic view later, *a la* Marx, resulted in dialectical materialism. (By the way, the University of Berlin was then a global center for the study of political science. Given the shift to the view that the state was sovereign, there was no discipline more significant at that point in time than political science.)

Ludwig Feuerbach (1804-1872), a pupil of Hegel's, had become an influential German intellectual. In 1841, ten years after Hegel's death, he published his very influential analysis, The Essence of Christianity, in which he proved to his satisfaction and that of the vast majority of the intellectuals of that day the mythology or non-existence of God and the mythology of Biblical Christianity. Engels later wrote, "We all at once became Feuerbachians."[5]

The conclusion that God is mythological left Feuerbach with a vacuum, of course, for how are we to understand the what-is-ness-of-what-is if not on the basis of the existence of the Biblical God? Feuerbach became a thorough-going materialist. Indeed, he finally came to the conclusion that, in effect, man is what he eats. You cannot be much more materialistic than that!

BOTH MARX AND ENGELS FOUND EVANGELICAL CHRISTIANITY WANTING

Before we trace the presuppositions of dialectical materialism and examine their consequences, we must share a very sad story, indeed, a tragic story, which will wrench the heart of any Biblical Christian. Many people do not realize that both Karl Marx and Friedrich Engels, his major collaborator, were born and raised in Evangelical Christian homes.

Karl Marx (1818-1883) was born and raised in the city of Trier in the Rhineland of Prussia. Karl's parents, both descended from lines of rabbinical scholars, had become Evangelical Christians (Lutheran) before he was born.[6] The Marx family regularly attended the only Protestant church in Trier, in which Marx was confirmed in 1834. It must be noted, however, that both home and church were significantly influenced by rationalistic elements.

Friedrich Engels (1820-1895), Marx's supporter, collaborator, and editor, was also raised in a Christian home, and one which was thoroughly Evangelical. He went to the University of Berlin, where he studied political science, as did Marx, and where he also came under the influence of left-wing Hegelianism. Under the influence of rationalism and, in particular, Hegelianism, he began to question sincerely and seriously, not only his Christian faith, but Christianity in general.

During these years, Engels corresponded with two former classmates, brothers, both of whom had become Evangelical pastors. Engels wrote to one on more than one occasion, setting forth that he was beginning to embrace left-wing Hegelianism and pleading with his friend to refute what he was being taught. He was obviously hoping that his pastor friend would be able to convince him that what he was being taught and was coming to believe was wrong. Tragically, however, it appears that the pastor was incapable of rising to the occasion. Not being a Biblical Christian, he would not know how to think Biblically and, therefore, could not understand what was taking place within the intellectual community.

How many people like Karl Marx and Friedrich Engels have we lost in Evangelical Christendom because we have not gone all the way with God, finally becoming Biblical Christians and mastering Biblical Christian thinking, learning to think beginning and ending with God? Indeed, it has been a lamented reality for years in the United States among Evangelical Christians that only a small percentage of youth born into Evangelical Christian families remain Christian into their early twenties.

THREE PRESUPPOSITIONS OF DIALECTICAL MATERIALISM

Marx, then, was thoroughly converted to non-theism at the University of Berlin and embraced left-wing Hegelianism, having come under the influence of Ludwig Feuerbach, who was as thoroughgoing a materialist as one can imagine. Attempting to fashion a worldview consistent with non-theism, Marx took the dialectic from Hegel (one could say that he stole it), fused it with the materialism of Feuerbach, and derived from this his presupposed dialectical materialism.

Inherent in dialectical materialism are three presuppositions, each of which will be examined in turn.

1. Progess is inherent in change

The first presupposition is that progress is inherent within change. All change is progressive. That is, there is no change that occurs that does not constitute progress. This explains why, of course, a person caught up in this mentality always favors change. How many discussions have we had with people who assume for no reason that change will be beneficial? Later we will examine this presupposition with regard to death; what does one who has such a mentality do with the reality of death?

2. Nature acts dialectically

The second presupposition is that nature acts dialectically. Marx, of course, was a thoroughgoing naturalist. He did not believe, however, with the eighteenth century Rationalists, that nature acts mechanistically or statically on the basis of presupposed immutable, indestructible law (the so-called Newtonian universe). Nor did he believe, with the nineteenth century Romanticist-Transcendentalists, that nature acts organologically in the manner of a permanent abode of an all-pervasive cosmic mind. Nor, for Marx, does nature act evolutionarily. Rather, nature acts dialectically.

The dialectical process of nature (and history, which is driven thereby) can be illustrated by considering the manner in which a person might move from one point to another. One would not move in a linear, straight-line fashion, nor would one move in a progressive spiraling fashion, nor would one move in a random, drunken zigzag fashion. One would move in a sequence of forwards, backwards, forwards, backwards motions. Indeed, the Maoist communists of China once taught the children of China the dialectical mentality by having them march three steps forward, two back, three forward, two back. The presupposition is, again, that nature acts dialectically.

3. Conflict is the essence of change and the dynamic of progress.

The third presupposition, which is without question the most significant, is that **conflict** is the essence of change and the dynamic of progress. Marx, borrowing from Hegel at this point, held that there is in every situation an established force and direction or thesis which, in turn, generates its interpenetrating opposite, or antithesis. There cannot be in without out, up without down, over without under, wet without dry. As the established force and direction or thesis generates its interpenetrating opposite or antithesis, there is conflict between these two forces. This conflict, then, constitutes the dynamic of progress.

Thus, there is in every situation an established force and direction or thesis which generates its interpenetrating opposite or antithesis; the two conflict with one another giving rise to gradual change, which accelerates to more rapid change, finally reaching a critical nodal point; at this point, the antithesis negates the thesis, there is a transformation from quantity to quality and the emergence of a new force and direction, known as the

synthesis. This synthesis then, in turn, becomes the established force and direction or thesis, generates its interpenetrating opposite or antithesis. There is conflict, gradual change, rapid change, acceleration to a critical nodal point, negation of the negation, transformation from quantity to quality, the emergence of a new force and direction or synthesis, which becomes the established force and direction or thesis, and the process is repeated again and again. [See the diagram of Hegelian Dialecticism below.]

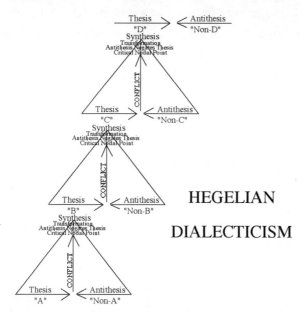

THE ESSENCE OF MARXISM: DIALECTICAL MATERIALISM APPLIED TO AN ANALYSIS OF HISTORY

Having said the above, we have said nothing, for if this were the essence of Marxism, it would not have endured to the present day with sufficient significance to be discussed. The essence of Marxism, and this is highly significant, is not in his theoretical abstract construct, but in his meticulous application of dialectical materialism to an understanding of the process of history: **the Marxist analysis of history**.

So significant was and is the Marxist analysis of history that 99.44 percent of the people who attempt to think today, including most Christians, are Marxist without even being aware of the nature of their thought-forms and conclusions. Indeed, I can tell in five minutes' time in serious conversation with any person whether that individual is of a Marxist orientation or not, and most are. If a person is not, it is a consequence of deliberately having learned how to think Biblically because, otherwise, if only inadvertently, most people are Marxist. The Marxist analysis of history is so pervasive that it is not possible today to be non-Marxist in one's thinking simply by default.

Why is this true? It is true for the following reason. Man, unlike any other creature, has been blessed with a memory. Accordingly, this being the case, it is not possible for man as an individual, nation, civilization, or race to think and, accordingly, act without drawing from and interpreting memory. We must employ some analysis of history.

Therefore, the question emerges, "How do we understand and make use of our memory as individuals, nations, civilizations, or a race?" We do so either Biblically, consciously beginning and ending with God, or on the basis of that which is substituted for God as the starting point and the terminal point of our understanding of the what-is-ness-of-what-is.

Now, follow me, because this is so fundamental. When we who have been holding on to what remains of Biblical Christianity in the West abandoned Biblical Christianity as a consequence of the shift to Evangelical Christianity, we also, if only inadvertently, abandoned the Biblical Christian worldview. That is, we no longer recognize God as applicable to all of life, having accepted the dichotomistic mind of sacred and secular. Therefore, we no longer have Biblical Christian thinking and an understanding of history beginning and ending with God! We abandoned a Biblical Christian philosophy, if you will, of history. (We recall that, in the West, it was Augustine who first introduced a Biblical Christian philosophy of history in The City of God.)

This, then, left a vacuum. If there is no Biblical Christian worldview, there can be no Biblical Christian understanding of history. If there is no Biblical Christian understanding of history, there is a vacuum and we must have some other understanding of history substituted for the Biblical Christian understanding of history. Someone's philosophy of history would come to fill the vacuum. Finally, Karl Marx's view came to do so with his attempt to understand history on the basis of presupposed dialectical materialism. The vacuum was so effectively filled that, as we have said, almost all people who attempt to think today do so on the basis of the Marxist analysis of history.

The Marxist Analysis of History Described

Let us, then, examine the Marxist analysis of history. How did Marx put flesh and blood on his so-called theoretical framework?

Marx, borrowing from Hegel, believed that history was moving inevitably and inexorably in a dialectical fashion through five stages on its way to ultimate perfection: from, in his terms, **primitive communalism**, through the **ancient slavocracy**, through **feudalism**, into **capitalism**, and on to **socialism**, at which point the dialectical process will terminate and, ultimately, history will blossom forth evolutionarily into the utopian society which Marx called **communism**.

In an effort to summarize these stages, we will begin with feudalism. Marx argued that during every historical stage there is a dominant class. For Marx, we will recall, it is the **economic** component of the material constituency which is determinative and, therefore, in each historical stage there will be a dominant economic class. What, then, will be the conflict which will bring about change (or "progress")? It will be that of class warfare.

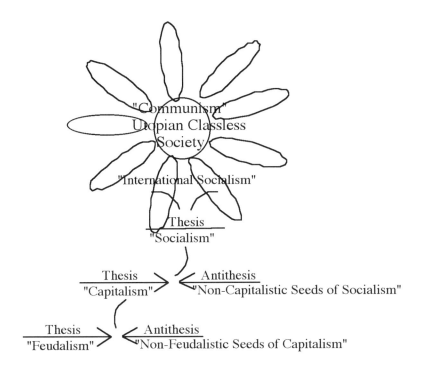

Thus, during the stage of feudalism, the dominant class according to Marx was the **landed aristocracy**. Feudalism, as the established force and direction, generated its interpenetrating opposite, there was conflict, gradual change, rapid change, critical nodal point, negation of the thesis by the antithesis, transformation from quantity to quality, and the emergence of a new force and direction or synthesis, which would become the established force and direction or thesis—which Marx argued was capitalism.

The dominant class during the capitalist stage, according to Marx, was the **bourgeoisie**. In turn, capitalism, as the established force and direction, would generate its interpenetrating opposite; there would be conflict, gradual change, rapid change, a critical nodal point, the negation of the thesis by the antithesis, transformation from quantity to quality, and the emergence of a new force and direction or synthesis which would become the established order, direction, or thesis which, according to Marx, would be socialism. The dominant class during the socialist stage would be the **proletariat**.

With the advent of socialism on an international scale, however, according to Marx, the dialectical process would terminate. Thereafter, history would not move dialectically by force, violence, and bloodshed, on the basis of conflict; rather, history would simply blossom forth evolutionarily into the utopian society of communism in which there would be no poverty, disease, ignorance, or war. Every person would think first of the other person and would take, accordingly, only to meet his or her own needs. No man would raise his hand against his brother and, hence, there would be no need for the police, no need for the military, even the international state would eventually wither away and die, and we would witness the advent of a utopian classless society.

This was the vision of Karl Marx, the Marxist analysis of history. And this is where we are today (evidenced, for example, in the title of a recent American First Lady's book: It Takes A Village.) Why has the Marxist analysis been so influential? As we have said, it is because of the shift within the intellectual community from the supernatural to the natural, from theism to non-theism. A vacuum resulted, and something had to fill that vacuum, for man **must** have a faith and a vision, a reason for living and a reason, if necessary, for dying.

MARXISM: SCIENCE OR RELIGION?

Marx believed that he had arrived at his analysis of history rationalistically or scientifically; he considered himself to be a child of the Enlightenment and a scientist. He referred to his system as **scientific socialism**, and to himself as a scientific socialist. He believed that he had finally unlocked the key to history, i.e., dialectical materialism, and that his work was uniquely scientific whereas all alternative explanations were not.

Was Marxism, indeed, a product of science? The Biblical response is immediate, "Absolutely not!" Marxism was and is a **religion.** That is what gives it its dynamics. It begins with an article of faith and it ends with an article of faith.

Marxism, however, is more than merely a religion. Indeed, it is a point by point perversion, plagiarism, and parody of Biblical Christianity. It is a standing of Biblical Christianity on its head. Which is to say that there never could have been Marxism as we know it had there not first been Biblical Christianity. This relationship could be explored in depth, which we cannot do here. Marx, rather than anticipating a perfect spiritual kingdom coming, into which man can gain entrance on the basis of the shed blood and finished work of God-in-Christ, anticipated a perfect material kingdom coming, into which man can gain entrance on the basis of the shed blood and the almighty works of collective man in cooperation with the impersonal process of history.

What we have in Marxism is the most intense effort to date to be absolutely consistent with the presuppositions of process philosophy, the religion of non-theism. We have in Marxism the convergence of the inescapable conclusions flowing from the presupposition of the non-existence of God. If we presuppose the non-existence of God, we inescapably end up with naturalism, materialism, historicism, and socialism; this is the pervasive thinking which dominates the West and world today. Marxism is simply a conglomerating of these: naturalism, materialism, historicism, and socialism. Marx, probably more thoroughly than anyone else, welded together the presuppositions and the conclusions of process philosophy, fashioning the most universally applicable statement of process philosophy to date.

Indeed, we can have the greatest respect for Karl Marx in terms of his commitment. Marx was more committed than anyone else; and that is why we have Marxism. Marx was a rather despicable character as a husband and a father, and his wife is to be greatly admired for staying with him. He was so preoccupied with his thoughts that he spent most of his time in the library or writing and working at his desk. Indeed, he died writing at his desk! I have met very few Christians who have had the same level of commitment as did Karl Marx in terms of his having attempted to think through the answers to the basic questions beginning with his presuppositions, in his case, the nonexistence of God. He was attempting to be absolutely consistent with the presuppositions of the religion of non-theism.

First Article of Faith: All change is progressive

Marxism as a religion, then, begins and ends with an article of faith. The point of departure is the presupposition, relative to dialectical materialism, that all change is progressive. One cannot empirically demonstrate that! Moreover, it would appear to be difficult to maintain such in the face of the ultimate reality of this age: death. Nevertheless, if you ever want to be exposed to tortured logic, ask a committed Marxist to explain death as progressive change. They will do so, of course, as long as you will listen. One who is committed to a religion will attempt to force the pieces to fit.

This initial article of the Marxist faith, that all change is progressive, is one reason for the reality that whenever Marxists come to power, there is wholesale destruction of life. Indeed, this is why the Marxists and, particularly, the Marxist-Leninists, put to death during the twentieth century countless millions of people, as we shall see, in the name of applied social science. They really believe that this is progressive change, because we are in the process of eliminating the bourgeoisie mentality. Death is viewed as prerequisite to progressive change and ultimate utopia.

Last Article of Faith: The dialectical process will terminate

The terminal point of dialectical materialism, which is the theoretical essence of the religion of Marxism, is also an article of faith. It is presupposed that with the advent of the presupposed international socialist order, the dialectical process must terminate. Even if one accepts the existence of socialism as defined by Marx, which the Biblical Christian most certainly would not, and accepts the existence of the dialectical process, which the Biblical Christian most certainly would not, the idea that the dialectical process will terminate with internationalized socialism can be nothing more than an article of faith. First of all, there has never been an international socialist order; therefore, how can we empirically demonstrate that, with the advent of a presupposed international socialist order, a presupposed dialectical process must terminate? Again, it is nothing more than an article of faith, but that is what gives Marxism its dynamics. It is a religion.

In all fairness to Marx, however, if he were alive and present with us, we could ask him a very logical question for which he would have an immediate response. The logical question would be, "Why must the presupposed dialectical process terminate with socialism on an international scale?" Marx would propose something along the following lines. The reader will recall that Marx proposed that with each critical nodal point there was a *transformation* (a word which, by the way, also comes from Biblical Christianity) from quantity to quality. This is more significant than at first appears. Marx was saying that, with every successive historical stage, we are moving from the less perfect toward the more perfect.

This is why, by the time we reach socialism, while we will not yet have arrived at perfection, socialism will contain within itself the seeds of perfection. Therefore, it will not be necessary to move dialectically, i.e., by force, violence, and bloodshed, into the next and final utopian stage. *Socialism*, containing the seeds of perfection, will simply blossom forth evolutionarily into perfection, in which no man will raise his hand against his brother, etc. Marx was presupposing, as it were, that we have moved from the jungles of savagery to the plains of civilization, that we are moving from the plains of civilization to the plateau of socialism, and that we will move from the plateau of socialism to the pinnacle of communism. That is the Marxist analysis.

Marxism Spawns a Movement of Revolutionaries

Marx believed that this process was inevitable and inexorable. There was nothing that man could do by taking thought or action, individually or collectively, to accelerate the process. Man could only recognize the process, applaud the process, and fall in step with the process, accepting force, violence, and bloodshed as the only means to the next stage. Marx argued that the stage that prevailed in his lifetime was that of capitalism and that we were moving, ultimately, into the next stage of socialism which would blossom forth into the utopian society of communism.

Marxism, however, and this is the important point which we shall discuss in the next chapter, spawned a movement of revolutionaries, the likes of which the world had never seen before. We have already discussed the revolutionaries who emerged out of the rationalist faith and the French Revolution. We have observed how the revolutionaries were given greater impetus as a result of Romanticism-Transcendentalism. However, from the brief analysis above, we can begin to appreciate the reality that, with Marxism, which is the most consistent derivative of process philosophy to date, revolutionaries are given greater impetus than ever before.

There have been many Marxists who, like the right-wing Hegelians, have refused to part with the pattern of limited government and the "democratic procedure" which flowed from Biblical Christianity. An influential group of these individuals organized in England (1883) under the name **Fabian socialists**, whom we will later discuss. There are other Marxists, however, who have sold themselves completely to the new faith and vision, concluding that no price is too great, including force, violence, and bloodshed, if necessary, to bring in the new age. One of the leading revolutionaries among them was the Russian, Vladimir Ilich Ulyanov (1870-1924), more commonly known as Lenin. As we shall see, it was the Party of Lenin which ultimately came to be known as the Communist Party.

Only in Recent Years Has the Marxist Faith Begun to Be Reexamined

The Marxist faith and analysis of history so completely won over the intellectual community of the modern world (from the mid-nineteenth century onward) that it has only been in very recent years that it has been challenged in the minds of leading intellectuals. Some who are reacting against Marxism are gravitating to the so called New Age movement— which, of course, is not new, being simply the latest restatement of the oldest religion in existence. The New Age Movement, as an expression of irrationalism [or, we could say, anti-rationality], retains elements of Marxism, but with a varied twist. Unlike an earlier expression of irrationalism known as Existentialism, which produced, for the most part, pessimism, the New Age movement is, like Marxism, very optimistic.

Indeed, there is talk in some circles today of re-spiritualizing Marx. That is, some are coming to conclude that Marx did not, after all, understand Hegel. Hegel never anticipated that matter would become perfect, only spirit. To Hegel, the only perfection is in the *zeitgeist* as it comes to be absolute. Hegel, as we know, drew his views largely from the ancient Greek philosophers (including, for example, Parmenides, from whom he drew his conception of the absolute). Marx had de-spiritualized the Eastern-influenced Hegel. Now, some say, Marxism has failed because it was too materialistic, so the need is to redefine and, as it were, re-spiritualize Marxism.

NOTES

1. Citation: Feuerbach, Ludwig, <u>The Essence of Religion</u>, 1848/49, quoted on the web page of the German Ludwig Feuerbach Society-Nuremburg: http://www.ludwig-feuerbach.de/lfg_eng.htm, last updated July 9, 2002.

2. <u>Author's Note</u>: Schwarz, Fred, <u>You Can Trust the Communists (to Be Communists)</u>. (Prentice-Hall, Inc., 1960). Schwarz, a successful medical doctor, became convinced that Marxism was a greater threat to humanity than any physiological disease and devoted his life to exposing its nature. See his autobiography, <u>Beating the Unbeatable Foe,</u> by Dr. Fred Schwarz, Regnery Publishing, Inc., 1996.

3. Compiler's Intellectual Background Note: Hegel, of Stuttgart, who had lectured and published his philosophy for many years, taught for the last thirteen years of his life: 1818-1831 at the University of Berlin, then the most highly regarded university in the world. Young people interested in the intellectual challenges of the day devoured his writings and flocked to study with him. By the time of his death, he was the most prominent and influential philosopher in Germany. Marx, who studied at the University of Berlin in the mid-1830s, wrote of being won to Hegelianism in 1837 when he was 19. Engels, who had already become acquainted with Hegel's writings, became identified with the "Young Hegelians" when he spent a year in Berlin in 1841 at the age of 21.

4. Citation: The quote and summary of Marx' response is taken from Chapter 10 of Fred Schwarz' book, <u>You Can Trust the Communists (to Be Communists)</u> (Prentice-Hall, Inc., 1960), 7th paper edition: Christian Anti-Communist Crusade, Longbeach, California, 1972, pp. 149-150.

5. Compiler's Note: Engels later wrote of Feuerbach's book, published in 1841: "Then came Feuerbach's Essence of Christianity. With one blow it pulverized the contradiction, in that without circumlocutions it placed materialism on the throne again... Enthusiasm was general; we all at once became Feuerbachians." (Engels, quoted in Aikman, David Barrington Thomson, The Role of Atheism in the Marxist Tradition (Diss., Univ. of Washington, 1979), p. 309. Available from University Microfilms International.)

6. Compiler's Biographical Additions: **Karl Marx** (1818-1883) was descended from lines of rabbinical scholars on both sides. The family regularly attended Trier's only Protestant church, whose pastor, Johann Kupper (1779-1850), was a personal friend of his father's. Kupper had been highly influenced by Kantian rationalism in his youth but now propounded what Aikman describes as "a pietism streaked with rationalist elements." Marx was instructed by Pastor Kupper and confirmed in 1834. There is no question that Marx was instructed in Christian faith, life, and history, but there is not enough evidence to determine with certainty the level of the sincerity of his faith. (Information adapted from Johnson, Paul, Intellectuals, Harper & Row, p. 53, and Aikman, David Barrington Thomson (1944-), The Role of Atheism in the Marxist Tradition (Diss., Univ. of Washington, 1979), Chapter 2, p. 104.)

After completing his work at the University of Berlin, Marx sought to teach philosophy in a Prussian university, but as a leading member of the revolutionary Young Hegelians, was not allowed to do so by the government. In 1842, he began editing a paper which criticized government suppression of revolutionary ideas. After this was censored in 1843, he married his childhood sweetheart and they moved to Paris. There Marx was exposed to various brands of socialism, became committed to international socialism, and met Engels, with whom he thereafter collaborated. Their writings were noticed by a group of German exiles and emigrants which had branches in many European cities. This organization was renamed "The Communist League" in 1847, and Marx and Engels were invited to write a "statement of faith" for it. The Communist Manifesto was soon translated and distributed into many nations.

Early the next year, the revolutions of 1848 took place in Paris and across Europe. Marx and Engels traveled widely to encourage the revolutionaries. He settled in Cologne and began editing a revived paper which, once again, was censored. Marx returned to Paris and, finally, moved to London, where he remained for most of his life. His weekly writings for the NY Tribune provided his only regular income from 1851-1860. He published Eighteenth Brumaire of Louis Bonaparte in 1852, Critique of Political Economy in 1859, and his influential Das Kapital ("Capital"), often called the "bible of socialism," in 1867. Marx regularly promoted revolutionary activity. In 1864, at a public meeting in London, he proposed an International Workingmen's Association. He also supported the Social Democratic Labor Party, founded in Germany in 1869. [Above information drawn from Ergang, Robert, Europe Since Waterloo, 3rd ed., Boston: D.C. Heath & Co., 1967, pp. 100-104 and Webster's Biographical Dictionary, p. 982.]

10 MARXISM-LENINISM: COMMUNISM (1903–PRESENT)

> *"Political power, properly so called, is merely the organized power of one class for oppressing another... [I]f, by means of a revolution, [the proletariat] makes itself the ruling class and sweeps away by force the old conditions of production, then... In place of the old bourgeouise society, with its classes and class antagonisms, we shall have an association in which the free development of each is the condition for the free development of all."*
>
> Karl Marx and Friedrich Engels, The Communist Manifesto[1]

We will now begin our discussion of communism, because communism, understood in connection with the Communist Party, is not only Marxism, it is Marxism plus Leninism.

As we noted in the previous chapter, Karl Marx (1818-1883) believed that the historical process was inevitable; therefore, it was not necessary for men to take thought or action individually or corporately to strive to influence the historical process. Man should simply recognize the process, applaud the process, and fall in step with the process, recognizing that force, violence, and bloodshed were necessary and prerequisite to progress and to ultimate perfection.

There were, however, as would be expected, revolutionaries spawned by the "gospel according to Marx" who came to believe that the historical process could be accelerated; that we could, by taking thought and action individually and corporately, move more rapidly to effect the international socialist order, from which the utopian society of communism could emerge. Foremost among these revolutionary disciples was Lenin.

Vladimir Ilich Ulyanov (1870-1924), more commonly known as Lenin,[2] was a Marxist who, believing that man by taking thought and organized action could and should accelerate the process of history, coordinated a group of revolutionaries who convened in Brussels, Belgium, in 1903. They were discovered by the Belgian police and forced to adjourn, after which they relocated and reconvened their meeting in London.

During their three-week-long meeting, the revolutionaries continued to debate, as they had been doing in their numerous underground writings, the best methodology for organizing to accelerate the process of history. Lenin argued that the best method would be on the basis of a disciplined *cadre*. He said, in so many words, "give me a small number of individuals who are absolutely committed to the enterprise and we will, with them, turn this world upside down." The opposition argued that anyone should be allowed to participate in the enterprise at will, volunteering, as it were, and drifting in and out on something of a semi-voluntary basis.

At this point a vote, theoretically, was taken and a majority of revolutionaries agreed with Lenin. The Russian word for "majority" is akin to *bolshevik* and, thus, the so-called Bolshevik Party or "Party of Lenin" was born, later to become known as, simply, the Communist Party. The Russian word for "minority" is akin to *menshevik*, thus those who opposed the Bolsheviks methodologically became known as the Mensheviks.

THE "PARTY OF LENIN" OR COMMUNIST PARTY: ITS MAKEUP

The makeup of the Communist Party, which came into existence in 1903, can best be visualized as an iceberg. The real work of the movement has not been accomplished by the visible one-eighth of the Party, the so-called card-carrying communists but, rather, has been done by the invisible seven-eighths: the so-called underground. It has not been possible for one to "join" the communist underground; one must be invited in. On what basis has one been invited in? On the basis of having demonstrated an understanding of the process of history and a total commitment thereto.

What has been the cost of being invited into the communist underground? It has been oneself. (In this we see, again, a perversion of Biblical Christianity). The communists have referred to themselves as "dead men on furlough." When a person has become a member of the underground, that person has ceased to exist as an individual for all intents and purposes and has simply become a cog in the party machinery. This, by the way, is one reason why a communist party line could be completely reversed in a 24-hour period and the whole party would swing from having been moving in one direction to suddenly moving in the opposite direction.

The Communist Party has viewed itself as the "vanguard of history," the "brain" of the proletariat. It is the "midwife," destined to deliver the international socialist order from the decadent, dying womb of capitalism.

The Communist Party: Its Objectives

What was the objective of the Party of Lenin, the Communist Party established in 1903? The objective of the party was not and has never been to effect communism. The objective of the Communist Party is to effect the international socialist order, that is, socialism on an international scale. Therefore, the objective is global conquest to smash the remaining bourgeoisie society as Marx defined it and replace it with an international socialist order which, then, it is presupposed, will blossom and flower into the utopian society of communism.

Many people today have proclaimed that communism has failed, that communism is dead; however, can something be said to have failed if it has not even been tried? Can something be said to be dead if it has never yet been brought into existence? On the basis of the Marxist analysis of history, communism has not yet emerged and, therefore, to contemplate the death of communism would be premature until long after all other systems are historical relics. Therefore, when people declare that communism does not work, they are only displaying their own ignorance.

Many people to this day do not understand this reality; they say, "Look at former Soviet Russia, look at Cuba, look at China; communism does not work." They even go so far as to say that communism has failed. Communism? Again, according to the Marxist analysis, communism has never yet existed. All we have ever had is pockets of socialism. Russia was the U.S.S.R. (the Union of Soviet Socialist Republics); China is the "People's Republic of China," the word "people's" being a euphemism for socialist. Thus, those nations were or are under the control of the Communist Party, but they were or are not communist nations; they are, in the Marxist analysis, socialist nations. For this reason, communists will scoff when a non-communist makes the observation that communism does not work. Communists believe that communism cannot and will not emerge until the entire world is first socialistic.

The objective of the Communist Party, then, was not and is not communism. The objective of the Communist Party was and is global conquest to effect the international socialist order, from which (and from which alone in the Marxist analysis) the presupposed utopian society can emerge.

The Communist Party: Its Phenomenal Success

How successful have the Marxist-Leninist Communists been? The Party of Lenin came into existence in 1903 with approximately seventeen supporters. In 1917 it came into power in Russia (at that time the world's leading emerging power) with approximately 50,000 supporters. By the 1960s the Party of Lenin had overrun more than 50 percent of the world's land mass and more than 50 percent of the world's population! It is not possible to find any other movement in all of recorded history that has enjoyed such phenomenal success. Indeed, the communists overran more people from 1917 to the 1960s than have heard the name of Christ.[3] The Party remained in control of Russia for 75 years, when it finally collapsed in 1991. Communist parties continue to prevail today in several nations, most notably, of course, China; other nations have strong communist parties within them vying for control.

The overwhelming success of the communists was recognized by the late Whittaker Chambers (1906-1961), who was for many years (in the 1930s) a member of the Communist underground in the United States. As such, Chambers worked closely with ranking members of the different departments of the United States government.   One of his co-workers— and a friend—was Alger Hiss who, during the final years of World War II (1939-45), was probably the most significant advisor of President Franklin Roosevelt relative to international politics. He was certainly the key advisor relative to the advent of the so-called United Nations, as attested by a photograph of Alger Hiss advising Roosevelt at the Yalta Conference. Chambers worked with Hiss in espionage activities.

Chambers describes, in his monumental autobiography, <u>Witness</u>,[4] how he became disillusioned with communism.   Once, when admiring the intricate design of his daughter's ear, he was struck by the recognition that there must be a Designer. Gradually, he abandoned atheism and, finally, broke with Communism and became a Biblical Christian. He and his wife immediately went into hiding. Later, in the mid-1950s, he emerged to bear witness to the Truth, standing against the pro-socialist, pro-international socialist spirit of the age, finally having to supply evidence toward convicting his former friend, Hiss, amid a nationally broadcast uproar of offended socialist sensibilities.

Chambers well understood the weakness of the West and the extent to which the disease of Soviet-led communism was infecting the world. He told his wife at the time that he was convinced that, by defecting from communism, he was leaving the winning side for the losing side as far as Western/American Civilization was concerned. Indeed, not long after his death in 1961, the West did come within an eyelash of destruction; however, by the grace of God, the West found the strength to resist and, as a result, the revolutionary effort as led by the Soviet Union collapsed. Whether the

West will be able to withstand the next strain of the revolutionary disease remains to be seen.

Witness is a life-changing book. I would urge every person to read it. Indeed, I believe it is the most powerful book that has been written in distilling the conflagration of truth and error in our age. I have read the introduction to Witness more than twenty times and it never fails to move me deeply. Chambers is an extraordinarily gifted writer, a person who is capable of turning himself, as it were, inside out. Yet, he delineates very clearly what is taking place and why it is occurring in the modern world. I have received lengthy letters from individuals around the world who have read Witness informing me how much it has altered their thinking and their living.

In the final analysis, then, Communism is best defined as a movement of atheists organized, for the first time in recorded history, on an international scale conspiratorially to drive the very idea of God from the mind of man. As we know, although Soviet-led communism has collapsed, this continues to be the goal of communist revolutionaries world-wide, and it is presently the goal of the leadership of the most populous nation on earth: communist-controlled China.

THE LENINIST FORMULATION FOR GLOBAL CONQUEST

Who, then, was the architect of the Communist Party strategy and tactics for global conquest? It was, of course, Lenin. Lenin's formulation for global conquest involved three basic tactics: 1) First, he taught that because the communists think dialectically they should, accordingly, act dialectically. 2) Secondly, he advocated the tactic which became known as 'peaceful co-existence'. 3) Finally, in the effort to effect global conquest, Lenin came to target the United States specifically as the last great bastion of capitalism.

Tactic 1. Thinking and Acting Dialectically

First of all, Lenin argued that the communists think and, accordingly, should act dialectically, recognizing that one often approaches one's goal by appearing to move away from it. This dialectical mentality and methodology can be illustrated both analogically and historically.

Probably the best analogy which has been used is that of the driving in of a nail with a hammer. Anyone who is familiar with the process of driving nails will recognize that it would be a very foolish person who would bring a hammer crashing down on a nail and simply continue to push. On the other hand, a person not familiar with the totality of the process of driving nails, happening upon a scene in which a hammer is being **withdrawn** from a nail might conclude that anyone who believes those two objects have any relationship one with the other is foolish. One who is familiar with the totality of the process, though, recognizes that the withdrawal of the hammer from the nail is just as basic to the ultimate objective as the downward thrust.

Similarly, Lenin proposed that, thinking and acting dialectically, communists should push toward their objective as far as they can go and, when they reach resistance, begin withdrawing. They should withdraw until the time is ripe to push again. Indeed, they employed this strategy with notable success. Time and again, when they were withdrawing, people would conclude, "Oh, they are mellowing, they have changed their mind, they are returning to (so-called) capitalism." Such, however, was not the case. They were simply thinking and acting dialectically, recognizing that one often approaches one's goal by appearing to move away from it. Many historical illustrations of the application of this methodology could be cited.

The Magnitude of the Destruction Wreaked by Communism

The statistics relative to the effect of the communists' coming to power during the twentieth century are mind-boggling. They are so overwhelming that, once a person grasps them, that person will never be the same. As long as I live I will never recover from having heard these statistics, from the magnitude of human suffering they represent. Following are the statistics relative to only three of the many nations which have been taken over by the revolutionaries since 1900.

Since overrunning **Russia** in 1917 and before the collapse of Soviet Russia in 1991, the communists put to death in that nation between **100-150 million people**. Alexander Solzhenitsyn, who spent years of his life in a slave labor camp in Soviet Russia, estimates that between 1917 and 1959 more than 66 million people perished there in slave labor camps alone.

Since overrunning **China** in the late 1940s, the communists have put to death in that nation, by conservative estimates, a minimum of **150 million people**. To bring it closer to where we are chronologically, we are told that before the communists overran the nation of Cambodia in 1975, there were approximately 8 million people in that nation; however, after four years of genocide, starvation, and flight, there were only 6 million people left alive in Cambodia.

Alexander Solzhenitsyn, who was denounced by the Soviet leadership when his book, <u>GULAG[5] Archipelago</u> was published in the West in 1974, said of the communists ". . . nowhere on the planet, nowhere in history, was there a regime more vicious, more bloodthirsty, and at the same time more cunning . . . than the Bolshevik; . . . no other regime on earth could compare with it . . . in the number of those it had done to death."[6]

Can we begin to comprehend these statistics? These are, in reality, not statistics, but [innocent] people—individuals such as ourselves. These are parents, mothers and fathers, sons and daughters, aunts and uncles, grandparents. They are flesh and blood people, just as you and I are.

Tactic 2. Peaceful Coexistence

The second component of the Leninist formulation for global conquest came to be known as "peaceful coexistence." Lenin argued that the communist victory to effect the international socialist order, which is historically inevitable, would be all the more rapidly assured if the non-communist-controlled world could be induced into believing that it could indefinitely peacefully co-exist with the communist-controlled world. This was a brilliant strategy.

The drive for peaceful coexistence took many forms and many terms were used to describe it. One expression, in use for a number of years was *détente*, a French word meaning "relaxation of tensions."[7] The most recent expressions, in use immediately before the collapse of Soviet Russia, were *perestroika* and *glasnost*.

Tactic 3. Target the United States, the Last Great Bastion of Capitalism

The third and most significant component of the Leninist formulation for global conquest was Lenin's targeting of the United States. Lenin referred to the United States as the last great bastion of capitalism. He believed that, were it not for the United States, the communists could, as it were, march across the rest of the world like boy scouts on parade. Consequently, targeting the United States, Lenin devised the following formulation for global conquest (paraphrased):

> The external encirclement of the United States,
> combined with the internal demoralization thereof
> will produce a gradual or progressive surrender.

He proposed, first, that the United States be externally encircled in every conceivable dimension: geographically, demographically (that is, in terms of population), politically, economically, militarily. He announced, more precisely, that first they would overrun Eastern Europe, then the masses of Asia, then the Southern hemisphere; then, surrounded and isolated, the United States would fall into their hands like an overripe fruit.

The internal demoralization was much more significant. By internal demoralization, he did not mean to propose that the people of the United States be brought to a point of conscious despondency or despair. Rather, he proposed that the communists do everything possible to effect a reduction of the will of the American people to resist communism. He implemented what came to be known as "fourth dimensional warfare," thinking beyond warfare in its classic military dimensions—which, at that time, involved land, sea, and air. Fourth dimensional warfare was paramilitary warfare, covert, invisible warfare, ranging through an entire spectrum—from economic warfare on the one hand, to psychological cybernetic warfare on the other. (Cybernetic warfare involves the control and/or manipulation of the flow of information, the assumption being that a person's judgment is no better than his or her information.) The objective was to bring about imperceptibly a shift of power from one's opponents to oneself until one enjoyed such a preponderance of power that one could simply assert one's will over one's opponent.

NOTES

1. Marx, Karl and Friedrich Engels, The Communist Manifesto (1848), New York, NY: Simon & Schuster, 1964, p. 95.

2. Compiler's Biographical Note: "**Lenin**" was one of a number of pseudonyms used by **Vladimir Ilich Ulyanov** (1870-1924) in his published writings from 1901. (Many revolutionaries used pseudonyms to avoid arrest.) All the Ulyanov children were revolutionaries. Lenin's older brother was hanged in 1887 for conspiring to assassinate the Tsar. Lenin completed a law degree in St. Petersburg (Leningrad) and helped establish a Marxist party in Russia. Leaders were arrested in 1895. While he was in exile, in 1899, a number of secret Marxist groups joined to form the Russian Social Democratic Labor Party; they organized their first congress in Minsk, after which, however, most of the leaders were arrested. In 1900, Lenin moved to Munich, Germany, where, with others, he founded the party newspaper, *Iskra*, which attracted many more Russians into the party. It was this party which attempted another congress in Brussels in 1903. [Information distilled from www.top-biography.com 3-10-2003.]

3. Citation and Compiler's Note: This comparison is found in Dr. Fred Schwarz' You Can Trust the Communists (to be Communists), Prentice Hall, Inc., 1960, Chapter 3, p. 38.

   Additional Details Regarding Soviet Expansion: Lenin led the Bolsheviks in 1917 to consolidate their power quickly and more ruthlessly in Russia (a nation of 262 million people). The royal family was put to death in 1918 and, during the civil war 1918-1920, some ten million people were put to death to insure that no enemies of the regime could come to power. Solzhenitsyn estimates that 300 church bishops were killed and 287,000 Orthodox priests died, many murdered in mass shootings. Some 790 monasteries and 53,500 churches were destroyed. An additional eight million people died of privation in civil dislocation. Others, an estimated twelve million people were sent to Russian labor camps, where they died more gradually. Some camps—such as Kami, Karaganda, and Vorkuta—were deliberately designed to kill their laborers.

To provide global Marxist-Leninist leadership, Lenin and the Bolsheviks founded the Communist International or Comintern (1917-1919?) later renamed the Communist Information Bureau or Cominform (1919-1956). The Comintern was intended to be the "iron fist" toward the global implementation of the communist faith. The Lenin School in Moscow attracted communist leaders from many nations who sought to learn Marxist-Leninist objectives and techniques for organizing, carrying out underground and conspiratorial operations, and effecting revolution and civil war. See The Secret World of American Communism, by Harvey Klehr, John Earl Haynes, and Fridrikh Igorevich Firsov, New Haven and London: Yale University Press, 1995), and Basic Communism: Its Rise, Spread, and Debacle in the 20th Century, by Clarence B. Carson, American Textbook Committee, P.O. Box 8, Wadley, Alabama 36276, 1990, pp. 1-482.]

4. Bibliographical Note: Witness by Whittaker Chambers, New York: Random House, 1952.

5. The word GULAG, an acronym for the name of Soviet Russia's prison system, was used by Solzhenitsyn in the title of his 1974 3 vol. book, The GULAG Archipelago 1918-1956: An Experiment in Literary Investigation. The word is introduced at the beginning of his book while referring to Kolyma, "the pole of ferocity of that amazing country of GULAG which, though scattered in an archipelago geographically, was in the psychological sense fused into a continent, an almost invisible, almost imperceptible country inhabited by zek people [prisoners]." The book exposed to the world in agonizing detail the extensive network of slave labor camps in Soviet Russia, several of which were deliberately designed to kill. [See the excellent abridgement of The Gulag Archipelago, approved by Solzhenitsyn, by Edward E. Ericson, Jr. (London: Collins Harvill, 1986).]

6. Alexander Solzhenitsyn, The Gulag Archipelago, London: Collins Harvill, 1986, p. 219.

7. Author's Bibliographical Note: An excellent book on this topic, by the Frenchman Jean-Francois Revel, is entitled How Democracies Perish, Harper & Row, 1985.

11 MARXISM IN AMERICA AND THE WEST:
FABIAN SOCIALISM (1883–PRESENT)

From the credo of the Fabian Society:

"For the attainment of these ends the Fabian Society looks to the spread of Socialist opinions, and the social and political changes consequent thereon. . . . It seeks to achieve these ends by the general dissemination of knowledge as to the relation between the individual and Society in the economic, ethical and political aspects."[1]

As we continue to discuss the third major stream of process philosophy, Marxism, we now shift our attention to the non-communist-controlled world. Has Marxism had any influence in America and the West in forms other than the Marxist-Leninist? If so, how significant has it been? We will be noting that, rather than Marxist-Leninist. most Marxists in America and the West became Fabian socialists.

From the first, Marxism had very profound touching points with the thinking of most Western-American intellectuals. First of all, Marxism is evolutionary with a vengeance, holding that we are moving from lower to higher, from savagery to civilization, from the primitive to perfection–ultimately toward the perfection of the presupposed utopian classless society, which Marx called "communism."

Secondly, most Western and American intellectuals came to accept the primacy of matters economic, believing that if we revolutionize along economic lines, we will have progress, if not ultimately perfection. Most of the analyses to which I was exposed in graduate school were essentially neo-Marxist in that regard. Thus, the presuppositions and conclusions of Marxism, including an economic determinism and the Marxist analysis of history, were readily accepted by the intellectuals of America and the West.

Most of the many intellectuals who came under the influence of Marxism in the West, and in America, did not, indeed, become Marxist-Leninists. They did not accept the proposition that socialism can only be brought into existence dialectically by force, violence, and bloodshed, smashing existing institutions in order, presumably, to prepare the way for new ones. Rather, they became *Fabian socialists*, believing that the best way to institutionalize socialism is evolutionarily, peacefully, gradually, "democratically" through the ballot box, and legislatively (not militarily) through the existing institutions. With regard to the three stages or methodologies for implementing revolution, they subscribed to education and coercion by law, but not coercion by force of arms.

FABIAN SOCIALISM OR "DEMOCRATIC SOCIALISM" (1883-PRESENT)

Those who came to take this position organized significantly in England in 1883 under the rubric of the Order of Fabian Socialism. Please note that, while it is an effort to implement the Marxism of the generation which preceded it, it also predates Marxism-Leninism (1903) by an entire generation. The Fabian Society, as it was also known, was the enterprise of such leading intellectuals as the socialist activists and writers Beatrice (1858-1943) and Sidney (1859-1947) Webb, and the playwright, George Bernard Shaw (1856-1950). The Fabian socialists, as we have said, agreed with Marxism and even with Marxism-Leninism, on the need for revolution and the need to implement socialism but they disagreed methodologically.

Where does the term "Fabian" Socialist come from?

What, then, is the origin and meaning of the term Fabian socialist? To answer that question, we must return to ancient history to the time of the three wars between Rome and Carthage known as the Punic wars. The best remembered of these was the Second Punic War (218-202 B.C.), which featured the courageous Carthaginian general, Hannibal (247-183 B.C.), and his doubly incredible feat. At that time, Rome was largely a land power and Carthage was almost entirely a sea power, centered in the north of Africa with possessions in the Iberian Peninsula (now Spain) and elsewhere.

Hannibal's first feat was to raise an army, which was nothing short of incredible for Carthage, which was largely a sea power. Secondly, he then conveyed that army across the north of Africa, across Iberia, over the Pyrenees mountains, across southern Gaul, over the Alps, which was an incredible engineering feat, and into the Italian peninsula. On three successive occasions in pitched battles (218-216 B.C.), outnumbered anywhere from 2:1 to 10:1, Hannibal defeated the Roman armies. At that point, he held Roman civilization, as it were, in the palm of his hand.

Hannibal could have followed up any of those victories with a march against Rome, destroying that civilization. He did not do so, however, because his objective was not the destruction of Rome, but what we today would call "peaceful co-existence." He wanted to bring the Romans to the point of a willingness to "live and let live."

Recognizing this, one of the two consuls to the Roman Senate named Fabius Maximus (d. 203 B.C.) counseled the Roman Senate to stop engaging Hannibal in pitched battles. Such decisive conflicts could only decimate the Roman armies and, ultimately, place Rome at Hannibal's mercy. Instead, he counseled guerrilla-like tactics and harassing operations directed, for example, against Hannibal's lengthy supply lines. This strategy (thereafter termed *Fabian*) was adopted and it worked. In time Hannibal was worn down and, finally, forced to flee.

There is a tragic sequel as far as Carthage is concerned. One of the outstanding orators of all time was Cato the Elder (234-149 B.C.) who, subsequent to the Second Punic War, ended every oration in the Roman Senate with these words: *Carthaginem esse delendam.* Carthage must be destroyed. He literally burned this into the minds of his countrymen and, accordingly, when the Third Punic War broke out, as it inevitably would, the Romans not only defeated Carthage; they razed (which is to say, lowered) the city and, furthermore, they plowed it under and poured salt over the furrows and Carthage ceased to exist. So much for "peaceful co-existence."

The Fabian socialists, taking their name from Fabius Maximus, argue that the best way to effect socialism (not only nationally but internationally) is gradually, democratically, through the ballot box, through the existing institutions, legislatively, not on the basis of force, violence, and bloodshed, nor dialectically as the Marxist-Leninists taught and practiced. For this reason, of course, Fabian socialists often refer to themselves as **democratic socialists** or their system as **democratic socialism**.

FABIAN SOCIALISM DOMINATES WESTERN POWER CENTERS: 1900 TO PRESENT

In order to understand what took place during the twentieth century and what is taking place today, we need to recognize that it was the Fabian socialists who came to dominate the power centers in Europe during the first few decades of the twentieth century (1900-1930) and who came to dominate all of the power centers in the United States during the 1930s. Thus, throughout the twentieth century, it has been the Fabian socialists who have dominated the intellectual community, the academic community, the media, the mainline denominations, the labor unions, the courts, the bureaucracies, the legislative assemblies and, for the most part, the executive leadership.

How Fabian Socialism Came to Dominate the United States

The Fabian socialists came to the United States in 1900 in the form of the I.S.S., the Intercollegiate Socialist Society. This was an effort to recruit student intellectuals on our major university campuses into the Fabian socialist enterprise; however, it was not significantly successful because the American people do not respond favorably to socialism. This is why, to this day, the U.S. does not have a party known as a *socialist* or labor party.

Thus, in 1920, following World War I (1917-1919), the Fabian socialists in the U.S. reorganized under the title, League for Industrial Democracy (LID). In reality, this was the league for Fabian socialism, but who could be opposed to industrial democracy? The graduates and alumni of the LID would come to command the power centers in the U.S. during the next two decades. This included all the power centers which we have enumerated above. Most significantly, they took over the Democrat Party during 1930s, making of it their political vehicle and have dominated it ever since.[2]

In addition, they started the industrial unions, such as the United Auto Workers, and they gained control of the CIO (Committee for Industrial Organization) unions. Interestingly, however, in the late 1930s, they temporarily lost control of the unions to the communists. They regained control of the industrial unions in the early 1940s under the Fabian socialist labor leadership of Victor and Walter Reuther. In 1947 they regained control of the trade unions and, in 1948, they started the Americans for Democratic Action (ADA). This, of course, should be translated: Americans for Socialistic Action. It was an effort to recruit academicians into the Fabian socialist enterprise and, with them, push the Democrat Party further to the "left," further toward a revolutionary mentality and procedure. During the 1960s, they started the Students for a Democratic Society (SDS). This, however, broke into two factions, one of which, the Weatherman faction, resorted to bombings and violence. Thus, Fabian socialism had come, as it were, full circle.

When we discuss the history of the last hundred years, therefore, we are not talking, and please note this, about Marxism-Leninism. We are talking about Fabian socialism. It is Fabian socialism, not Marxism-Leninism, which has been in the driver's seat and, therefore, it is Fabian socialism which has been responsible for what has taken place. Many people fail to recognize this, blaming Marxism-Leninism alone for the horrors of the twentieth century. All that has taken place, however, is a consequence, primarily, of Fabian socialism. Indeed, who were the first to export the gospel according to Marx into many nations, including Soviet Russia? The Fabian socialists.

In 1991, after the collapse of Soviet Russia, many who blamed the Marxist-Leninist-Communists rather than the Fabian socialists, concluded that, because the so-called Cold War was over, the world would become a hospitable place and went along with the proposition that the West should disarm and relax. This was to fail to recognize the nature of the struggle. Soviet Russia, as we have said, came into existence in the first place because of Fabian socialism, and in 1991 the Fabian socialists still occupied the power centers in the West and, indeed, most of the world! They follow the same presuppositions and seek to implement the same policies.

The Relationship Between Fabian Socialism and Communism

What, then, has been the relationship between the Fabian Socialists and the Marxist-Leninists? Again, we must keep in mind as we explore this relationship that the Fabian socialist form of process philosophy (which subscribed to the Marxist analysis of history) came into existence in 1883, a generation before the Marxist-Leninists emerged in 1903.

Although they subscribe to the same basic analysis of history and have the same objective—an international socialist order—they differ methodologically. As we have said, the Fabian socialists contend that socialism can be advanced peacefully through the existing institutions, whereas the Marxist-Leninists believe, teach, and practice that the international socialist order can only be brought into existence dialectically, using force, violence, and bloodshed, as they phrase it, to smash the capitalist bourgeoisie society.

The Fabian socialists recognize that they have the same large objective as the Marxist-Leninists. They believe that if they show "good faith" to the communists, if they love them a little, if they subsidize them, they can persuade them to change their minds concerning their brutal, bestial, barbaric tactics. They believe that it is possible literally to tame or domesticate the communists. To that end, of course, they have been very instrumental in the preservation and perpetuation of Marxist-Leninist control in nation after nation after nation by subsidizing to the tune of billions of dollars the communist control of those nations, in the hope that such subsidies will bring about the domestication of communism.

On the other hand, the communists believe that the Fabian socialists are hopelessly, indeed incredibly, naïve relative to an understanding of the process of history. Anyone who supposes that socialism can be brought into existence on an international scale gradually and peacefully, non-dialectically, does not understand the historical process. Nevertheless, the Marxist-Leninists have been more than willing to allow the Fabian socialists, not only to pave their way to conquest of nation after nation, but to subsidize them once they come to power.

Different Methodologies: The Nature of the Cold War

In fact, to trace the history of the Marxist-Leninist conquests during the twentieth century is to discover that in most nations they did so on the strength of the Fabian socialists leading the way for them. Russia is a case in point. Keep in mind that there were two revolutions in Russia in 1917, the first in the spring of that year and the second in the fall. In the spring revolution (February 1917) the Fabian socialists, led by Prince Georgi Lvov (1861-1925) and Kerensky (1881-1970) overthrew the Tzar. Then, in the fall revolution (November 1917), Lenin and his Marxist-Leninist revolutionary followers overthrew the Fabian socialists by propagandizing the organized workers' and soldiers' soviets, exploiting them so as to win sufficient support.

What, then, was the Cold War? The Cold War was not a war between communism and anti-communism, because anti-communism did not control the power centers of the world. It was a struggle between the Fabian

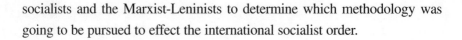

socialists and the Marxist-Leninists to determine which methodology was going to be pursued to effect the international socialist order.

Both Oppose Anti-Communism

Recognizing this relationship between Fabian socialism and Marxism-Leninism, we can also begin to understand why, throughout the Cold War, the Fabian socialists were **anti**-anti-communism. While a communist was a problem for them methodologically, a far worse threat to them was a person who was anti-communism. Why? Well, for good reason. A person who has become anti-communism is very likely to become what? Anti-socialism! Ronald Reagan is an excellent case in point.

Anyone who opposed communism more than methodologically, even in the face of the potential destruction of the West by the Marxist-Leninists, invariably went through the Fabian socialist meat grinder. This is why in 1964, when the communists were escalating activity in Vietnam, presidential nominee Barry Goldwater went through the meat grinder. This is why Ronald Reagan was *persona non grata* and they did everything possible to keep trying to destroy his presidency.

Indeed, it should not escape our notice that, when Marxist-Leninist Soviet Russia began to crumble, the Fabian socialists went to great lengths to try to keep Soviet Russia alive—even up to the very last minute. They cheered Gorbachev to the end even selecting him as *Time* magazine's "Man of the Decade" in 1990. Europeans worshipped Gorbachev, a Marxist-Leninist, a master dialectician for whom *glasnost* and *perestroika* were nothing more than a dialectical move to buy time to gain more subsidies to keep Soviet Russia afloat, thus to enable Soviet Russia to be the first to develop and deploy space weaponry and, also, to gain control of Middle-Eastern oil, in order to be able to have the non-Communist-controlled West at their mercy. These are the realities.

Even though Soviet Russia has collapsed and, with it, the Soviet-led thrust toward international socialism, we cannot breathe easily today, for there is no substantive change. Oh yes, we are glad to see Soviet Russia go, but the greatest menace still exists—that which brought Soviet Russia into existence: Fabian socialism still commands the power centers.

A Similar Attitude Toward War

We understand that Marxist-Leninists view war as a necessary instrument for bringing about the next stage of history. What, however, has been the Fabian socialists' attitude toward war? That is, what has been the attitude of those who have largely controlled the power centers of the West, including the flow of information, those who have set the agenda for discussion, determining what people were going to think about, talk about and, ultimately, do?

The Fabian socialists' attitude toward war is very apparent:

Any war which advances international socialism is a good war, whereas any war which threatens to impede the advancement of international socialism is a bad war.

Thus, the war against Nazi Germany (WWII 1939-1946) was a good war because, as we will later note, Nazism is not international socialism, but national socialism and, therefore, Nazism threatened to impede the advancement of international socialism. The Vietnam war (1964-1975) was a bad war because it threatened to impede international socialism.

When the Communists overran Nicaragua from their Soviet Russia-funded base in Cuba during the final years of the Carter administration (1977-1980) to advance international socialism, we heard nothing from the Fabian socialist-dominated media; there was no "hue and cry." Yet, when President Reagan attempted to prevent the Marxist-Leninist revolutionaries who had gained control of Nicaragua from exporting their revolution into El Salvador, Honduras, Guatemala, and beyond, suddenly, that was a bad war because it threatened to impede the advancement of international socialism. There was an unmistakable "hue and cry" against his efforts to fund the anti-communist *Contras*.

We should note, parenthetically, that the silence of the Fabian-socialist dominated media is often deafening, just as the cacophony of sound is often most instructive. No people have been more surfeited with information than have the people of the West during the past century, yet no people have understood less about what was going on. If Western civilization goes under, those who later make their way through the ruins will doubtless be amazed that such a magnitude of information could be yoked with such an appalling paucity of knowledge and understanding.

In America, particularly after the Reagan administrations and since the tragedy of 9-11, there is evidence of increasing dissatisfaction with Fabian socialism, and some promising inroads have been made into the media and other power centers. Nevertheless, the Fabian socialists still dominate and have a powerlock on most power centers. Consequently, the efforts of revolutionaries [and terrorists], both from within and globally, are not presuppositionally opposed. Indeed, revolutionaries are taking advantage of technology in an effort to maintain and expand their influence and use Fabian socialists to achieve their objectives. This will continue until we have the implementation of Biblical Christianity, with people penetrating the power centers to bring them back into captivity unto God that they might fulfill their God-created and God-intended functions.

A Biblical Christian Response to the Ideological Drive for International Socialism

What is a Biblical Christian response to the process philosophy drive toward international socialism and, in particular, the employment of military means toward such, as has been and is the case with Marxism-Leninism-Maoism? First, let me indicate what a Biblical Christian response is not. It is not the adoption of an ostrich-like mentality. As instruments of salt and light in this age, we cannot choose to remain oblivious to the realities. Secondly, it is not the adoption of a blind faith mentality, assuming that the violence and destruction we have witnessed elsewhere in the world could not happen here.

Nor should Biblical Christians adopt a last days "death wish" mentality. How many Evangelicals have I met in recent years who are reasonably well informed about these issues but, when asked what we should do about them, have no response beyond, "We should welcome these events because they are further evidence that we are in the very last days."

The answer to Fabian socialism and Marxism-Leninism-Maoism, and this applies to the religion of Mohammed, as well, is the applicability of God to all of life! Any effort to implement an ideology, if only inadvertently, renders its adherents into revolutionaries motivated by hatred. A revolution of hate is what Marxism-Leninism-Maoism has been about, as the adversary has poured himself into and through this intense form of opposition to the way and will of the Biblical God. Historically, however, Biblical Christianity produces reformers committed to implementing the way and will of God, and God, we are told, is love. We have, then, an alternative to revolution: a reformation of love. Men and institutions are restored to God, who alone is able to effect perfect love which, as we have said, is inextricably wedded to perfect justice.

We will never be able to defeat Marxism or any other ideologically rooted threat on the basis of a commitment to what Schaeffer called our own "personal peace and affluence." As Marvin Olasky put it, we will never prevail with a mentality of *sosporism*, motivated only by a determination to "save our swimming pools." The only response powerful enough to overcome our determined enemies is, once again, Biblical Christianity and the application of God to every area of life. The issue is not "right" or "left," "conservativism" or "liberalism;" it is truth or error! It is not an ideology or religion; it is the Infinite, Personal, Trinitarian, Sovereign, Creator God, who is Alpha and Omega and everything in between.

NOTES

1. Martin, Rose L. <u>Fabian Freeway: High Road to Socialism in the U.S.A.</u>, Santa Monica, CA: Fidelis Publishers, Inc., 1968, quoted on p. 19.

2. <u>Author's Bibliographical Note</u>: For an excellent history of Fabian socialism and its control of the Democrat Party, see <u>The Democrat's Dilemma: How the Liberal Left Captured the Democratic Party</u> by Philip M. Crane (Chicago: Henry Regnery Company, 1964).

12 THE INSTITUTIONAL STRUCTURE AND PROCEDURE OF PROCESS PHILOSOPHY

"I believe that we are at the threshold of a fundamental change in our popular economic thought... Do what we may have to do to inject life into our ailing economic order, we cannot make it endure for long unless we can bring about a wiser, more equitable distribution of the national income... **It is common sense to take a method and try it. If it fails, admit it frankly and try another. But above all, try something..."**

President Franklin Delano Roosevelt, 1932[1]

We now to shift our attention to the very significant theoretical analysis of the institutional structure and procedure of process philosophy. Having already discussed the institutional structure and procedure of the Biblical Christian and Rationalist worldviews, we will also be able to compare and contrast them with the institutional structure and procedure of process philosophy.

How has process philosophy, as the prevailing intellectual current in the West worked its way into the fabric of our society? How has it affected the way we live right up to the present hour? How has it worked its way out through the various institutions: civil-social (family, government), legal (courts), economic, international political, ecclesiastical (church), educational (schools), and aesthetic? (As we know, we are addressing only the first four in this book.)

First, we need to recognize that, during the final quarter of the nineteenth century (roughly from 1875 to 1900), most intellectuals in the West and, indeed, the world, led by the United States, came under the influence of process philosophy in one or more of its expressions and, accordingly, adopted a process view of life. To differentiate these relativistic thinkers from the erstwhile absolutist thinkers, we will refer to the process thinkers as the "neo-intellectuals."

PRESUPPOSITIONS OF THE PROCESS PHILOSOPHY "NEO-INTELLECTUALS" (1875-1900)

These neo-intellectuals influenced by process philosophy reached one of three conclusions concerning God: 1) He does not exist, 2) if He exists He cannot be known, or 3) if He exists He has no personal relationship with man and existence. In short they became, theoretically, atheistic or agnostic or were, at best, deistic.

With respect to the anthropological question, the neo-intellectuals have been forced to conclude that man is of **material** origin and nature. Moreover, if man has problems, which he most certainly does, such as poverty, disease, ignorance, and war, they can only be materialistically defined. Presupposing that there are solutions to these problems, they can only be materialistically addressed, that is, by rearranging the material constituency or "environment."

Finally, the neo-intellectuals conclude that the best way to effect the positive change they envision is to concentrate power in some central instrument (which, in the modern West and world has become the institutional state) so as to amass sufficient power (which, ultimately, has to be total power on a global basis) so as to be able to rearrange the material constituency on a global basis so as to be able to ameliorate or alleviate—if not altogether eliminate—those materialistically defined problems, such as poverty, disease, ignorance, and war.

Activist Disciples: A Shift in Approach to Man and Life

These presuppositions and conclusions on the part of the neo-intellectuals gave rise to a host of activist disciples, most of whom have simply accepted the presuppositions into which they were born. These activists have engaged their energies in the effort to shift us from a spiritual, individual, and personal approach to man and life to a material, collective and social approach to man and life.

Indeed, if there is no Biblical God--no Infinite, Personal, Trinitarian, Sovereign, Creator God—man cannot be a unique creation, a person, an individual. The best man can possibly be, as we will be discussing, is a social animal. Man is only, as it were, the product of some impersonal materialistic process. If that is the ultimate reality, differentiation is an illusion. That is, if all we have, ultimately, is the impersonal + time + chance, everything is at root the same, coming from the same impersonal, materialistic process. Thus, in the final analysis, there can be no qualitative differentiation between and among that which exists, including man.

The Categorical Imperative of Process Philosophy

Therefore, if the ultimate reality is equality, the imperative becomes the egalitarian society. When man recognizes his true nature, that is, his materialistic nature, he will recognize that differentiation is only an illusion. He will also reach the logical conclusion that it is the false presupposition of differentiation held by those who subscribed to previous worldviews which has been the source of all manner of strife and oppression down through history.

Thus, the categorical imperative of process philosophy becomes the egalitarian society. We must disabuse ourselves of all differentiation, which is mythological. We must eliminate the illusion of differentiation, whether economic, political, social, ethnographic, or even biological. To achieve what we presume will be a harmonious, egalitarian society, which is the imperative of the religion of non-theism, we must eliminate **all** differentiation, ultimately even sexual differentiation. Thus, we have the unisex mentality, followed by those who logically move on into feminism and homosexuality. This, indeed, is the nature of the modern homosexual movement.

As we pause to consider this, we begin to understand the nature of homosexuality and feminism: they are an effort to eliminate sexual differentiation; they are anti-sex sex! Homosexuality has been in existence virtually since the fall, but in its modern form it is a very profound theological statement. It is not simply an "alternative life-style;" it is not simply a philosophical statement; it is a theological statement. It proclaims that ontologically all things are equal, therefore we must eliminate all differentiation.

Today, homosexuality is the very cutting edge of the flow of the religion of non-theism. This is why it is so politically incorrect to speak against it. Feminism and the unisex mentality are cut out of the same intellectual cloth.

By the way, if we were to succeed in eliminating biological differentiation, what would this do to the human race? Could we preserve and perpetuate the race on the basis of sodomy? Obviously not. This is another example of the reality that, to the extent we live in this age, we must do so on the basis of beginning and ending with the truth of what-is. When we begin and end with a lie, the result is invariably destruction and death.

The Three Revolutionary Methods

How, then, are we going to achieve the egalitarian society? The first method to be attempted, once again, is the **educational method**. This is why education is so greatly emphasized today. All man needs to do to eliminate differentiation and ultimately achieve the egalitarian society is to be educated to his true materialistic nature. It is assumed that, if man can only come to realize his true nature, he will act in concert therewith, and the result will be ever greater, if not, ultimately, complete equality. This has not worked, but this is why educators and others are refusing to give up on the failed public school system; they continue to strive with religious zeal to move us into the egalitarian society.

The failure of the educational method brings us to the **political method**. It is now believed that, if we are to have the egalitarian society, it must be coerced by force of law. We must legislate equality. Indeed, if we stop to think about it, this is what most legislation in the United States since 1913 has been about; very little legislation has been passed that has not been designed to effect the egalitarian society. The political method has not worked and will not work, which brings us to the third and final method.

Those who embrace the third method are those who have concluded that, if we are ever to have the egalitarian society, it must be coerced, if necessary, by force of arms: the **military method**. This method is, in the final analysis, what Marxism-Leninism-Maoism (as but one expression of **process philosophy**) is all about.

THE RELIGION OF NON-THEISM: WHAT IS SUBSTITUTED FOR GOD AS SOVEREIGN?

If there is no God, He cannot be sovereign over all of life, including the institutions. There is a vacuum. Therefore, something else must be substituted for God as the final authority. To be more explicit, if there is no supernatural, the final authority over man and the institutions of life will not be the Trinitarian God of the Bible (whose sovereignty allows unity and diversity, a holy commonwealth, without anarchy or tyranny). Nor, in the post-Christian West, will it any longer be nature and the immutable, indestructible natural law discovered by rationalistic man. Nor will it be pantheistic organological nature within man, which was also found wanting. Thus, there is a vacuum. What is left to replace God as sovereign, as the final authority over all of life, including the institutions? Without question, that which comes to be sovereignized is the state, that is, man in social relationship.

We must be very, very careful here because this has been the prevailing view and, as one who used to be a proponent of process philosophy, I recognize that the process philosophy view is a logical and consistent view, given its presuppositions. Allow me to reiterate, therefore, what was just stated.

Having abandoned the supernatural, we have abandoned the Biblical God, deistic nature, and pantheistic man as sovereign. What is left? Man in social relationship. Thus, what has modern man substituted for God as sovereign? Man in social relationship is sovereignized and absolutized. Very gradually, the sovereignized state necessarily and inescapably becomes the redemptive state. Ultimately, it becomes god for, given our worldview, we cannot and do not exist apart from the state. In the state we live and move and have our being! All of life comes to be subsumed under the state and nothing can, accordingly, be understood excepting in relationship with the state.

What is Socialism?

This brings us to what is called socialism. Socialism is usually defined very superficially as, theoretically, a system in which the state owns and operates, whether directly or indirectly, all the means of production. That is not socialism; it is but a manifestation of socialism. Socialism is, very simply, the absolutizing (if only inadvertently) of the social approach to man and life. Given the presuppositions of process philosophy, in the absence of the Biblical God, man, in the final analysis, cannot be an individual, but can at best be a social animal. Thus, the only approach to man, ultimately, becomes the social approach which, when absolutized, brings us to socialism. Inherent in socialism is non-theism! Socialism is a consequence of non-theism; in fact, I would argue that socialism is an imperative of non-theism.

The Institutional Arrangement: The Civil-Social Area is Central

Because all of life is subsumed under the state and can only be understood ultimately in relationship with the state, it is obvious that the civil-social area now becomes central.

We recall that, for the Biblical Christian, the institutional structure and procedure was one of a holy commonwealth, in which God was central and all institutions are directly responsible to God. Thus, there was no central institution. There was neither an anarchical nor hierarchical institutional arrangement. This view, with the shift from God to man, was temporarily derailed by ecclesiasticism as there was a gravitation toward looking to the church (the institution which God had created) instead of to God.

For the Rationalists, education was the institutional focus, given the centrality of the human intellect. Romanticist-Transcendentalists sought to impose the liberty and equality mandated by pantheism on all institutions by means of centralizing power in the civil-social area.

Now, for those who subscribe to process philosophy, the civil-social itself has been absolutized and, thus, logically, becomes the focal point in the institutionalization of process philosophy. Man is now central, so the primary institution will become that institution which man first believed himself to have created: the state. A focus on the state will, it is presupposed, produce a better if not perfect society. Ultimately, the state will become the redemptive state; this, in turn, will bring us to the authoritarian state and, unhappily, as we have witnessed in the twentieth century, we end up with the so-called totalitarian state.

CIVIL-SOCIAL AREA

What, then, is the socialist system in the civil-social area? It is a system of pragmatic, freewheeling, limitless government wherein the state, as substituted for God, has the prerogative and the imperative of assuming any and all powers deemed necessary to effect the egalitarian society.

If one understands what has just been said, one understands the institutional structure and procedure of the modern world. Given the emphasis on and, if only inadvertent, absolutizing of the state, a process philosophy view seeks to understand all other institutional areas ultimately in relationship with the state.

What is the Biblical response to this? The previous reformation addressed the reality that the church, if only inadvertently, had been absolutized (ecclesiastical absolutism) and had interposed itself between God and man, not only as regards so-called "salvation" but as regards all of life. Everything was subsumed under the church and could only be understood in relationship with the church. We often think of the Reformation only in terms of its restoring justification by faith, but the much more significant consequence was the restoration of the sovereignty of God. Today, with the religion of non-theism, it is the state which has been interposed between God and man, not only as regards redemption, but as regards the totality of what-is. Biblical Christians need, once again, to reaffirm, restate, and reapply the sovereignty of God.

By the way, we should not think of the authoritarian state in the model of a Hitler or a Stalin; it is not usually so crude. Indeed, it is much more subtly implemented in much of the West today. The state indirectly regulates the means of production, then rakes off the proceeds; it also deliberately, as a procedural necessity, keeps an underclass dependent upon the state, which it uses to stay in power and to continue to control the population.

Let us, then, look at all the other institutional areas as they exist in relationship with the central institution: the state. How do the other institutions exist on the basis of this reinstitutionalization and restructuring in which everything is ultimately understood in relationship with the state which is, in effect, god?

Marriage by Man's Standard: Anarchy or Hierarchy?

By the way, before we leave the civil-social area, we noted in our discussion (Chapter 5) of Rationalism that marriage is cut away from God and that, without God's sovereignty providing the necessary community, the only alternatives would be anarchy or hierarchy in marriage.

Perhaps, now that we have discussed process philosophy, we can better understand why a presupposed marital union apart from communion is mythological. Why do we suggest that a marital union apart from God does not exist and has never existed? The reason is that union presupposes a relationship between two equal parties, but there cannot be any such thing as two equal parties apart from equality under God. Why? Because, if God is cut away, no basis for a presupposed equality remains. On whose terms is such a presupposed equality established? Yours? Mine? By what standard? by whose standard? We end up, then, with anarchy and with the only possible order being provided, not by a presupposed unity, but by either conformity or compulsion.

In marriage, as in any and every area of life, the only alternative to anarchy apart from Biblical Christianity is hierarchy, an arrangement in which one party must be rendered subordinate to the other. Even Evangelical Christians are falling into this trap. To escape the anarchy of presupposed egalitarian marriage, they are opting for hierarchical marriage. In a hierarchical marriage, one party must submit to the other, and we all know which party is subordinate: wives must submit to their husbands! Such is not the Biblical arrangement.

Today, we are trying to effect community with a presupposed *union* which becomes anarchistic and, then, necessitates authoritarianism. We will actually reach the point where we will look to the state to dictate (indeed it already is, and Marxist-Leninist-Maoist China is also an excellent example) who will live with whom, how many children couples will have, and all other manner of decisions which belong, Biblically, to God and to those united in *holy matrimony* under God.

ECONOMICS: A PLANNED ECONOMY

In the area of economics, we will shift from a market-oriented economy toward a planned economy, as the state seeks to become the dominant force in the market, in the economy, and in the whole of society.

This, of course, has profound consequences. One of the most significant consequences will be a debauched currency.

Why? It is soon concluded that the easiest way to enable the state to control the market, the economy and, indeed, the whole of life is through a manipulated banking and currency. In the United States, this began significantly in 1913 with the institution of the Federal Reserve system. State-manipulated currency makes possible a bogus, debauched currency, that is, a currency which is no longer backed by any valuable commodity for which it can be exchanged.

This, then, will lead to so-called inflation as the government takes advantage of its control over an unbacked currency to devalue the currency in order to repay its debts with less than it owes. Thus, the government systematically "rips off" its debtors and we have institutionalized inflation.

This, from a Biblical perspective, is institutionalized theft. The state institutes systematic theft as a way of life (or, to be more accurate, as a way of death) and the greatest thief becomes the government. Consequently, evil and corruption become pervasive, for how can a state which institutionalizes crime and thrives on theft effectively oppose crime or pursue justice?

Another obvious effect of process philosophy on economics will be an effort to destroy private property and increase so-called public property. In the United States, so-called conservation and environmental regulations, along with extensive hidden taxation, have been widely used to bring land, labor, capital, and the fruit of production under state control.

By the way, the market provides an excellent example of the reality that man can only pervert, but cannot destroy what God has created. To cite an extreme example, former Soviet Russia's attempt to replace the market with a planned economy was a failure. We could have visited former Soviet Russia at any point in time and purchased virtually anything we desired, provided we were able and willing to pay the price. On what basis? The black market. What was the black market? It was simply the God-created market rendered illegal by the absolutized state.

LAW: SOCIOLOGICAL JURISPRUDENCE

In the area of law, with process philosophy, we will shift from a presupposed absolute or changeless law and a resulting precedental jurisprudence to a presupposed relative law and a resulting sociological jurisprudence.

Formerly, it was held that law derives from that which is fixed, absolute, and changeless, whether the Biblical God or a presupposed immutable, indestructible Natural law. Accordingly, it was possible to discover that which is fixed and that which is derived therefrom, and order life on that basis. The immutable law constituted the "cement" that held everything together.

Accordingly, for many centuries of Western civilization, and largely in America from the founding of the English colonies through the early twentieth century, the procedure relative to jurisprudence was precedental. We had an emphasis on *stare decisis*, which is to say that if one studied law, one did so largely on the basis of case study or case history, not absolutized, but viewed in relationship with immutable law. It was presupposed that one could discover truth (immutable law and that derived therefrom), learn that truth, and act consistently on the basis of such. In fact, this presupposition is embodied in the language in which, to this day, the majority opinion of the United States Supreme Court is introduced. The opinion always begins with the following two words: "**We find** . . ." the presupposition being that there is that which is discoverable and universally and perpetually applicable.

Thus, one studied law to learn what had been discovered and how, then, the truth had been applied in previous cases. If one became an attorney, one would argue from a commonly held body of information. If one became a judge, one would rule on the basis of that same commonly held body of information. In other words, the presupposition was that legal judgments were derived from that which was fixed and, thus, cases should be turned on the basis of precedent (that which had already been learned and applied). We had a **precedental jurisprudence**.

We recognize, of course, that if we drive ourselves all the way back to the seventeenth century (1600s), we find that God and the Bible are the underlying key to law as formerly understood. This was apparent in the English colonies in American civilization. We had Biblical law.

In addition, we had a body of common expectation and experience based on Biblical law and/or Biblical principles which came to be known as "common law."[2]

When we shift from a presupposed absolute law and resulting precedental jurisprudence to a presupposed relative law, the result is **sociological jurisprudence**. Law, like everything else, is plasticized and relativized. Therefore, we no longer turn cases on the basis of precedent; we turn cases on the basis of sociological data.

The first evidence of this procedure at the United States Supreme Court level was in 1908 with the case *Muller vs. Oregon*. The case itself was relatively inconsequential, having to do with whether an Oregonian law which allowed women to work a ten-hour day was Constitutional. Louis Brandeis (1856-1941), in his famous brief, marshaled sociological data and attempted to win his case on the basis thereof. The Supreme Court agreed with Brandeis and, thus, we had the advent of sociological jurisprudence at the Supreme Court level. Brandeis was later appointed by President Woodrow Wilson, who was a proponent of process philosophy, as a justice to the United States Supreme Court.

Sociological jurisprudence necessarily has the effect of politicizing the courts. Decisions are turned, not on the basis of precedent, but on the basis of sociological data—which, correctly translated, means the political preferences or whims, as it were, of the judges or the justices in question. This, of course, carried to its ultimate, brings us to anarchy and, then, authoritarianism.

Consequences of Sociological Law

If a person who has been arrested, tried, and found guilty of a crime by a jury of his peers, is brought before a judge steeped in process philosophy for sentencing, that person will probably be given a light or a suspended sentence. Why? The judge, steeped in process thinking, will presuppose that the person is a product of his or her environment or material constituency, and, therefore, that the person cannot, in the final analysis, be held responsible for his or her behavior or, most certainly, cannot be held responsible to the point of being punished, or punished severely. Thus, rarely is anyone found guilty and rarely is anyone punished or punished severely.

If we adopt this procedure, we will inevitably have a rising rate of crime. In a fallen world, if there is no punishment, people are not going to be discouraged from a given line of behavior. Those who have researched this realize that most felonious crimes are committed by repeat offenders. An obvious example is murder in the first degree, most of which are committed by second, third, fourth, and fifth time offenders.[3]

How, then, are we "coming to grips" with rising rates of crime? We are told that some "progressive" nations, such as Sweden, are experiencing falling rates in crime. What, however, have they done? They have legalized crime! This is, actually, very logical. Why? Because, given the presuppositions of process philosophy, can there be, in the final analysis, any such thing as **crime**? There is no such thing as crime because there is no truth in any absolute sense. Nothing is ultimately right or wrong.

In recognition of this, if one takes a degree in sociology in the modern university, one is much less likely to study a course in **criminology** as one is to study a course in **deviant behavior**. We have reached the conclusion that we are, at worst, social deviants—not criminals. We have "alternative lifestyles," and one person's lifestyle may deviate from the norm and dictate that he or she occasionally take the life of someone else. If so, what is needed is understanding, not punishment.

Ultimately, this will produce anarchy. Civilization cannot be maintained without a law order and it is not possible to have a law order on the basis of presupposed relative law and sociological jurisprudence.

Anarchy, of course, will ultimately result in an imposed order; relative law will bring us back to absolutized law. This, however, will not be the absolute law provided by the Biblical God of love and justice or by a presupposed Nature, but an absolutized law rooted in the fiat, arbitrary, capricious law of whatever group has succeeded in coming to power.

AREA OF INTERNATIONAL POLITICS

Finally, in the area of international politics, which has reference to relationships between and/or among civilizations or nations, the process philosophy view is that of so-called **collective security**. Before discussing this view, however, inasmuch as we have not yet discussed the ramifications of any worldview relative to international politics, we need to catch up. We will discuss the Biblical Christian view and the Rationalist view, after which we will proceed with the process philosophy view thereof.

Area of International Politics: A Biblical Christian View (abridged)

The Biblical Christian recognizes that there is nothing wrong with the existence of nations, for the Bible makes it clear that God Himself raises up nations and puts down nations. Additionally, it is recognized that nationhood can be of God as long as the nations do not come to consider themselves to be sovereign, for God alone is sovereign. (Accordingly, by the way, Biblical Christians can and should be **patriots** sincerely appreciating their nations, particularly insofar as they are fulfilling their God-given purpose, but not **nationalists**, because nations are not to be absolutized.)

Indeed, if all nations and all peoples would look to God and acknowledge God as sovereign, there would be relative international order, harmony, and peace. There would not be perfection, for there will be no perfection until the return of God-in-Christ and the institution of God's kingdom in its full power and glory over all that is, but there would be relative international order, harmony, and peace.

Given, however, that man is fallen, not all peoples or nations will look to God and recognize Him as sovereign. Therefore, there will be times when one nation will attempt to overrun another nation or, indeed, all other nations. What, Biblically, should be the response of one nation when another nation attempts to overrun some other nation or, indeed, all other nations? What, we are asking in effect, is the Biblical view of war?[4]

The prevailing view today, flowing logically from process philosophy, is that war is evil and that we should be working to eliminate it. Biblically, however, the notion that it would be possible to eradicate war in this fallen world is recognized as being contrary to reality. The most lucid, profound, and influential statement of the Biblical view of war to date is found in Augustine's The City of God (426). This Biblical view prevailed in Western civilization for centuries. Augustine made it plain that, Biblically, a good man would certainly prefer, if possible, to do away with war.

> Surely, if he will only remember that he is a man, he [that is, a good ruler] will begin by bewailing the necessity he is under of waging even just wars. A good man would be under compulsion to wage no wars at all, if there were not such things as just wars. A just war, moreover, is justified only by the injustice of an aggressor… [which] ought to be a source of grief to any good man, because it is human injustice. It would be deplorable in itself, apart from being a source of conflict. Any man who will consider sorrowfully evils so great, such horrors and such savagery, will admit his human misery.[5]
>
> Aurelius Augustine

A just war flows out of our responsibility to address injustice as Biblically defined. The Biblical view of war is, in short, that offensive wars, with one exception [addressed elsewhere], are inadmissible and that defensive wars, without exception, are imperative.[6] Why are defensive wars imperative? Because when a nation attempts to overrun another nation or, indeed, all other nations, that nation has interposed itself and is attempting to play God in the life of the other nation or nations and, thus, by substituting itself for God or even purporting to be God, once again, is engaged in blasphemy; and it is not possible to have Biblical Christian order and society if blasphemy is permitted. Thus, defensive wars are imperative.

This prompted C. S. Lewis to make a very profound observation: If there is a **just war**, there must simultaneously be an **unjust peace**. How true that is! Can we advocate peace when there are significant powers striving to overrun all the peoples of the world for ideological or religious reasons, oppressing and killing innocent people, even shaking their fists in the face of the Biblical (Trinitarian) God?

Pacifism in Christian circles comes from the Anabaptist tradition, which holds that all institutions excepting the church are **secular** and profane. Accordingly, the posture is a desire not to be entangled in the evil affairs of this age but, rather, to strive only to serve God and His kingdom through the church. The reason I do not hold this view is because I do not believe that the institutions of this age are by nature diabolical but, rather, that they have been perverted to one degree or another by those in service of the adversary and that Biblical Christians are called, as reconciled to God-in-Christ and led and empowered by God-the-Spirit, to implement the way and will of God in all the institutions of life, seeking to bring everything that He created back into captivity under God to make it serve its God-created and God-intended function.

I believe, for example, that President Ronald Reagan practiced the Biblical view of war. He declared the former Soviet Union to be an "evil empire" and engaged in a defensive or "just war" against it. His whole objective was to get rid of it. Thanks to Margaret Thatcher and Ronald Reagan, Soviet Russia and the Soviet-controlled empire, which put to death millions and millions and millions of innocent people in the name of applied social science, are history.

When a Christian favors disarmament, a simple observation will usually cause that person to rethink his or her position. That observation is, very simply, "Oh, I understand, you are opposed to the police." I live in a community of about 30,000 people. If, suddenly, we did away with the police in Marion, Indiana, everyone in that community would be aware of it, and some people rather painfully so. Why do we have police in a fallen world? Why do we arm the police? So that they can engage in lawlessness, chaos, disorder, and violence? No. In a fallen world, we have police so that they can, theoretically, discourage those who would be inclined to lawlessness, chaos, violence, and disorder from acting upon their inclinations.

Why do we have the military? The military is simply the police turned outward. The police are to provide for internal order, dealing with the threats to that order which arise from within. The military is to maintain order, dealing with threats to that order which arise from without. In a fallen world, both the police and the military are necessary. Indeed, one does not need to be a Christian to understand this; one only needs to be rational, for without both, no nation or civilization can be preserved or perpetuated.

Given, then, the necessity for every nation to maintain a strong defense, we recognize Biblically the responsibility of every nation to maintain a disciplined military, under God. This would necessarily include an effective **weapons system** [as we discuss elsewhere], being ever mindful that our confidence is never to be placed, ultimately, in our own strength or arms, but in the Almighty, and that, with respect to weaponry, the ultimate question in a fallen world is never the quantitative question, "How many," but always the qualitative question, "What system?"

Area of International Politics: A Rationalist View (abridged)

What is the view of international politics and war which flowed out of the Enlightenment and the Rationalist worldview? As we will recall, the Rationalists believed in a deistic God who is no longer applicable to life. He is no longer sovereign, nor is He the cement of the international political order; nature is now the cement.

The Rationalists believed in the existence of nations and, moreover, in the so-called *sovereignty* of nations. For the Rationalist, there was no power higher than the nation state. This was, in effect, a polytheistic arrangement.

The Rationalists, however, faced a serious dilemma. Given a diversity of sovereign nations, how would it be possible, theoretically, to maintain order? How would it be possible to prevent a presupposed sovereign state or a world made up of separate entities of presupposed sovereign states from engaging in competition, conflict, and war? The answer? Ah, nature, of course! Nature comes to our rescue! It is presupposed that everything operates naturalistically and that nature has provided a system which makes possible international political "checking and balancing," resulting in relative order, harmony, and peace. Isn't nature thoughtful?

The system which, presumably, nature provides, came to be known as the **Balance of Power System.** This system has "naturally" provided, first, that the world will divide into a multi-polarity of powers replete with a **balancer nation**. The balancer nation is to be powerful enough to "check and balance" any other nation or combination of nations, but not so powerful as to be able to overrun all other nations. Therefore, this system, which nature has provided, makes possible international political checking and balancing to maintain relative order, harmony, and peace.

The Balance of Power System

How does it work? Let us hypothecate that three nations (nations 1, 2, and 3) attack two others (nations 4 and 5). What happens? Naturally, the balancer 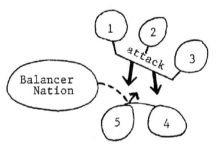 nation comes to the rescue of the two under attack, and checks and balances the other three, and we have continuing relative order, harmony, and peace.

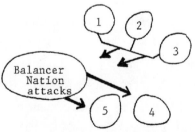

Conversely, let us hypothecate that the balancer nation attacks nations 4 and 5. What happens? Naturally, the other three nations come to the aid of the two under attack, thus checking and balancing the balancer nation, resulting in relative order, harmony, and peace.

The Rationalists concluded that the classic example of a balancer nation was Great Britain which, upon the defeat of Napoleonic France, effected the *Pax Britannica,* a century of relative British-policed peace during which time (from 1815-1914) there were no wars on the magnitude of a world war. Biblically, however, we know that England emerged as the leader, not on the basis of any naturalistic schematics, but as a consequence of a restated and reapplied Biblical Christianity. Nevertheless, this was the Rationalistic analysis. Later, of course, it was scrapped as we had the advent of process philosophy, which, as we know, was itself a derivative of Naturalism and Rationalism.

Area of International Politics: A Process Philosophy View (abridged)

The process philosophy view of international politics is, simply, that "one rotten apple spoils the barrel." Socialism cannot work on a national scale; it can only work on an international scale. That is, in order to have the egalitarian society, we must first have international socialism. We must have enough power concentrated so as to be able to change the material constituency worldwide and hence, ultimately eliminate the materialistically defined problems such as poverty, disease, ignorance, and war. Therefore, the imperative of process philosophy is the world-state system; the nation-state system is no longer sufficient.

As we have already discussed, there are basically two methodologies, both of which were played out during the twentieth century. The first, the more widespread view, has been Fabian Socialism (1883-Present), the view that socialism on an international scale can be brought into existence gradually, peacefully, evolutionarily, and democratically through the ballot box and through existing institutions. This is known as "collective security." Nations, led by Fabian socialists, will voluntarily, gradually, surrender their presupposed sovereignty to a central agency which, ultimately, will become the world state. We have seen the germ of the world state in the League of Nations (1920-1945) and, now, the United Nations (1945-Present).

Once power is sufficiently concentrated in the world state, it will be possible to change the environment globally in order to virtually eliminate all of the materialistically defined problems, such as poverty, disease, ignorance and war, and usher in the international socialist order culminating in the egalitarian society. This is the faith which has driven the Fabian socialist efforts to implement process philosophy in international politics, beginning with Woodrow Wilson's presidency (1913-1921).

The other methodology, as we know, is that of Marxism-Leninism-Maoism, which holds that the only way we can effect the world state and the international socialist order is through force, violence, and bloodshed. The dictatorship of the proletariat, the so-called communist party, using the dialectical procedure, must smash the capitalist bourgeoisie nations in order to effect the international socialist order out of the decadent, dying womb of capitalism. Thus, we will effect the dictatorship of the proletariat which, of course, will ultimately wither and die, leaving us with the egalitarian or "classless" utopian society.

The Difference Between Communism and Nazism

What, by the way, is the difference between Communism and Nazism? Fascism is a combination of nationalism and socialism, and Nazism (a word derived from "National Socialism") is fascism with one added ingredient: racism. Nazis believe that there is a **super race** (the so-called Aryan or Teutonic race) which is capable of effecting a super state to show the world the way. Nazism, then, including its racism, is one logical expression of the presuppositions of process philosophy.

The Marxist-Leninists-Maoists, on the other hand, do not absolutize race as do the Nazis. Marxism-Leninism-Maoism, as another expression of process philosophy, holds that the ultimate differentiation is not race, but class. They believe that there is a *super class* which, being led by the Marxist-Leninists-Maoists who are the vanguard thereof, will bring about the dictatorship of the proletariat. This **super class** will institute the **super state**, the international socialist order, which it will dominate and which, then, by some miracle, will eventually wither away and die, giving way to the utopian classless society of communism.

It is said, by the way, that the Nazis are on the **right** and the Communists are on the **left**. It is also assumed that anyone who is on the right is at least a semi-Nazi. Nothing could be further from the truth, however, from a Biblical perspective. The truth is that both Nazis and Communists are cut from the same intellectual cloth: process philosophy. They are both on the left. The only difference is national vs. international socialism.

One could say that the Nazis are on the right of the left and the Marxist-Leninists-Maoists are on the left of the left, but there is no right left—in more ways than one! The Biblical Christian, again, is not interested in right and left but in **right** and **wrong**, **righteousness** and **unrighteousness**. We need to learn to think and speak in terms consistent with underlying presuppositions rather than using terms, such as right or left, liberal or conservative, which are, all too often, a substitute for thought.

So, then, the imperative of process philosophy in its predominating expressions, with regard to international politics, has become the world state. It follows that the process philosophy view of war, as discussed in Chapter 11 when we discussed the relationship between Fabian Socialism and Communism, is that any war which advances international socialism is a good war, and any war which threatens to impede the advancement of international socialism is a bad war.

Successive International Political Arrangements in Western Civilization

Let us summarize, in general, the successive international political arrangements of the West. Western civilization has moved from the **city-state system** of the so-called ancient world—which was transcendental, man and divinity being brought together in the state, to the **imperial state** of Rome—which was the city-state of city-states, a system in which one worshipped the state and the ruler thereof as God, to the **feudal state**, which derived in significant measure from Biblical Christianity with its divided authority and diffused power, presupposing that God is sovereign and man is depraved, to the **nation state** which, under the impact of Rationalism, was absolutized and became the sovereign state or **nationalistic state**, to the **world state system**, which is the imperative of process philosophy, needed in order to have the realization of the egalitarian society or the utopian classless society. (By the way, the so-called New Agers would like to take us to yet another level, to the **cosmic state** in which, it is presupposed, man will be able to realize not only material but "spiritual" perfection.)

NOTES

1. Citation: From Roosevelt's address at Oglethorpe University on May 22, 1932, as printed on the Franklin and Eleanor Roosevelt Institute web site July 20, 2006, http://www. feri.org/common/news/ details.cfm?QID=2065&clientid=11005

2. Compiler's Note: Russell Kirk explains, "The word *common* here signifies that this body of laws is recognized and enforced throughout all the land, rather than being merely local law or custom; also it signifies that 'the law is no respecter of persons,' all orders and classes, including kings, being subject to its rules— 'equality before the law.'" Russell Kirk, America's British Culture (Transaction Pubs., New Brunswick USA, c1993, 1994, p. 29.)

3. Compiler's Note: Biblically, we are told that God established capital punishment for murder in His covenant with Noah after the flood, giving his reasoning as follows: *Whoever sheds man's blood, by man his blood shall be shed, for in the image of God He made man.* (Genesis 9:6)

4. Compiler's Note: War, by the way, as the brilliant Von Clausewitz noted, could be defined as "diplomacy by other means." (In Dr. Martin's course (which he considered his best course, by the way) American Foreign Relations, he deals in depth with the question of war. One volume students read is On War, the classic analysis of war reflective of a Biblical view by Karl von Clausewitz (1780-1831), a Prussian army officer.)

5. Citation: Augustine, Aurelius, The City of God, Book 19: Chapter 7. Found in Bourke, Vernon J., ed. Saint Augustine: The City of God, an abridged version from the translation by Gerald G. Walsh, Demetrius B. Zema, Grace Monahan, and Daniel J. Honan. New York: Image Books, a division of Doubleday & Company, Inc., 1958, p. 447.

6. Compiler's Bibliographical Note: Loraine Boettner has written an excellent short treatment of the Biblical Christian View of War: The Christian Attitude Toward War, Presbyterian & Reformed Publishing Co., 1985 (First ed., 1940).

The 1985 edition contains a chapter which is taken from sermon given on February 13, 1983—*The Unholy War*—by Dr. D. James Kennedy, Pastor of Coral Ridge Presbyterian Church, Fort Lauderdale, FL.

13 CONSEQUENCES OF THE INSTITUTIONALIZATION OF PROCESS PHILOSOPHY (1920s–PRESENT)

"Whither is God," he cried. "I shall tell you! We have killed him—you and I! All of us are his murderers."

"The time is come when we have to pay for having been Christians for two thousand years. We lose the support which gave meaning to our lives."

Friedrich Nietzsche[1]

Without question, process philosophy became the established order in the West during the twentieth century and continues as such. The Fabian socialist variant of process philosophy was institutionalized, coming to control Europe by the 1920s and the United States by the late 1930s. In this chapter we will summarize how this came to pass and discuss the process philosophy establishment. In which of the institutional areas has process philosophy become dominant? How much power has it enjoyed and does it enjoy, and why?

The Term "Liberal" (Redefined)

First, however, we must clarify the use of the term **liberal**, for **liberalism** will have no meaning for us if we do not recognize its twentieth century derivation. The twentieth century men and women who bought into process philosophy came to call themselves liberals.

Earlier, during the nineteenth century, the term liberal had gained respectability in the intellectual community as having reference to a libertarian—one who, theoretically, proposed to absolutize liberty. Libertarian liberals were those in the rationalist flow who had been on the crest of the wave of Romanticism-Transcendentalism. They presupposed that man is part and parcel of God and, accordingly, absolutized liberty.

The twentieth century neo-intellectuals, however, had abandoned Romanticism-Transcendentalism for process philosophy, yet they retained the name liberal. Unlike the libertarian liberals of the nineteenth century who absolutized liberty, the twentieth century liberal absolutizes equality. Thus, the twentieth century liberals are egalitarian rather than libertarian and their imperative is not liberty, but the egalitarian society. The term liberal has been redefined and it is with this understanding that we use the phrase **process philosophy egalitarian liberal**.

In Europe, the process philosophy thinkers and their activist disciples tended to call themselves **socialists** right off the bat: the Fabian socialist party on the continent is known as the Social Democrat Party. [The party which reflects what remains of Biblical Christianity is called the Christian Democrat Party.] In England, they call themselves the Socialist or Labor Party, as you would prefer.

In the United States, however, the term socialist never sold. They first called themselves **populists**, then **progressives**, then **liberals**. In 1932, the Fabian socialists took over the Democrat Party, making it their political vehicle and, therefore, in the United States, it is the Democrat party which is the vehicle for socialism. The other major party, which reflects what remains of Biblical Christianity, is called the Republican party. A Biblical Christian, who begins and ends with God, is neither an egalitarian nor a libertarian, recognizing that the only liberty we have is liberty within God and His established order, and the only equality we have is equality before God, which is the only way in which there can be any equality.

PROCESS PHILOSOPHY DOMINATES EUROPEAN POWER CENTERS 1900-1930 TO PRESENT

During the first three decades of the twentieth century, roughly from 1900 to 1930, the process thinkers and their activist disciples *a la* Fabian socialism came to dominate all the power centers in Europe and in the commonwealth nations (including Russia until the revolution in 1917). This domination included the intellectual community, academia, the media, the mainline ecclesiastical denominations, the labor unions, the courts, the bureaucracies and, for the most part, the legislative assemblies.

Thus, during the first three decades of the twentieth century, most European nations came under, not only the influence, but the **control** of those fired by process philosophy and the institutional structure and procedure flowing therefrom.

PROCESS PHILOSOPHY DOMINATES UNITED STATES POWER CENTERS 1930s-PRESENT

In the United States, such was not the case. From 1900-1930, the process thinkers and their disciples gained dominance only in the areas of education, religion, and the arts. They did not yet dominate the civil-social, economic, legal, and international political areas because of what remained of the Biblical Christian base. There was an effort to implement process philosophy in what was known as the Progressive Era, beginning with the first administration (1901-1905) of President Theodore Roosevelt (1901-1908) and running until 1919, but it proved to be abortive, though seeds were planted which would later bear fruit.

The New Deal: The Second American Revolution 1930s

The implementation of process philosophy in the remaining areas was occasioned (not caused, but occasioned) by the Great Depression, beginning in the late 1920s. The Great Depression was caused by government policies (most notably by the Federal Reserve system which had been established in 1913), but was blamed erroneously on the market. The Fabian socialist revolutionaries and their activist disciples seized upon this to come to power during the 1930s.

This, known as the *New Deal*, brought about, during the administrations (1933-d.1945) of Franklin Delano Roosevelt (1882-1945), the implementation of process philosophy in the civil-social, economic, legal, and international-political areas. It also constituted the second American revolution, which culminated in a sovereignized national executive. The sovereignizing of the nation state had occurred during the Lincolnian revolution. We now have the sovereignizing of the national executive. (For an excellent summary of this *New Deal* revolution, see Garet Garrett's monograph, *The Revolution Was.*[2])

Thus, the process philosophy egalitarian liberals succeeded in establishing process philosophy in Europe, the commonwealth nations, and the United States. The process thinkers and their activist disciples became the established order, the ruling class, the new elite of Western-American civilization.

THE SEMANTICS OF SOCIALISM

Whenever there is a change in presuppositions and worldviews, there is an accompanying shift in the definition and use of words. Thus, there is a semantics of every worldview: socialism/process philosophy, Biblical Christianity, Rationalism, or Romanticism-Transcendentalism, as examples. When there is a semantic shift, one of three things will happen to words: some words will be rendered anachronistic or archaic, no longer useful. Theoretically, some new words are "coined." Most commonly and significantly (which is what we will be discussing), the same words continue to be used but they are redefined. The person who fails to understand that certain words have been redefined is easily manipulable, not recognizing that the words are being used to refer to something altogether different than was the case formerly.

Today, because the process philosophy egalitarian liberal establishment is manning the power centers, we need to be aware of the linguistic shift to the "semantics of socialism." We could spend hours describing example after example after example, but will discuss only the following: democracy, public welfare, public interest, public funds, civil rights, and common man, looking at each in turn.

"Democracy"

Suddenly, after World War I (1871-1919) America became a **democracy**. That had not been the case before. The word democracy did not even exist in our primary documents. As a matter of fact, when I taught briefly years ago in the state-controlled schools, I had a standing offer with my students: if they could find the word democracy in any of our primary documents, it would be worth $25.00. I included in our primary documents the United States Constitution, all state constitutions prior to 1900, and the Declaration of Independence. I even threw in, for extra measure, the Gettysburg Address. I never lost $25.00 on that basis, because the word democracy did not, at that time, appear in those documents.

Why, then, after World War I did America become known as a democracy (and this applies to other nations, as well)? Democracy is the idea that the majority, as educated by the state, is right, and that the minority must submit to the majority, to avoid obstructionism. The United States, however, had never been, was not, and would never have chosen to be such a democracy, which would have been a very fickle government of man and not of law. We were a republic with a written constitution, a constitutional republic.

In fact, a democracy has **never** existed in practice, only in theory. Theoretically, it is a government in which every person participates directly in every decision relative to governance. This would be difficult, if not impossible, to practice! Theoretically, I suppose, we could all be wired together and punch a button relative to every question of state, but such would be very fickle, very unstable. Moreover, it would give rise to mobocracy, which would give rise to dictatorship.

What, then, according to the semantics of socialism, is meant when the word democracy is used? We have shifted in American history from the view that government is of God, by God, for man under God (the holy commonwealth arrangement), and from the view, theoretically, that government is of, for, and by man (the Rationalistic social contract view), to the view that government is of, for, and by the state (the process philosophy view). Thus, when you hear the word *democracy* today, think socialism, and you will know exactly what is being said. When we read, therefore, that the United States is a democracy, we should translate that to read, "the United States is a socialistic nation," and so with the other nations of the West. The so-called *democracies* have reference to Fabian-socialist dominated nations. If you and I do not understand that, we are simply being manipulated.

"Public Welfare"

A semantic analysis of public welfare or public interest is most instructive. Notably, the framers of the United States Constitution were not interested in public welfare but in the general welfare or interest, by which they meant the welfare of individuals in free association in the aggregate. From a Biblical Christian perspective, there is no such thing as public. For the process thinker, however, there is no alternative, for there is nothing private. Given the presuppositions of process philosophy, there is no such thing as an individual, a person. We are part and parcel of the same impersonal process. Therefore, everything is public. It is not possible to have individuality or personality. The **only** approach is the public approach.

Thus, we have **public interest** and **public welfare**, but what do we mean by these terms? What, finally, do we mean when we state that something is in the public welfare? We mean that it is in the interest of and for the welfare of the **state**, for in the state we live and move and have our being. The state is ultimately god. We do not exist apart from the state, for there is, ontologically, no individuality or differentiation. There is only the impersonal, materialistic process of which we are only but one expression. So "in the interest of the state" and "for the well-being of the state" is what is being said when we talk about the public welfare and the public interest. What is yours is mine, and what is mine is yours, and what is ours belongs to the state. We owe the state everything. A Biblical Christian understands that, in reality, of course, we mean "in the interest of those who are in control of the state."

The tragedy that over one and one half million individuals have been put to death each year in the United States alone underscores the supremacy of the state and the insignificance of the individual in the process view.

The Biblical Christian, on the other hand, opposes special interests, and is concerned for the general interest, the interest of individuals in free association in the aggregate. Indeed, American statesmen used to speak in terms of the general, not the public interest.

"Public Funds"

We also have, of course, **public funds**. How often do we hear, "We will finance this with public funds." For the Biblical Christian, there is no such thing as public funds. We have individual taxpayers' dollars, not public funds. Not so for the process thinker. Why? Because there is nothing individual. What is yours is mine and what is mine is yours and what is ours is the state's. Biblically understood, public funds are taxpayers' dollars which are confiscated by an authoritarian state. Indeed, most taxation today is confiscatory, not revenue-raising. We speak of public funds as though wealth grows on trees in the nation's capital.

From a Biblical perspective, however, there is no difference between a state legislator, who discovers that you have two radios and I have none, forcibly entering your property, taking one of your radios and giving it to me, and that same legislator sitting in a legislative assembly and voting wealth from your pocket into mine in a program of confiscatory taxation designed specifically for the redistribution of wealth. This is to recognize that Robin Hood was not a Biblical Christian! Once, while lecturing in Olde England on this topic, a gentleman with whom I had become acquainted during the week groaned audibly. I had just shot down his hero, for he was from Nottingham!

Biblically, nevertheless, we know that, one day, a legislator who sits in a legislative assembly and votes wealth from one person's pocket to another will stand before Almighty God and give an account for theft. A person does not suddenly cease to be responsible to God when he finds himself in a legislative assembly!

"Civil Rights"

The framers of the U.S. Constitution were not interested in **civil rights**, that is, rights granted by government. They were interested in **civil liberties**, what the government could not do. Government could not abridge the privilege of speaking freely, worshipping freely, assembling freely, and bearing arms freely. These were civil liberties. Today, however, we have only civil rights, rights granted by government. There is a flip side to civil rights, however, which we must never forget: what the government can grant, it can also take away or deny! Today, government is sovereign. For the Biblical Christian, God alone is sovereign.

"Human Rights"

Then, of course, we have **human rights**. Human rights? What are human rights? Like the Rationalists' so-called natural rights, human rights are imaginary, an ideological construct. Biblically we are told that man is born, not with rights, but with wrongs or, as you would prefer, with responsibilities. When one accepts the Saviorhood of God-in-Christ, one is delivered from one's wrongs, and when one accepts the Lordship of God-in-Christ, one is delivered from any imagined rights!

"Common Man"

Another expression regularly used is that of the **common man** or, rather, the common person. Who is a common person? Are you? Am I? From the process philosophy perspective, what we have is, indeed, common. Everything is ultimately the same; we are only under the illusion that it is unique. Karl Marx used the expression, "mass man." We have all heard the expression, the masses (of people). The Biblical Christian does not believe in masses of people. We are talking about individuals, about persons. This is fundamental. Biblical Christians must guard against using language that depersonalizes.

A Renewed Mind Renews Our Vocabulary

Having begun to explore the semantics of socialism, we can see more clearly how our worldview influences our vocabulary. Those of us who are Biblical Christians can see that, as we learn to think Biblically (and, of course, we are never going to be perfect in this regard), we will begin and end with God in our thinking, which will affect our vocabulary, both in terms of the words we use and the words we do not use and in the way that we use the words that we use, that is, the definitions.

THE PROCESS PHILOSOPHY EGALITARIAN LIBERAL ESTABLISHMENT IN THE U.S. 1930S - PRESENT (ABRIDGED)

We now complete our discussion of process philosophy by examining very briefly the present process philosophy egalitarian liberal establishment which, as we noted, became the ruling elite in the West and, consequently, the world during the early decades of the twentieth century. As we do so, we will be exploring the anatomy of an establishment for, without question, the process philosophy egalitarian liberals have been established, indeed, entrenched in power in the West, the United States, and the world during most of the twentieth century and on into the twenty-first century.

Those who are a part of this establishment are not able to see beyond their presuppositions to propose alternative solutions to the issues before us, many of which have been exacerbated by their proposed solutions and programs. (We are not suggesting, of course, that they are responsible for man's dilemma in the large sense which, Biblically understood, is a consequence of the Fall of man.)

Let us review, once again, what they presuppose. 1) First, almost without exception, they presuppose the non-existence of God or the non-applicability of God (which are one and the same). Thus, they are atheistic, agnostic or, at best, deistic. 2) Secondly, they are of the conclusion that man is of material origin and nature, a product of his material constituency or environment. Accordingly, if man has "problems" such as poverty, disease, ignorance, and war, these can only be materialistically defined and addressed. 3) To solve these materialistically defined problems, it is necessary to concentrate greater power in some central instrument (preferably the state) so as to be able to ameliorate, alleviate, if not to eliminate those problems. Thus, the process thinker is committed, ultimately, to limitless government for, if any god is to be successful, it must have limitless power. It is no accident that the twentieth century has witnessed wholesale the advent of the authoritarian state in a variety of expressions, including destructive attempts to establish a total (totalitarian) state.

Labeling the Opposition: What is a "Conservative?"

Every ruling establishment will determine what its opposition is labeled or called. The process philosophy egalitarian liberal establishment (which, as noted above, accepted as a designation for themselves the word liberal, which had had favorable connotations) has chosen to refer to its opponents as *conservatives*. This is a pejorative term; a conservative is opposed to progress, holding on unreasonably and obstructionistically to old, outdated patterns of thinking and living.

Thus, if one is asked to define the word conservative, an adequate response would be, simply, a non-liberal. A conservative is one who does not accept either the presuppositions and/or the conclusions of process philosophy, the present establishment. Almost without exception, so-called conservatives begin with 1) the presupposition of the existence of God and, accordingly, believe 2) that man is of spiritual origin and nature and of infinite, eternal value. Additionally, although they draw their inspiration from a variety of intellectual traditions, their view of the institutions includes the view that 3) government should be limited in power.

Indeed, the difference between the liberal and the non-liberal is their attitude towards government. I can tell in five minutes' time in serious conversation with any person whether that person is of a liberal or a non-liberal orientation, regardless of what they may call themselves. What is the person's view of the state? Do they begin and end with the state, if only inadvertently, or do they not? It is as simple as that. Today, because we have had the sovereign state becoming the redemptive state becoming the authoritarian and even (as we have witnessed) the totalitarian state, every person in the modern West and world is either bowing to the new Baal, if only inadvertently, or refusing to bow to Baal. We cannot serve two masters, no matter what we may say.

CONTROL FROM THE INTELLECTUAL COMMUNITY TO PODUNK CENTER, USA

We noted in chapter 1 that there are levels of application of a worldview. Here, we would ask, "How did process philosophy (or how does any worldview) work its way from the so-called intellectual community into the local community?" This is not difficult to trace. First, the worldview works its way from the so-called intellectual community into our most sophisticated or prestigious centers of higher learning, which in the States include the institutions on the East and West coasts, such as the Ivy League universities on the East coast and universities such as Stanford in the West. The graduates of these leading institutions of higher learning come to chair (and, hence, dominate) the leading departments in the leading universities in the hinterlands, such as, for example, the Big Ten universities.[3]

The graduates of the leading universities in the hinterlands come to dominate the lesser universities in the hinterlands, such as the universities on the plains, in the mountains, and in the South as well as the emerging state universities. The South has been perceived, in general, as being intellectually depressed, a view which reflects opposition to its Biblical Christian traditions. Finally, the graduates of the emerging state universities come, in turn, to teach K-12 in "Podunk Center," anywhere and everywhere, USA.

This is how a worldview works its way from the intellectual community [which, in the United States, has embraced process philosophy for the last 150 years] through the prestigious institutions of higher learning, through the lesser institutions of higher learning, down through the emerging state universities, and into the local community. The prevailing worldview is what is then taught as gospel. In this way a worldview penetrates into the fabric or warp and woof of a civilization.

Control of the Flow of Information

We also need to understand that, historically speaking, the process philosophy establishment in the United States and the rest of the world has dominated the flow of information more thoroughly than any previous establishment to date, and many previous establishments have been extremely powerful in this regard. Virtually everyone for many years has been manipulated.

> **A person's judgement is no better than his or her information**

We must keep in mind that a person's judgment is no better than his information. Therefore, if I can **manipulate** the information you receive, I can manipulate, for all intents and purposes, your thinking and behavior; if I can **control** the information you receive, I can control, for all intents and purposes, your thinking and behavior. The process philosophy egalitarian establishment has for decades essentially controlled the flow of information, setting the agenda for discussion, determining what people think about, what they talk about, and what they do, including the way they vote.

This is, my friends, inordinate power. In fact, this power is so inordinate that, as a result, we no longer have freedom of expression worthy of the name remaining in the modern West, including the United States. The reason I say this is, as we must ever be reminded, freedom of expression has always been and always will be in this age a two-sided privilege. It is both the privilege of speaking and, secondly, the privilege of being heard.

We still have a relatively large measure of freedom in terms of freedom of speaking. A person can preach a sermon or go out on virtually any street corner and begin speaking on any topic and, probably, will be allowed to continue. This, as we know, such was not the case in former Communist-controlled Russia, where those who spoke out often "disappeared," never to be seen again. Clearly, there was little freedom of expression there.

The point is, however, that in the United States we have virtually lost the privilege of being heard. When the print media dominated discourse, anyone who chose could start a newspaper, magazine, or periodical and, therefore, could write and be read. Any person's views could be heard. Since the advent of television newscasting, however, the process philosophy egalitarian liberal establishment has dominated the flow of information. As we discuss elsewhere, the print media and publishing houses have also been dominated by the process philosophy establishment.

I submit that one of the most profound consequences of a Biblical Christian reformation in the United States, as well as in Europe and other countries, would be the recovery of freedom of expression. Government controls would be removed from the media; freedom of enterprise would lead to freedom of expression. Ultimately, we would abolish the FCC (the Federal Communications Commission, instituted by President Franklin Roosevelt in 1935) and allow the market to function.

Anyone who wanted to speak, whether theist or nontheist, could speak and be heard. Truth would be made known; people would have access to accurate and useful information. Costs would go down as the market would be allowed to function, including the cost of advertising (which is presently exorbitant, and is being paid for by consumers who pay higher prices for products so advertised). Programming would improve under the influence of competition.

Today, however, across the world, the process philosophy egalitarian liberal establishment, though it is less powerful than it was prior to the Reagan era, still controls the flow of information, setting the agenda for discussion and determining what people think about, talk about and, ultimately, do.

CONSEQUENCES OF THE INSTITUTIONALIZATION OF PROCESS PHILOSOPHY

We have explored the nature of process philosophy, one of its four major streams—Marxism—and its institutional structure and procedure. We have noted briefly its prevailing influence in the thinking and living of the world from the early 1900s to the present. In conclusion, let us turn our attention to its consequences. What has it produced and what have been the reactions to what it has produced?

As we consider the consequences of process philosophy during the past century, we would first call attention to the prophetic work of Friedrich Nietzsche (1844-1900). Nietzsche, in my analysis, was the most perceptive so-called intellectual of the last three centuries.

Probably the most influential intellectual of the last three centuries was Friedrich Hegel (1770-1831) who, as we recall, introduced to the West the profound shift in thinking from the absolute-antithetical-Biblical to the synthetic thought form. As a consequence, people do not tend to think today any longer in terms of truth in an absolute sense. As a result, even in their thinking, they find it difficult to comprehend even the possibility of there being truth in an absolute sense. In fact, I would estimate that only one percent of the people that I have met believe in truth in any absolute sense. People talk about truth, but they do not believe it absolutely. If we did believe in truth, our lives would be radically different.

The most perceptive intellectual in recent centuries, however, in my analysis, was the brilliant German philosopher-poet, Friedrich Nietzsche.[4] It was Nietzsche who first anticipated and advocated irrationalism, which has, indeed, become the hallmark of twentieth and twenty-first century man.

Sadly, Nietzsche is best remembered superficially by Evangelical Christians for having declared that "God is dead."[5] He said this, however, not because he wanted God to be dead, but simply in acknowledgement of what had long since been the case within the intellectual community–and, in a very real sense, within the general culture of his day. He was making an observation, not an assertion.

He should be better remembered, not for having derided what the Roman Catholics had come to call the "immaculate conception," but for having derided what he came to call the "immaculate perception."[6] Nietzsche argued, not only that God or the supernatural is mythological, but that rationalistic man is mythological as well.

If we stop to consider this, we recognize the reality of it. If there is no Biblical God, then man cannot be rational! Where is the standard for rationality? Man's rationality is anchored in who-God-is, because man is who-he-is because of who-God-is, Biblically speaking. So, Nietzsche was being quite consistent with the presupposition of the non-existence of God.

Nietzsche, unlike many of his contemporaries who were buoyed up in a gigantic bubble of optimism, argued that rationalistic man, far from producing a better not to mention perfect world, would produce the worst of all possible worlds imaginable, and he recoiled against the chamber of horrors which he saw coming.

Many people accuse Nietzsche of advocating irrationalism because he was suffering from syphilis. That venereal disease does, if allowed to run its pathological course, eventually render a person mentally incapacitated, and so it was with Nietzsche. He spent approximately the last ten years of his life mentally deranged. However, Nietzsche was not advocating irrationalism because he was suffering from syphilis; he was doing so because of his brilliant perception. Given the conclusions of the non-existence of God and the mythology of rationalistic man, he could see no other alternative or hope than in a non-rational or irrational realm. Nietzsche, then, anticipated Existentialism, as well as Occultism and the so-called New Age movement.

Without question, as Nietzsche had foreseen, the twentieth century was characterized by a chamber of horrors flowing from process philosophy. Indeed, the horrendous consequences of process philosophy during the twentieth century cannot be exaggerated. They include totalitarianism in the forms of Nazism and communism, two world-wide holocausts, an international depression of unprecedented magnitude (from which we have yet to fully extricate ourselves), and a cold war, replete with classicide, genocide, and megalomania, during which countless millions of people were put to death in the name of applied social science. These horrors were, if you will permit me, the fruit of Rationalism.

Moreover, process philosophy is continuing to bear its bitter fruit as the new millennium dawns; in the name of applied social science millions of innocent people are still being put to death every year in our so-called modern age.

The intellectual impact of these realities has been devastating, indeed, shattering. Western intellectual man, as a consequence, has given up on Western civilization as having any particular significance, even becoming anti-Western. He has also given up on any possibility of unity, of "getting it all together," or finding a coherent worldview.

Western intellectual man has given up on man himself as having any uniqueness or any ultimate meaning or significance. Finally, Western intellectual man has given up on rationality, and on man as being a rational creature. On this point, Nietzsche was a harbinger of things to come.

Therefore, process philosophy has disintegrated. There is, of course, a considerable hangover of process philosophy among so-called secondary intellectuals and lesser activistic minds. In terms of the cutting edge, however, process philosophy has resulted in intellectual anarchism, subjectivism, and despair. Indeed, the hallmark of intellectual man in the wake of the consequences of process philosophy during the twentieth century has come to be a pervasive intellectual despair.

Today, people are looking to the irrational and, once again, to the unseen realm, for answers. Elsewhere we discuss this in detail along with the alternatives for the West and world the rest of the today.

Here, we will close by noting that Biblical Christians have a tremendous opportunity today, because there is a vacuum, and when there is a vacuum, it is there for the taking. If, indeed, we would have a renewal of Biblical Christianity and the implementation of the Biblical Christian worldview, as we have only been able to summarize it in this book, a small number of people, reconciled to God in Christ and led by God the Spirit, allowing God to flow through their lives in His limitless power, could move into and fill that vacuum in every sphere of existence. It would not take very many people.

A reformation will occur, however, only if the people of God, to begin with, will fall on their faces before God and repent. God owes us nothing. We owe Him everything. He will never save Western civilization, including the United States of America, as an end in itself. If we are preserved from destruction, it will only be as a means to the end of the exaltation of God and the pointing of all peoples to God on the basis of His finished work in Christ and His lordship over all of life.

Reformation, of course, would not produce perfection. Indeed, those who are seeking a system which will produce perfection would be well advised to throw Biblical Christianity out the window as an alternative, for Biblical Christianity presupposes that there will not be perfection until the return of God-in-Christ and the implementation of His Kingdom in its full power and glory over all that exists.

In the final analysis, in any nation or civilization, we will either have revolution, which can only be destructive, or reformation, which does make for a substantial difference, including a relative order, community, liberty, justice, charity, and productive activity.

NOTES

1. Nietzsche, Friedrich, from The Gay Science (1882-1886) and Unpublished Notes, as quoted in Pfeffer, Rose, Nietzsche: Disciple of Dionysus, NY: Cranberry, NJ: Associated Univ. Presses, Inc., 1972, p. 73, 78-79.
2. Bibliographical Note: The Revolution Was by Garet Garrett, The Caxton Printers, Ltd., Caldwell, Idaho, n.d.
3. Compiler's Note: The eight private, well-endowed Ivy League schools, which have enjoyed a long history of academic prestige and influence, include (with their founding years) Harvard in Cambridge MA 1636, Yale in New Haven CT 1701, University of Pennsylvania in Philadelphia PA 1740, Princeton in Princeton NJ 1746, Columbia in New York City NY1754, Brown in Providence RI 1764, Dartmouth in Hanover NH 1769 and Cornell in Ithaca NY1865. Undergraduate numbers are small (4,000-10,000 each), but the schools also control many well-populated and well-funded postgraduate programs and research organizations. Stanford was founded in 1891 as a "progressive" school–co-educational, non-church-affiliated, and based on the German model like Johns Hopkins and Cornell. Other schools which enjoy high rankings are MIT, Duke, Rice, Caltech, UC Berkeley, UCLA, Virginia, and North Carolina
4. Biographical Note: Friedrich Nietzsche (1844-1900) was the son of a Lutheran minister and was educated in the Classics at Leipzig and Bonn. At the age of twenty-five, he was appointed professor of Classical philology at the University of Basel (1869-79). He wrote on philology, music, Greek antiquity, and, particularly, philosophy, including Thus Spake Zarathrustra (1883ff.), which proclaimed the "gospel" of the superman, A Genealogy of Morals (1887), and The Will to Power (1888).
5. Compiler's Note on Nietzsche's statement that God is dead: Walter Kaufmann notes that "Nietzsche invented a parable from which some eighty years later, a few American Protestant theologians derived inspiration–and this slogan [that God is dead]." The parable was, apparently, first published in 1882 in Nietzsche's book, Die Fröhliche Wissenschaft [The Gay Science]. The statement is also found in a later book of Nietzsche's, Thus Spake Zarathrustra (1883/84). [Nietzsche: Philosopher, Psychologist, Antichrist by Walter Kaufmann, 3rd. ed., Princeton Univ. Press, 1968.]
6. Compiler's Note; The Immaculate Perception is subtitle and a phrase used in the second part of Nietzsche's Zarathrustra [found 3-30-03 at www.thecry.com/existentialism/nietzsche]

APPENDIX A

Word Definition List from Oxford/Webster's Dictionaries
*Indicates the definition is taken from Dr. Martin's material rather than the dictionary

Abolition: Ending the existence of.

Abolitionist: One who aims at the abolition of any institution [such as slavery].

Absolitionsim: *The absolutizing of the view that an institution must be abolished; viewing slavery, for example, as an absolute evil which must be abolished by force of arms if necessary.

Absolute: Existing without relation to any other being; self-existent; self-sufficient.

Absolutize: To make absolute; convert into an absolute.

Aesthetic: Belonging to the appreciation of the beautiful, of the arts.

Alpha* and *Omega: "A" to "Z"; the first and last letter (O) of the Greek alphabet. In the Bible, God refers to Himself as the Alpha and the Omega.

Ameliorate: To make better or more tolerable.

Analogy: Process of reasoning from parallel cases.

Anarchy: Absence of government; disorder, confusion.

Anthropological: Of or having to do with man (Greek word for man: *anthropos*)

Anthropoligical Question: *What is the origin, nature, role, and destiny of man?

Antithesis/Antithetical: Things which are in opposition to each other, in contrast.

Apostasy: Abandonment of religious faith. *Subtraction from Biblical truth.

Aribitrary: 1) Derived from mere opinion or preference; not based on the nature of things. 2) To be decided by one's liking; dependent upon will or pleasure.

Atheism: Disbelief in, or denial of, the existence of God.

Authoritarian: Favorable to the principle of authority as opposed to that of the individual.

Authoritarianism: Authoritarian principles. *Rendering some authority, as government, absolute.

Automaton: A living being whose actions are purely involuntary or mechanical.

Autonomous: Right of self government, freedom of the will [*freedom from responsibility to authority]

Axiology: Theory of value. What is the ultimate value?

Biblical Christian: *One who accepts the Bible as the absolute Word of God and views God and His Word as applicable to all of life.

Blasphemy: That which takes place when someone or something which is not God, sets itself up in the place of God.

Bourgeoisie: The middle class. [*Also, a component of the Marxian construct]

Capital: Money, property, or stock employed in trade, manufactures, etc.; the sum invested or lent, as distinguished from the income or interest.

Capitalist: One who has capital, money for investment or money invested; esp. a person of large property, which is employed in business. (Webster).

Capitalism: Possession of capital or wealth. Dominance of private owners, of capital and production for profit. [*A component of the Marxian construct which views history as economically determined. The definition is widely accepted by Marxists as being consistent with reality.]

Christendom: That portion of the world in which Christianity prevails, or which is governed under Christian institutions, in distinction from heathen or Mohammedan lands.

Christian-Rationalist Conglomerate: *Dr. Martin's term for American society in the 1700s which was a profoundly intertwined admixture of Christianity and rationalism.

Communion: Intimate fellowship or rapport. *Communion is only possible under God Who, as the "glue," is the source of all fellowship.

Communism: A theory which advocates a state society in which there should be no private ownership, all property being vested in the community and labour organized for the common benefits of all parts; the professed principle being that each should work according to his capacity, and receive according to his wants. [*A theory held and articulated by Marx; the word is applied, in particular, to Marxism-Leninism as formulated by Lenin and followed by the Communist Party established in 1903.]

Conservative: *A non-liberal; one who does not accept either the presuppositions and/or the conclusions of process philosophy.

Constitution: Body of fundamental order according to which a State or other organization is governed.

Cosmological Question: *What is the origin, nature, and destiny of the cosmos?

Cosmos: All that exists, the limits of which limited man does not know.

Deism: Belief in the existence of God without accepting revelation. *Belief in a God who created the universe but has no ongoing relationship with man.

Democracy: A state having government by all the people. *A theory of government based on the presupposition that man, not God, is the author of government, which imagines that all people can and ought to participates directly in human governance; majoritarianism.

Democratic Procedure: *The idea flowing out of Biblical Christianity that, God being no respecter of all persons, all persons can participate in governance under God in their respective spheres of responsibility.

Demoralization: Destroy the morale of, corrupt the morals of.

Depravity: Moral perversion, innate (inborn, natural) corruption of man. *Man is completely dependent upon the work and will of God for his deliverance from the dilemma into which he was born.

Developmentalism: Unfold; to go through a process of natural evolution or growth, from a less perfect to a more perfect or more highly organized state.

Diabolical: Having to do with, proceeding from, externally like the Devil; devilish, inhumanly cruel.

Dialectical Materialism: Marxist theory of political events as due to conflict of social forces caused by man's material needs. [*The basis of the Marxian construct which combined the dialectic of Hegel with the materialism of Feuerbach.]

Dichotomy: Division into two. *A false division which arises in the mind of a person who tries to understand something without beginning and ending with the Trinitarian God in his or her thinking.

Dualism: 1) State of being dual or twofold; a twofold division. 2) A system which accepts two gods, or two original principles, one good and the other evil.

Ecclesiastical: Of the church or of the clergy.

Ecclesiastical Absolutism or Ecclesiasticism: *The church has become sovereign in the place of God.

Egalitarian: Of, relating to, (person) holding, the principle of equal rights for all persons. *A principle or position derived from the ontological view that all things which exist are of the same substance and, therefore, are equal by nature.

Empirically: Based on or acting on observation or experiment, not on theory. Deriving knowledge from experience alone.

Environmentalism: Everything is produced by the environmental and constituent forces.

Epistemology: Theory of the method or grounds of knowledge. How do we know?

Evangelical Christian: *One who holds the Bible to be the Word of God. (May or may not believe that God and His Word are applicable to all of life; may, instead, accept a dichotomy between sacred and secular.)

Exacerbate: Aggravate, make worse, irritate.

Exploit: 1) To utilize, to make available, to get the value or usefulness out of. 2) To draw an illegitimate profit from.

Exploitation: The act of exploiting or utilizing.

Extrapolate: Estimate from known values, data etc.

Fabian: Employing cautious dilatory (given to delay) strategy to wear out an enemy.

Fascism: A one-party system of government in which the individual is subordinated to the state, and control is maintained by military force, secret police, rigid censorship, and governmental regimentation of industry and finance.

Federal: Of a system of government in which several states form a unity but remain independent in internal affairs.

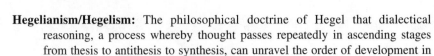

Hegelianism/Hegelism: The philosophical doctrine of Hegel that dialectical reasoning, a process whereby thought passes repeatedly in ascending stages from thesis to antithesis to synthesis, can unravel the order of development in which human consciousness and reality participate.

Heresy: Opinion contrary to the orthodox doctrine of the Christian church. *Addition to Biblical truth.

Humanism: Devotion to human interests, system concerned with human (not divine) interests.

Hypothecate: *Dr. Martin uses this word for a supposition, based on a selection of alternatives, used as a basis for reasoning.

Hypothesis: Supposition made as basis for reasoning, without assumption of its truth.

Ideology: Science of ideas. Manner of thinking characteristic of a class or individual. *A construct spun from the mind of man without reference to the revealed mind of God in an effort to understand reality and solve man's dilemmas.

___ism: *The postfix "ism," added to any term, usually indicates that whatever precedes it is being absolutized (that is, rendered, if only inadvertently, the ultimate integration point).

Inadvertently: Without proper attention, negligently. *Without being conscious of what one has done or is doing.

Intellectual Content: *That part of a communication which is rational in nature and able to be understood intellectually by man.

Irrational: 1) Not rational; void of reason or understanding. 2) Not according to reason; absurd, foolish.

Legislate: Enact laws, make provision by laws.

Materialism: Belief that nothing exists but matter and its movements and modifications, excluding that which is supernatural

Modern: 1) Being at this time; now existing. 2) Of or pertaining to the present and recent times, as distinguished from the remote past. [*A component of the naturalists' structuring of history.]

Nationalism: Patriotic feeling, principles, or feelings; policy of national independence. *The absolutizing or sovereignizing of a nation (in the place of God).

Naturalistic: View of the world that excludes the supernatural or spiritual. Action based on natural instincts; moral or religious system on purely natural basis.

Nomenclature: 1) A name, appellation, designation. 2) The system or set of names for things, etc., commonly employed by a person or community.

Non-Theism: *A theology and anthropological religion, popular among Western intellectuals, which has dispensed with even the consideration of God's existence.

Ontology: Branch of metaphysics dealing with the nature of being. How do we exist?

Pantheism: Doctrine that God is everything and everything is God; "all"-theism.

Perpetuate: Preserve from oblivion.

Perversion: A perverted or corrupted form of something.

Philosophical Questions: *"Philo" is Greek for "love of" and "soph" means "wisdom," so we have the love of wisdom with regard to the origin, nature, and destiny of life.

Philosophy: Seeking after wisdom or knowledge especially that which deals with ultimate reality.

Polytheism: Doctrine that there are many gods.

Presupposition: Thing assumed beforehand as a basis of argument or discussion. That which is required as a prior condition.

Pretension: The act of pretending or laying claim.

Pretext: That which is put forward to cover the real purpose or object; the ostensible reason or motive of action.

Progressivism: Movement from lower to higher; simple to complex. Continuously increasing in severity or extent.

Proletariat: The lowest class of a community.

Rationalism: Practice of explaining ultimate reality in a way consistent with [human] reason.

Relative: Comparative, in relation to something else. *Not absolute.

Relativism: Doctrine that knowledge is relative, not absolute. *The assumption that there is nothing absolute, absolutized.

Right Reason: *The idea (John Locke and others) that right thinking exists and can be discovered apart from the Word of God.

Scholasticism: The attempt to provide an intellectual basis for something on the ground of the human intellect without reference to the Word of God; usually in terms of logical analysis.

Semantics: Branch of philosophy concerned with meanings.

Socialism: *The absolutizing of the social approach to man and life.

Sovereign: 1) Of or belonging to, characteristic of supremacy or superiority. 2) Having supreme rank or power.

Subsidiary: Serving to help, assist, or supplement.

Subsume: To state as a minor proposition or concept under another.

Synthesis: Combination, putting together, building up of separate elements, especially of conceptions or facts into a connected whole. [*Here, a component of the Hegelian dialectic, the revolution in thought forms.]

Teleology: Doctrine of final causes, destiny, where are we going?

Temporal: Lasting or existing only for a time; passing, temporary.

Terminal: 1) Belonging to or lasting for a term or definite period. 2) A terminal degree is the highest in one's field.

Theism: Belief in the existence of God (or of gods).

Theocentricism: Having God as the central interest and ultimate concern.

Theology: The study or science which treats of God, His Nature and attributes, and His relations with man and the universe.

Thesis: Proposition, statement, to be maintained or proved.

Transcendental: Philosophy explaining matter and objective things as products of the subjective mind regarding the divine as guiding principle in man.

Trinitarianism: Doctrine of the union of the three in one Godhead: Father, Son and Holy Spirit.

Tyranny: 1) The government of a tyrant or absolute ruler. 2) Arbitrary or oppressive excercise of power; unjustly severe use of one's authority.

Utilitarianism: 1) The doctrine that actions derive their moral quality from their usefulness as means to some end, as happiness [theory held by Jeremy Bentham and John Stuart Mill]. 2) Devotion to mere material interests.

Utopia: Ideally perfect place with perfect social and political systems.

APPENDIX B
FOR FURTHER READING AND BIBLIOGRAPHY

MOST HIGHLY RECOMMENDED:
All of the writings of the following individuals; particularly significant works listed:

Augustine, St. Aurelius (354-430) (trans. from Latin)
The City of God. Hutchins, Robert Maynard, ed. in chief. Great Books of the Western World. Vol. 18: Augustine, pp. 127-618. Chicago: Encyclopedia Britannica, Inc., 1952.

Dooyeweerd, Herman (1894-1977) (trans. from Dutch)
In the Twilight of Western Thought: Studies in the Pretended Autonomy of Philosophical Thought. Nutley, NJ: Craig Press, 1975; Roots of Western Culture: Pagan, Secular, and Christian Options. Toronto: Wedge Pub. Foundation, 1979.

Kuyper, Abraham (1837-1920) (trans. from Dutch)
Christianity as a Life System: The Witness of a World View. (Pub. as Lectures on Calvinism. Eerdmans, 1976.)

Lewis, C.S. (1898-1963)
Mere Christianity. New York: Macmillan, ©1952, 1981; The Abolition of Man. Riverside, NJ: Macmillan, 1962; The Problem of Pain. Macmillan, 1962.

Schaeffer, Francis A. and Edith
The Complete Works available from Westchester, IL: Good News Pub., 5 vols. paper
The God Who Is There: Speaking Historic Christianity Into the Twentieth Century. Downer's Grove, IL: InterVarsity, 1968.
He Is There and He Is Not Silent. Wheaton, IL: Tyndale, 1972.

Escape From Reason. Downer's Grove, IL: InterVarsity, 1968.
How Should We Then Live? The Rise and Decline of
    Western Thought and Culture. Good News, 1976.
A Christian Manifesto. Good News, 1981.
With C. Everett Koop, Whatever Happened to the Human Race. Revell, 1979.
True Spirituality. Tyndale, 1971.
Pollution and the Death of Man: the Christian View of
    Ecology. Tyndale House, 1970.
Genesis in Space and Time: The Flow of Biblical History.
    Downers Grove, IL: InterVarsity Press, 1972.

Solzhenitsyn, Alexander
Warning to the West. NY: Farrar, Straus & Giroux, 1976; Nobel Lecture
on Literature. Trans. by Thomas P. Whitney. NY: Harper & Row, 1972;
Gulag Archipelago (Abridged, 3 vols. in one: Harper & Row, 1985)

FURTHER READING RECOMMENDATIONS:

Aikman, David. The Role of Atheism in the Marxist Tradition. University Microfilms, Intl., 1979.

Alcorn, Randy. Pro-Life Answers to Pro-Choice Arguments. Portland, OR: Multnomah, 1994.

Bainton, Roland. Here I Stand: A Life of Martin Luther. Nashville, TN: Abingdon Press, 1978.

Bastiat, Frederick. The Law. Irvington-on-Hudson, NY: Foundation for Economic Education, 1950.

Blamires, Harry. The Christian Mind: How Should a Christian Think? Ann Arbor, MI: Servant Books, 1963.

Bunyan, John. The Pilgrim's Progress: From This World to That Which Is to Come. [classic fiction]

Burke, Edmund (1729-1797). Reflections on the Revolution in France. Buffalo, NY: Prometheus Books, 1987.

Burkett, Larry. The Coming Economic Earthquake. Chicago, IL: Moody Press, 1991.

Burnham, James. Suicide of the West. New Rochelle, NY: Arlington House, 1964.

Cairns, Earle E. Christianity Through the Centuries: A History of the Christian Church. Grand Rapids, MI: Zondervan Pub. House, 1981; God and Man in Time: A Christian Approach to Historiography. Grand Rapids, MI: Baker Book Co., 1979.

Calvin, John. ed., John T. McNeill. Calvin: Institutes of the Christian Religion. Philadelphia, PA: The Westminster Press, 1960.

Carden Allen. Puritan Christianity in America: Religion and Life in Seventeenth Century Massachusetts. Grand Rapids, MI: Baker Book House, 1990.

Chambers, Whittaker. Witness. New York: Random House, 1952.

Chesterton, G.K. (1874-1936). Orthodoxy. Garden City, NY: Image Books, 1959, ©1936.

Clark, Gordon Haddon. A Christian View of Men and Things. Grand Rapids, MI: Eerdmans, 1952; Religion, Reason, and Revelation, Jefferson, MD: Trinity Foundation, 1986.

Colson, Charles and Ellen Santilli Vaughn. Against the Night: Living in the New Dark Ages. Ann Arbor, MI: Servant Publications, 1989.

Colson, Charles. Born Again. Grand Rapids, MI: Chosen Books, 2004.

Coppedge, James F. Evolution: Possible or Impossible?. Northridge, CA: Probability Research in Molecular Biology, 1973.

Eliot, T.S. Christianity and Culture. NY: Harcourt, Brace, and World, 1940.

Epstein, Edward J. News from Nowhere: Television and the News. NY: Random House, 1973.

Evans, M. Stanton. Clear and Present Dangers: A Conservative View of America's Government. NY: Harcourt Brace Jovanovich, 1975.

Garrett, Garet. The Revolution Was. Caldwell, ID: The Caxton Printers, Ltd, 1944.

Geisler, Norman L. and William Watkins. Worlds Apart: A Handbook on Worldviews, 2nd ed. Grand Rapids, MI: Baker Book House, 1988.

Groen Van Prinsterer, Guillame. Lectures on Unbelief and Revolution; Van Dyke, Harry, ed. Groen Van Prinsterer's Lectures on Unbelief and Revolution. Ontario, Canada: Wedge Publishing Foundation, 1989.

Hodge, A.A. Outlines of Theology. Grand Rapids, MI: Zondervan, 1972.

Johnson, Paul. Modern Times: The World From the Twenties to the Nineties. NY: HarperPerennial, 1992.

Kirk, Russell. The Conservative Mind, from Burke to Eliot. New York: Avon, 1968.

Kuhn, Thomas. The Structure of Scientific Revolutions. Chicago, IL: University of Chicago Press, 1962.

Ladd, George Eldon. The Gospel of the Kingdom. Grand Rapids, MI: Eerdmans, 1971.

Langley, McKendree R. The Practice of Political Spirituality: Episodes from the

Public Career of Abraham Kuyper, 1887-1918. Ontario, Canada: Paideia Press, 1984.

Luther, Martin. Three Treatises. Philadelphia, PA: Fortress Press, revised edition., 1970.

Machen, J. Gresham. The Christian View of Man. London: The Banner of Truth Trust, 1965.

Marshall, Jr., Peter and D. Manuel The Light and the Glory. Old Tappan, NJ: Revell, 1977. (Effort to reinterpret early Amer. Hst.)

Muggeridge, Malcolm. The End of Christendom. Grand Rapids, MI: Eerdmans, 1980. Christ and the Media. Grand Rapids, MI: Eerdmans, 1977; Chronicles of Wasted Time. NY: Morrow, 1973.

Moberly, Walter. The Crisis in the University. London: S.C.M. Press, 1949.

Morison, Samuel Eliot. The Intellectual Life of Colonial New England. NY: New York Univ. Press, 1936.

Morris, Henry M. The Long War Against God: The History & Impact of the Creation/Evolution Conflict. Grand Rapids, MI: Baker Book House, 1989.

Nickel, James. Mathematics: Is God Silent. Vallecito, CA: Ross House Publishers, 1990.

Noebel, David. Understanding Today's Worldviews: Biblical Christian, Marxist-Leninist, and Secular Humanist Worldviews. Colorado Springs, CO: Summit Press, 1991; The Battle for Truth. Eugene, OR: Harvest House Publishers, 2001.

Olasky, Marvin and Herb Schlossberg. Turning Point: A Christian Worldview Declaration. Westchester, IL: Crossway Books, 1987;

Olasky, Marvin. Central Ideas in the Development of American Journalism: A Narrative History. Hillsdale, NJ: L. Erlbaum Associates, 1991; The Tragedy of American Compassion. Chicago, IL: Regnery Publishing, 1992; Renewing American Compassion: How Compassion for the Needy Can Turn Ordinary Citizens into Heroes. Chicago, IL: Regnery Publishing, 1997.

Pascal, Blaise (1623-1662). Pascal's Pensees. Introduction by T.S. Eliot. NY: E.P. Dutton, 1958.

Ramm, Bernard R. The Christian College in the Twentieth Century. Grand Rapids, MI: Wm. B. Eerdman's Pub. Co., 1963. Nashville, TN: Nelson, 1984.

Reagan, Ronald. An American Life. NY: Simon & Schuster, 1990.

Revel, Jean-Francois. How Democracies Perish. NY: Doubleday, 1984.

Richardson, Don. Eternity in Their Hearts: The Untold Story of Christianity Among Folk Religions of Ancient People. Ventura, CA: Regal Books, 1981.

Rookmaaker, H.R. Modern Art and the Death of a Culture. Downers Grove, IL: InterVarsity Press, 1970.

Rose, Tom. Economics: Principles and Policy from a Christian Perspective. Mercer, PA: American Enterprise Publications, 1986.

Rushdoony, Rousas. The One and the Many: Studies in the Philosophy of Order and Ultimacy. (Now available from Vallecito, CA: Ross House Publishers.)

Schlossberg, Herbert. Idols for Destruction. Nashville, TN: Thomas Nelson Publishers, 1983.

Schwarz, Frederick. You Can Trust the Communists to be Communists. Englewood Cliffs, NJ: Prentice-Hall, 1960. (Christian Anti-Communism Crusade, P.O Box 890, Long Beach, CA 90801 U.S.A.)

Singer, C. Gregg. A Theological Interpretation of American History. P & R Pub. Co., 1981; From Rationalism to Irrationality: The Decline of the Western Mind from the Renaissance to the Present. Phillipsburg, NJ: P & R Publishing Company, 1979.

Sire, James. The Universe Next Door: A Basic World View Catalog. Downers Grove, IL: InterVarsity, 1988.

Sproul, R.C. Lifeviews: Understanding the Ideas that Shape Society Today. Old Tappan, NJ: F. H. Revell, 1986.

Tansill, Charles C. Back Door To War. Chicago, IL: Regnery, 1952.

Treadgold, Donald. A History of Christianity. Nordland Pub. Co., 1979.

Van Til, Cornelius. Christian Apologetics. Phillipsburg, NJ: P & R Publishing Company, 1976.

Washington, George. Washington's Farewell Address. Noah Webster Library Reprint from 1800.

Weaver, Richard M. Ideas Have Consequences. IL: University of Chicago Press, 1948.

Zacharias, Ravi. A Shattered Visage: The Real Face of Atheism. Brentwood, TN: Wolgemuth and Hyatt, 1990.

BOOKS/TOPICS REFERENCED IN THE TEXT:

Bentham, Jeremy. <u>Introduction to the Principles of Morals and Legislation</u>. ©1789. (The Collected Works of Jeremy Bentham, USA: Oxford University Press, 1996.)

Blackstone, William. <u>Commentaries on the Laws of England</u>. ©1769. (A Facsimile of the First Edition of 1765-1769, IL: University of Chicago Press, 1979.)

Carson, Clarence B. <u>Basic Communism: Its Rise and Spread, and Debacle in the 20th Century</u>. Wadley, AL: American Textbook Committee, 1990.

Copernicus, Nicholas. <u>On the Revolutions of Heavenly Spheres</u>. ©1543

Crane, Philip M. <u>The Democrat's Dilemma: How the Liberal Left Captured the Democratic Party</u>. Chicago, IL: Henry Regnery Company, 1964.

de Tocquieville, Alexis. <u>Democracy in America</u>. ©1835, 1840.

Emerson, Ralph Waldo. <u>The Complete Essays of Ralph Waldo Emerson</u>. New York: The Modern Library, 1940.

Feuerbach, Ludwig Andreas. <u>The Essence of Christianity</u>. ©1841.

Freeman, Douglas Southall (1886-1953). <u>George Washington, a Biography</u>. NY: Scribner, 1948-57.

Friedman, Milton and Rose. <u>Free to Choose</u>. NY: Harcourt Brace Jovanovich, 1979.

Gaussen, Louis. <u>The Inspiration of the Holy Scriptures</u>. Chicago, IL: Moody Press, 1949.

Goldwater, Barry M. <u>With No Apologies: The Personal and Political Memoirs of U.S. Senator</u>. New York: Morrow, 1979.

Hamilton, Alexander (1757-1804), James Madison, and John Jay. <u>The Federalist Papers: A Collection of Essays Written in Support of the Constitution of the United States</u>. Garden City, NY: Anchor Books, 1966.

Hazlitt, Henry. <u>Economics in One Lesson</u>. NY: Arlington House Publishers, 1979.

Hickman, Randall J. <u>Justice for the Unborn</u>. Ann Arbor, MI: Servant Books, 1984.

Hutchinson, Thomas. <u>History of the Colony of Massachusetts Bay</u> (Research Library of Colonial Americana, Arno Press, 1971.) Boston, ©1764.

Kirk, Russell. <u>The Roots of American Order</u>. Malibu, CA: Pepperdine University Press, 1974; <u>America's British Culture</u>. New Brunswick, NJ: Transaction Publishers, 1993, 1994.

Klehr, Harvey, John Earl Haynes, and Fridrikh Igorevich Firsov. <u>The Secret World of American Communism</u>. New Haven, CT and London: Yale University Press, 1995.

Koop, C. Everett. The Right to Live, the Right to Die. Tyndale House, 1976.

Lebreton, Jules and Jacques Zeiller. A History of the Early Church. NY: Collier Books, 1962.

Marx, Karl. The Communist Manifesto. ©1848. Signet Classics, 1998. Das Kapital. ©1867. Washington, DC: Gateway Editions, 1999.

Newton, Sir Isaac. Principia. [Mathematical Principles of Natural Philosophy]. ©1687. Berkeley, CA: University of California Press, 1999.

Nietzsche, Friedrich. The Will to Power. ©1888. Vintage Publishers, 1968. Thus Spake Zarathrustra. ©1883.

Sartre, Jean Paul. Being and Nothingness: An Essay in Phenomenological Ontology. ©1943. Trans., Hazel Barnes, New York: Philosophical Library, 1956. No Exit. Trans., Stuart Gilbert. New York: Knopf, 1948.

Schwarz, Fred. Beating the Unbeatable Foe. Chicago, IL: Regnery Publishing, Inc., 1996.

Sowell, Thomas. The Economics and Politics of Race: An International Perspective. NY: Quill, 1985, ©1983.

Spinka, Matthew. John Hus: A Biography. Princeton: Princeton University Press, 1968.

Trevelyan, George Macaulay. England in the Age of Wycliffe. London: Longman, 1972.

Tyler, Alice Felt. Freedom's Ferment: Phases of American Social History to 1860. Minneapolis, MN: The University of Minnesota Press, 1944.

von Clausewitz, Karl. On War. ©1832. Penguin Classics, 1982.

Warfield, Benjamin B. The Inspiration and Authority of the Bible. Philadelphia, PA: The P & R Publishing Company, 1947.

INDEX